SELF-HELP

VOLUNTARY ASSOCIATIONS IN THE 19TH CENTURY

Studies in Economic and Social History

P. H. J. H. Gosden

Reader in Educational Administration and History
University of Leeds

SELF-HELP

Voluntary Associations in the 19th Century

B. T. BATSFORD LTD, LONDON

First published 1973
© P. H. J. H. Gosden 1973
Printed and bound by C. Tinling & Co. Ltd, Prescot
for the publishers B. T. Batsford Ltd,
4 Fitzhardinge Street, London W1H 0AH
0 7134 1387 5 (hardcover)
0 7134 1388 3 (paperback)

Contents

Acknowledgements

In writing this study I have become indebted to many for their help and assistance. I am grateful to the officers of a number of friendly societies, building societies and trustee savings banks for their kindness in making record material available. In particular I would like to acknowledge the assistance given by officers of the Manchester Unity of Oddfellows, of the Ancient Order of Foresters, of the Leeds Permanent Building Society and of the Building Societies Association. Members of the staffs of the Brotherton Library, Leeds University, of the Goldsmith Library, London University and of the London Library have been generous with their time in meeting my requests. Finally I would like to express my gratitude to Mrs. Edith Brass who transformed an untidy manuscript into a typed draft.

Preface

By far the most important of the voluntary associations concerned with the promotion of thrift and self-help in the 19th century were the friendly societies. As their name implied, these represented an attempt by working men to meet their social and convivial needs as well as to insure against the hazards of sickness and death. It was not merely the coming of Government old age pensions and national health insurance that led to the change in the character of friendly societies in the 20th century. It was also the shortening of the working week, the introduction of annual holidays and the consequent widening in the opportunities for recreation and social activities open to working men which gradually reduced their importance.

Building, cooperative and collecting societies were all forms of association which sought to meet a particular form of social need and served additionally as thrift organizations. The only form of purely thrift organization dealt with here are the savings banks which alone of all these associations were not legally under the control of their own members. Even members of the collecting societies were in a technical, legal sense supposed to possess powers of ultimate control—ineffective as they often proved.

Generally speaking these organizations were fiercely independent. But for various reasons some contact with the state was usually inevitable and for this purpose they came to be grouped under the Registrar of Friendly Societies. Philosophically, there was a conflict of opinion over the existence of the Friendly Societies' Registry between those who felt it was the duty of the state to encourage providence among the people and those who objected to the state undertaking any such paternalistic functions, for by apparently attempting to look after the affairs of individuals, the government was discouraging individual prudence. In these circumstances the considerable achievement of the Registry in improving the financial reliability and soundness of the voluntary associations was due more to the personalities of the three men who successively held office as Registrar in the 19th century—J. Tidd Pratt, J. M. Ludlow and E. W. Brabrook—than to any legal powers granted by Parliament.

Chapter One

Introduction: the position before 1800

In 1890 Gladstone recorded a message on Edison's new phonograph for a meeting of the Mutual Building Association of New York. He said 'The purpose of the meeting may, I conceive, be summed up in two words—self-help and thrift—and I cannot, although much occupied, refuse to send to it a few words of congratulation and goodwill. It is self-help that makes the man, and man-making is the aim which the Almighty has everywhere impressed upon creation. It is thrift by which self-help for the masses dependent upon labour is principally made effective. For them, thrift is the symbol and instrument of independence and of liberty, indispensable conditions of all permanent human good. . . .' The faith in the individual and a correspondingly low opinion of the potential of Government which was such a prominent feature of the ideas underlying this message was probably at its strongest in the middle years of Victoria's reign. By the time Gladstone recorded his message there was some questioning of this attitude.

The best known expositions of the Victorian philosophies of self-help and thrift are certainly those written by Samuel Smiles. *Self-Help* first appeared in 1859 and *Thrift* in 1875. In the preface of the 1866 edition of *Self-Help*, Smiles regretted that some had misunderstood and criticized him for eulogizing selfishness. This was the very opposite of self-help for 'the duty of helping one's self in the highest sense involves the helping of one's neighbours'. Certainly, mutual aid associations received the highest praise from Smiles. Cooperative societies and friendly societies cultivated the habit of prudent self-reliance amongst the people and were worthy of every encouragement. Mutual assurance was 'economy in its most economical form'. He took issue with those who criticized friendly societies for meeting in public houses where members wasted much money on drink, pointing out that the societies relied very much on the 'social element. The public house is everybody's house. The members can there meet together, talk together and drink together. It is extremely probable that had they trusted solely to the sense of duty—the duty of insuring against sickness—and merely required the members to pay their weekly contributions to a collector, very few societies of the kind would have remained in existence'.[1]

Voluntary provident associations flourished particularly in the period of greater prosperity following the 1840s. By far the most important class of associations were the friendly societies. They had many more members than any other type of association while the legal and administrative framework created to suit their needs was made to serve also the cooperative and building societies and savings banks. Moreover, in their typical form of clubs offering both good fellowship and mutual insurance, the friendly societies had rather earlier origins than the other forms of provident association. In essence many of them owed their origins to the need felt by working men to provide themselves with succour against the poverty and destitution resulting from sickness and death at a time when the community offered only resort to the overseer of the poor. The other forms of provident association met needs that were felt by many to be less pressing, and they came to flourish on a large scale only when a modest measure of relative prosperity began to diffuse itself more widely through society.

[1] Samuel Smiles, *Thrift*, 1875, pp. 114–18.

Friendly societies before 1800

The desire to advertise their longevity shown by 19th-century friendly societies was presumably partly due to an anxiety to impart to members and to prospective members a sense of the permanence of their institution. *Their* society had flourished for so long that there could surely be no question as to its financial health and future well-being; regardless of the fate of other societies *it* would be there to meet members' claims for sick pay or funeral benefit in years to come. Apart from this more or less consciously felt material desire for early origins, there also appear to have been somewhat romantic attempts by enthusiastic supporters of some of the better-known societies to discover links with antiquity. The Loyal Ancient Independent Order of Oddfellows was said to have had its origins in AD 55 in the reign of the Emperor Nero. The Antediluvians laid claim to even greater antiquity while there were Foresters who counted Adam as the 'first Forester'. Quite a number of the orders included the term 'ancient' in their titles, the largest and best-known being the Ancient Order of Foresters. Some of the other large societies which incorporated this adjective in their names were the Ancient Druids, the Ancient Britons, the Ancient Order of Buffaloes, the Ancient Fraternity of Gardeners and the Loyal Ancient Shepherds.[1]

At a more serious level, some 19th-century writers traced points of similarity between contemporary voluntary associations and fraternities of the pre-Christian era. H. Tompkins, a member of the staff of the Registrar's Office, reviewed these parallels as he saw them in his *Lecture on the Friendly Societies of Antiquity*. J. M. Ludlow, while serving as secretary to the Royal Commission on Friendly Societies in 1873 expressed his conviction that there was no historical gap between 'the gilds of old times' and modern friendly societies, 'that if we knew all, we could trace the actual passage from one to the other.'[2] The origins of 'the friendly society' in the accepted sense of that term seem to have been much more recent and perhaps more prosaic than these ideas might suggest.

[1] *The Quarterly Review*, vol. 116, 1864, pp. 321–2.
[2] *The Contemporary Review*, April, 1873, p. 748.

There is literary evidence of the existence of contemporary voluntary associations described as friendly societies from the end of the 17th century when Defoe wrote that 'Another branch of insurance is by contribution, or (to borrow the term from that before mentioned) Friendly Societies; which is, in short, a number of people entering into a mutual compact to help one another, in case any disaster or distress fall upon them'.[1] Defoe described the sailors' contributions to the chest at Chatham as really a friendly society and added that others might be named. Basing his suggestions on the evidence afforded by these societies, Defoe sketched out a proposal for founding pension offices. All sorts of people—beggars and soldiers excepted—'being sound in their limbs and under 50 years of age', were to go to the pension office and pay one shilling per quarter. In return they were to receive the following benefits:

—if they were sick, physicians were to treat them and provide prescriptions without charge,

—if they broke any bones, surgeons were to take charge and cure them gratis,

—those who were unable to work through injury or any kind of sickness were to be allowed subsistence pay or a pension for life if the affliction were permanent,

—the widows of seamen who died abroad, or who were drowned were to be given pensions during their widowhood.

Defoe summarised his proposals in these words, 'that all persons in the time of their health and youth, while they are able to work and spare it, should lay up some small inconsiderable part of their earnings as a deposit in safe hands, to lie as a store in bank, to relieve them, if by age or accident they should come to be disabled or incapacitated to provide for themselves; and that if God bless them, that neither they nor theirs come to need it, the overplus may be employed to relieve such as shall.'

As early as 1728, a pamphlet was published by an unknown author on the theme of the need for magistrates and the governing classes to encourage the formation of friendly

[1] Daniel Defoe, *Essays on Projects*, 1697, p. 118.

societies or 'box' clubs as a way of diminishing the burden of the poor on the rates.[1] The writer explained that in the opinion of many JPS there could be no more advantageous scheme than the creation of box clubs which already kept 'hundreds a year' from being burdens on the poor rates. By observing the calamities and disasters 'which daily happen' in a community and 'by seeing others in a bed of sickness' the members were stirred to a new 'view of providence'. In his work on the poor laws which was published in 1752, Alcock indicated that friendly societies then existed in one form or other especially in some parts of the West of England.[2] A little more than twenty years later Baron Maseres put forward a scheme by which the overseers of every parish should be empowered to grant annuities to such inhabitants as might wish to purchase them, the annuities being secured as a charge on the poor rates of parishes. The churchwardens and overseers were to invest the money they received in 3 per cent Bank annuities.[3] The scheme was formally drafted as a parliamentary proposal and passed the Commons but was rejected in the Lords. The principal effect of Maseres' proposals was to stir widespread interest in and discussion of friendly societies. A plan to enable the poor to maintain themselves by subscribing part of their earnings to a general or national society to be set up by Parliament was formulated by Acland, rector of Broadclist, Devon and published in 1786.[4] The subscriptions were to be compulsory and the whole scheme was in some respects akin to the National Health Insurance system of more recent years but was, of course, conceived in a totally different spirit. This might be seen from the treatment proposed for those classified as 'drones' who were to be returned to their place of legal settlement and restrained from ever leaving it again under penalty of being treated as rogues and vagabonds. This ferment of ideas on friendly societies in the later years of the 18th century led to the passing of Rose's Act

[1] *A method for the regular management of those societies called Box Clubs*, 1728.
[2] T. Alcock, *Observations on the defects of the Poor Laws and on the causes and consequences of the great increase and burden of the poor*, 1752.
[3] Baron Maseres, *A proposal for establishing life annuities in parishes for the benefit of the industrious poor*, 1773.
[4] John Acland, *A plan for rendering the poor independent of public contributions, founded on the basis of the friendly societies, commonly called clubs*, Exeter, 1786.

in 1793 which is discussed below.[1] It also led to some agricultural societies offering premiums for the formation of benefit clubs.[2]

The records of a few 17th- and early-18th-century societies survived in a sufficiently complete form for the Chief Registrar to be able to publish brief historical accounts of their origins and development in a memorandum annexed to his Report for 1906. Of these, the United General Sea Box of Borrowstounness Friendly Society was instituted in 1634. The first statement of accounts was made in 1634 and showed that the Society had £72 12s in its box. The port of Bo'ness enjoyed considerable prosperity and this was reflected both in the prosperity of this society and in the foundation of other societies which fused with it at different dates down to 1863. 'An event, perhaps unique in the history of friendly societies, took place in December 1884. This was the celebration of the fifth jubilee or 250th anniversary of the society at which the members and their friends to the number of over one hundred, sat down to a love feast.'[3] Another early Scottish friendly society founded by and for seamen was the Sea Box Society of St Andrews. This was established in 1643 'by several seamen in and about the City of St Andrews for the pious and benevolent purpose of relieving such of their number as in the course of Providence may happen to be visited with sickness, or the infirmities of old age, and of making a provision for the support of the widows and orphan children of deceased members'.[4] Two other very early Scottish societies were the Incorporation of Carters in Leith whose earliest documentation dated from 1661 and the Fraternity of Dyers in Linlithgow which was in existence before 1670.

A group of long-surviving societies formed by Huguenot refugees came into existence in the reign of Louis XIV. The revocation of the Edict of Nantes in 1685 and the ensuing

---

[1] *Infra*, p. 34.

[2] F. M. Eden, *The State of the Poor*, 1797, pp. 602–3. Eden singled out for commendation the agricultural society established at Bath which incorporated a condition disqualifying from eligibility for a premium any society which laid out any part of its funds in lotteries.

[3] P.P. 1907, LXXVIII, Report of the Chief Registrar for 1906, p. xiii.

[4] *Ibid.*, p. xiii.

persecution of French Protestants led to many of them fleeing to this country. According to John Ferry, secretary to the Norman Society in 1861, the districts of London where they mainly settled were 'Pancras, Battle Bridge, Soho and Spitalfields'. The energies of the immigrants became manifest in various ways, they seem to have grown moderately prosperous and to have formed friendly societies among themselves in order to ensure a system of relief for those who fell on hard times. The Norman Society itself was founded on 11 January 1703 by refugees from Normandy who had settled in Bethnal Green and Spitalfields with the object of promoting social intercourse and providing assistance in sickness and old age and the expenses of burial. Meetings were held fortnightly and contributions were at the rate of 1d weekly. By 1742 funds had accumulated to such an extent that weekly sick pay was raised to a higher scale whenever the capital remained above £100. A sliding scale arrangement by which benefits rose and fell with the increase or decrease of capital was a distinctive feature of societies of Huguenot origin. The books and accounts were kept in French until 1800 after which English came to be used, but even in the 20th century membership remained limited to descendants of French Protestant refugees.[1]

A similar friendly society was the Society of Lintot which was founded in Spitalfields in 1708, membership being limited to members and descendants of members of the Church of Lintot, which was a district in Normandy. As with other Huguenot societies, it flourished financially so that 200 years after its foundation this society of 60 members had a considerable capital of £2,846. It was paying 21 shillings per week in sickness and a pension of 6s 6d to members of 65 years of age and over. Other Huguenot friendly societies which thrived in the Spitalfields area were the Society of Protestant refugees from High and Low Normandy, the Society of Picards and Walloons and the Friendly Benefit Society held at the sign of the Norfolk Arms, Irving Street, Bethnal Green.

On two occasions during the 18th century, attempts were made to create friendly societies for particular groups of working men and to make membership compulsory. The first

[1] *Ibid.*, pp. xvii–xviii.

of these was in 1757 when an act was passed 'for the relief of coalheavers working upon the River Thames; and for enabling them to make a provision for such of themselves as shall be sick, lame or past their labour, and for their widows and orphans'. The legislation required the deduction of 2 shillings in the pound from the earnings of all registered coalheavers. The deductions were paid into a fund from which benefits were to be paid on the following scale: in sickness, 7 shillings weekly; in old age, 3s 6d weekly; funeral benefit, 40 shillings; widows benefit £5. If the funds available were inadequate to pay these sums, the benefits were scaled down.[1] According to the act itself the reason for its enactment was that the expense of maintaining sick and aged coalheavers and the widows of the dead 'fall heavily upon the parishes to which they respectively belong'. This legislative foray was not successful and in 1770 the act was repealed. There had been a series of frauds and the measure was said to have been ineffectual in dealing with the purposes for which it was designed.[2]

The second of these legislative essays was in 1792, when an Act was passed setting up a permanent fund for the relief of skippers and keelmen employed in the coal trade on the river Wear.[3] Here again, membership was compulsory and the income for the fund was to be levied on the quantity of coal transported, the maximum levy permitted being a half-penny per chaldron of coal carried in the keels. In discussing this Act, Eden felt that while it did not conform to what he called the first principle of friendly societies—that they should be governed by rules of their own devising to which the members had individually consented—it did at least allow the members the right to elect the stewards annually, and it was these who in their turn chose the guardians who ran the fund. He also pointed out that one of the most important functions of local friendly societies, for which the act obviously made no provision, was to bring men together to spend a convivial hour with their neighbours, and to hear what was often in Goldsmith's words 'much older than their ale' and generally as harmless,

[1] 31 Geo. II, c.76.s.4; Eden, *op. cit.*, pp. 605–7.
[2] 10 Geo. III, c.53.
[3] 32 Geo. III, c.29.

8

namely the news which had been collected by rustic politicians.[1] Eden was one of the very few writers on the problem of poverty at the end of the 18th century who saw strong objections to all compulsory schemes for friendly societies. Whatever benefit was intended for the poor, compelling them to subscribe was in effect taxing them. He added that in the existing difficult financial situation he could not imagine a severer tax 'than a twenty-fourth, or a thirty-sixth, of a man's daily earnings, imposed as a direct tax . . .' 'Why use force', asked Eden, 'when mutual convenience will probably make that palatable which legislative direction may render nauseous ?'[2]

By the end of the 18th century there may possibly have been several thousand local box clubs and friendly societies. Such evidence as there is indicates that there was a rapid growth during the last 40 years of the century. The increased rate of industrial development and the needs of a growing number of industrial workers may account for the quickening in the rate of growth.[3] There is no source of accurate statistical material relating to the societies in the 18th century but Eden's survey showed they had become very widespread. It is perhaps worth setting out Eden's conclusions in 1797 at this point. 'No institutions', he wrote, 'have ever made a more considerable progress in a short space of time than has been made within a few years by the benefit clubs or friendly societies. I regret that it is not in my power, to state either the number of such societies or the numbers of their respective members. This is an inquiry far beyond the powers of a single individual. As there, however, is not a district in the kingdom in which many societies are not found, the whole amount of their number must be very considerable. These societies do not owe their origin to Parliamentary influence; nor to private benevolence; nor even to the recommendations of men of acknowledged abilities, or professed politicians. The scheme originated among the persons on whom chiefly it was intended to operate: they foresaw how possible, and even probable, it was that they, in their turn, should ere long be overtaken by the general calamity of the

---

[1] Eden, *op. cit.*, pp. 614–15.
[2] *Ibid.*, p. 603.
[3] P. H. J. H. Gosden, *The Friendly Societies in England, 1815–1875*, 1961, p. 2.

times and wisely made provision for it. A stronger proof could not well be given to show that the great mass of the people, prompted only by what they themselves saw and felt, were convinced of the inefficacy of all legislative regulations and therefore resolved in at least one instance to legislate for themselves. Rejecting, as it were, a provision gratuitously held out to them by the public, and which was to cost them nothing (the Poor Law), they chose to be indebted for relief, if they should want it, to their own industry and their own frugality. And I would fain hope that I do not deserve to be set down as wanting in all due respect for Parliamentary wisdom if, in a case like this, I should declare my preference of the wisdom of the people. I cannot recollect any act of the legislature for many years that has either produced such important national advantages or been so popular as the institution and extension of friendly societies.'[1] Eden was convinced that the state should not attempt to regulate friendly societies, for if it did so 'the inclination of the labouring classes to enter them will be greatly damped, if not entirely repressed'.[2] In this he was entirely accurate in his observations, for in the next century even that mild form of state protection offered by registration was to be found objectionable by many members and even in the later 19th century, the Chief Registrar believed that there were probably as many members of unregistered as of registered societies.

[1] Eden, *op. cit.*, from the preface to vol. I.
[2] *Ibid.*, pp. 630–1.

Chapter Two

Friendly Societies in the early 19th century

I. The Local Societies

The most complete picture of the friendly societies in the nineteenth century is that given in the series of reports from the Royal Commission on Friendly and Benefit Building Societies which sat from 1871 until 1874.[1] The Commissioners classified friendly societies in seventeen groups of which the most significant were the affiliated societies or orders, the local societies in town and country districts, dividing societies and deposit friendly societies. The affiliated orders received most attention from the Royal Commission and during the middle and later years of the century were the predominant form of organization—although in the last two decades the deposit friendly societies grew very rapidly. During the thirty or forty years after 1800 the main form of friendly society organization was the local society.

[1] Four Reports from the Royal Commission appointed to inquire into Friendly and Benefit Building Societies, 1871-4 (Abbreviated hereafter as RCFS)
First Report, 1871, XXV.
Second Report and Evidence, 1872, XXVI.
Third Report, 1873, XXII.
Fourth Report, 1874, with Appendices, 1874, XXIII.
Reports of Assistant Commissioners, 1874, XXIII.

At no time in the nineteenth century is it possible to give entirely accurate figures for the total number of members of friendly societies or, indeed, for the total number of societies. Throughout there remained many societies which did not register and which made no returns of membership. The inquiries made by Eden in the course of his extensive survey of the condition of the poor and the replies sent in by parish overseers which were given in the Poor Law returns are the two most useful sources of information for the early years of the century. Eden estimated that there were about 7,200 societies with a total of 648,000 members in 1801.[1] Some confirmation of these figures is provided by the overseers whose returns produced a total of 9,672 friendly societies with 704,350 members in 1803.[2] Later figures from the same source show the growth of local friendly societies in the early part of the century. The overseers returned 821,319 persons as members of friendly societies in 1813, 838,728 in 1814, and 925,429 in 1815. These figures were said to indicate that nearly $8\frac{1}{2}$ per cent of the resident population were members of societies.[3] The somewhat fragmentary evidence which exists suggests that the average local society at this time probably had about a hundred members. Those with fewer than 40 or so appear to have been new foundations or clubs in a state of decline. According to the detailed information published by Eden in *The State of the Poor* very few societies had as many as 200 members. Local clubs usually had no rule limiting their size, but occasionally societies did specify a maximum number of members.[4]

[1] F. M. Eden, *Observations on Friendly Societies for the Maintenance of the Industrious Classes during Sickness, Infirmity, Old Age and other Exigencies,* 1801, p. 7. He found that 5,117 local clubs had been enrolled with magistrates under the Act of 1793 and added one-third (which was probably too small a fraction) to allow for unregistered clubs thus producing a total of 7,209. He also found that in 400 clubs there was an average membership of 97 and therefore took 90 as the average number of members for all societies—hence the total of 648,000 members.

[2] P.P. 1803–4, XIII, Abstract of answers and returns relative to the expense and maintenance of the poor.

[3] P.P. 1818, V, Report of the Select Committee on the Poor Laws, 1818, Appendix II. The figures returned by parish overseers need to be treated cautiously.

[4] Margaret D. Fuller, *West Country Friendly Societies,* 1964, p. 41.

By using both the Poor Law returns of 1815 and the percentage of persons in membership of the societies shown in the figures produced by the Select Committee of the House of Lords in 1831,[1] it is possible to get some idea of the distribution of friendly societies over the country as a whole. In view of its comparatively early industrial development it is not surprising to find that Lancashire had the highest proportion of its population in friendly societies, 17 per cent, taking the population at the 1821 census figure. The overseers' returns for 1815 had shown 147,029 members in that county, nearly twice as many as the next largest total, 80,684 for the West Riding. Apart from these two counties others where more than 10 per cent of the population belonged to friendly societies were Cornwall, Devon, Leicestershire, Monmouth, Nottingham, Shropshire, Staffordshire, and Warwick. Twelve counties had 5 per cent or fewer of their population in societies; Berkshire, Buckinghamshire, Cambridge, Dorset, Hereford, Kent, Lincolnshire, Norfolk, Oxford, Hampshire, Sussex, and Westmorland. The contrast between these two groups of counties helps to indicate the extent to which friendly societies developed more rapidly where there was at least some industry. An analysis of the situation in part of Nottinghamshire, for instance, in the early 19th century, showed that the friendly society movement spread outwards from the towns and industrial districts.[2] In the industrialized areas, working men were better able to afford the cost of friendly society membership and may have felt greater need to make this provision against sickness than those who worked on the land.

In the great majority of local societies, the members were drawn from a variety of occupations. An analysis of seven well-established societies in Sheffield about 1840 showed that the members were drawn from 79 trades, the largest group being 276 cutlers, and the next largest 107 grinders, but there were fewer than 20 members following any one of 63 of the trades listed.[3] In rural areas there was less variety in the occupations

[1] P.P. 1830–1, VIII, Report from the Select Committee of the House of Lords on the Poor Laws, 1831.

[2] J. D. Marshall, 'Nottinghamshire Labourers in the Early Nineteenth Century', *Transactions of the Thornton Society*, LXIV, 1960, p. 64.

[3] G. C. Holland, *The Vital Statistics of Sheffield*, 1843, pp. 211–13.

followed by members since the majority naturally were engaged in agriculture. Where a majority of the members of a local friendly society belonged to a single industrial occupation there was an obvious possibility that the society would become involved in industrial disputes. Some reports to the Home Secretary at the time of the Lancashire weavers' turn-out in 1808 claimed that in certain cases the weavers drew their financial support from friendly societies[1] although where they were in a minority they were evidently unable to do this.[2] Where for some reason local societies were confined to men of one particular trade, at times they developed into trade unions.[3]

The most important feature of the organization of the local societies was their complete independence. Each society had its own funds and was governed by its own rules as decided by the members. Even among those societies which registered in order to benefit from such advantages as the state offered, it proved impossible to enforce any strictly legal interpretation of their functions. Year after year Tidd Pratt, who was Registrar for much of the century, complained that the contributions of members in registered clubs were being spent on drink or on feasting so that financial stability was being undermined and the law broken. Many local societies never registered and if this put them outside the protection of the law, it also put their activities beyond the reach of magistrates and Registrar. Independent local societies were sufficiently flexible to meet the needs of members as they arose.

The officers of local societies were normally chosen by rotation, as in many early trade and working class organizations

---

[1] E.g. H.O. 42/95, 14 June 1808, R. A. Farington to Lord Hawkesbury, in Aspinall, *The Early English Trade Unions*, 1949, p. 102.

[2] *Ibid.*, 9 June 1808, R. A. Farington to Lord Hawkesbury, in Aspinall, *op. cit.*, p. 101.

[3] S. and B. Webb, *History of Trade Unionism*, 1907, p. 23; H.O. 42/133, Memorial respecting Combinations and Benefit Societies dated 27 May 1813 in Aspinall, *op. cit.*, p. 163. 'Your memorialists are fearful that much mischief has resulted from permitting any Benefit Society to be composed altogether of persons of one line of business to the exclusion of all other persons. It is by such exclusions that such Societies are enabled to promote illegal and dangerous measures with a safety and a secrecy that would never be attempted nor attained by mixed bodies.'

generally.[1] The period of office was frequently six months, sometimes a year and sometimes for less than six months. The Friendly Society of All Trades at Ryton, for instance, changed its stewards every twelve weeks.[2] Most of the management fell upon the two or four members designated as stewards. If a member refused to serve when his turn came round, the rules often provided for a considerable fine to be imposed. The custom of appointing the stewards by rotation continued in many local societies throughout the century. When the Armley Clothiers' Loyal and Friendly Society, a flourishing local club dating from 1860, revised its rules in 1894, the revised rules provided for eight stewards to be appointed annually 'who shall serve by rotation as they stand on the alphabetical role of members.' When a society had a president as well as stewards he seems usually to have been elected. The landlord of the alehouse at which the society met was often the treasurer in that he kept the box containing the funds. There was usually more than one lock so that no one key-holder could gain access to the funds on his own; typically there would be three locks, the key to one being held by the landlord and the keys to the other two by the stewards. The main exception to the principle of universal liability for service and appointment by rotation was for the office of clerk or secretary. Obviously this officer had to be able to read and write sufficiently well to keep the club's accounts. Sometimes it was necessary to appoint an outsider as clerk and a small honorarium was paid in some societies. As late as 1870 the Royal Commission noted the difficulty which many societies apparently experienced in finding a sufficiently literate secretary. Even among registered societies the state of the annual returns—or their complete absence year after year—indicated that many clubs had no one competent to act as clerk.[3]

The two financial benefits expected by a member from his local friendly society were a weekly allowance when he was sick, and a funeral payment for his widow. There are plenty of

[1] S. and B. Webb, *Industrial Democracy*, 1902, p. 7; Fuller, *op. cit.*, gives examples of the provision made by local friendly societies for the choice of Officers and their duties in the West Country.

[2] Articles of Agreement of the Friendly Society of All Trades, Ryton, Co. Durham, Article VI.

[3] P.P. 1872, XXVI, RCFS, Q.616, evidence of A. K. Stephenson.

examples of local societies founded in the late eighteenth century which survived until the twentieth, but there were also many which collapsed financially and left their members bereft of provision. Young's comment in 1874 about the local club, that 'as an organisation of thrift it has never been a healthy plant . . . ',[1] had plenty of evidence to support it. Most societies incorporated in their rules some sort of provisions to save them from the most obvious financial hazards. New applicants for membership had to be in good health at the time of joining, and they would not be 'free of the box' i.e. they would not qualify for benefit until they had paid contributions for a minimum stipulated period, often one or two years. Entry into the army or navy would naturally disqualify a man from benefit. No benefits could be claimed where a member was sick and unable to work as a result of his own folly, perhaps as a consequence of drunkenness or wrestling. It was quite usual for societies to exclude from membership men following occupations believed to have an unusually heavy incidence of sickness, such as coal-mining. The general practice was to offer full sick pay for a limited period such as three months followed by half-pay for another three months. The actual size of the weekly payment would depend on the contributions the members could afford and varied considerably from one society to another and from one part of the country to another. In general it was higher in industrial than in rural areas. The highest rate of sick benefit in rural areas often seems to have been about six shillings weekly while in some of the industrial centres ten shillings was usual. Similar variations occurred in the amount of funeral money. In the poorest societies this might be no more than £2 but in wealthier clubs in the larger towns as much as £10 was paid. As with sick pay, a minimum period of membership was normally required before a man became eligible for benefit while the rules of many societies did not permit the payment of funeral money where death was due to suicide.[2]

---

[1] P.P. 1874, XXIII Pt II, Report of Sir George Young, Assistant Commissioner to the R. C. appointed to inquire into Friendly and Benefit Societies, 1874, p. 16.

[2] The largest collection of rules of local friendly societies is that which the Registrar of Friendly Societies has accumulated over the years. When registration was transferred from local magistrates to the Registrar, many of the rules

The inability of many societies to pay the promised benefits, their financial exhaustion and collapse was the aspect of friendly society activity which probably most attracted the attention of statesmen, certainly by the middle years of the century. The financial stability of his society was obviously of vital importance to the individual member even though he expected non-financial benefits as well. Too many of those who joined local societies as young men found that by the time they reached middle age their society had broken up through lack of funds. Thus they had contributed during the years when they were unlikely to make any claim for benefit, only to find that when they most needed the help for which they had paid, there was no club to provide it. Once a man had passed the age of forty it was virtually impossible for him to join another society, since societies generally refused to admit new members who were unlikely to be able to contribute for some years before the increasing probability of sickness would make them a charge on the funds. The main cause of financial difficulty was simply a tendency to offer benefits larger than the contributions could support, even though contemporary accounts of the collapse of societies often set out accusations of mismanagement and improper expenditure of funds.

The two factors which governed the relationship between contributions and benefits were local custom and often a certain amount of competition. If a new society were to be set up where one or more clubs already existed it would need to appear to offer better value in order to attract members. The inducement to join sometimes took the form of offering full sick pay for a longer period, in other instances it took the form of spending a larger part of the monthly contribution in liquor on lodge night. It was undoubtedly of considerable advantage to an alehouse keeper to have a flourishing society meeting monthly at his house. There was the obvious profit which he made from supplying drinks on club night but there was also the value of

---

that had been enrolled with the J.P.s from 1793 were also transferred. Most of these are now in the keeping of the Public Record Office.

Two large collections which also include the rules of some unregistered societies are those in the British Museum and in the Goldsmiths' Library of the University of London.

ensuring that his clients did not need to go to a rival establishment in order to join a friendly society. If they had to do so, their custom might be lost not only on club nights but for the rest of the month as well to the inn at which their society met. Against this background it was hardly surprising that the Royal Commission reported that there were hardly any villages in the South of England where one or more clubs had not failed and disappointed their members within living memory.[1]

It was quite clear that when men joined a local society they were in no position to judge whether the relationship between its contributions and benefits was likely to make it financially sound. Since the society was run by the members it was equally clear that the management itself would have no clear understanding of likely liabilities. Faced with this situation, in 1819 the government required magistrates to refuse registration to any society until its tables and rules had been given a certificate of approval by 'two persons at least, known to be professional actuaries or persons skilled in calculations'.[2] This requirement was of little use. Those whose approval of tables was accepted by magistrates had insufficient understanding of what was or was not adequate. Six years later the Commons Select Committee on Friendly Societies described the requirement of the 1819 Act as useful in principle but difficult to apply because of the lack of data on questions of sickness and mortality, especially among the classes who joined friendly societies. In the absence of suitably qualified actuaries in the localities, the Committee reported that in many counties the magistrates had accepted the certificates of 'petty schoolmasters and accountants whose opinion upon the probability of sickness, and the duration of life is not to be depended upon'.[3]

The undeveloped condition of actuarial knowledge during the first half of the century meant that it was impossible to provide societies with safe tables. The earliest attempt at providing comprehensive tables of probability for sickness in the friendly societies had been made by Dr. Richard Price, a

---

[1] P.P. 1874, XXIII PE. I, RCFS, 4th Report, para. 227.
[2] 59 Geo. 3, c. 128, s.2.
[3] P.P. 1825, IV, Report of the Select Committee of the House of Commons on Laws respecting Friendly Societies, 1825, pp. 12–13.

mathematician and nonconformist divine, in the late eighteenth century.[1] These tables, sometimes called the Northampton tables, were much commended to local societies by the influential in the early years of the nineteenth century. Yet the rate of sickness assumed was much too low and societies adopting these tables did not thereby achieve financial stability. Further sets of tables prepared by Price's nephew, William Morgan, actuary to the Equitable Insurance Office and known as the 'Southwell' tables proved to be equally misleading.[2] In 1824 the Highland Society published tables based on its own experience and that of other societies dating back to 1751. Once more the tables were welcomed and commended for use as 'safe' by many of the influential. Yet there were fundamental differences between friendly society practices in Scotland and England which made the use of these tables a route to financial disaster for English societies whose actual sickness experience exceeded by from 32 to 37 per cent that provided for in the Highland Society's tables.[3] The Scottish societies were looked on largely as charitable organizations to which men did not turn for aid until their own private resources were exhausted. Moreover, many of them had very long waiting periods, sometimes as long as five years, before new members could claim sick benefit.

The Select Committee of 1825 warned that the adoption by societies of existing tables would be unlikely to guarantee financial safety. Members felt that the necessary data on which to base reliable tables for societies consisting of working men did not exist, and recommended that this problem should be referred to a new committee. The new committee recommended in 1827 that registered societies should be required to make returns of their experience at least every five years.[4] One section in the Act of 1829 dealing with friendly societies

[1] C. Walford, *Insurance Cyclopaedia*, 1870–78, vol. V, p. 386 summarises the assumptions on which these tables were based. The rate of sickness to the age of thirty-two was said to have been observed while the increase in the rate beyond that age was a matter for observation.

[2] J. Frome Wilkinson, *Mutual Thrift*, 1891, p. 83.

[3] F. G. P. Neison, *Contributions to Vital Statistics being a Development of the Rate of Mortality and the Laws of Sickness*, 1857 ed., p. 416.

[4] P.P. 1826–7, III, Report of the Select Committee of the House of Commons on Laws respecting Friendly Societies, p. 12.

adopted this recommendation by requiring registered societies to send a return of sickness and mortality experienced at the end of 1835 and after every subsequent period of five years to the Clerk of the Peace who had to transmit these returns to the government.[1] This became in retrospect one of the most important provisions ever enacted concerning friendly societies, replacing as it did the existing partial and incomplete material for the first time with data on which actuaries could base reliable tables.

Before this material became available, a set of tables based on information collected from English societies was completed by the actuary Charles Ansell in 1835. It was published by the Society for the Diffusion of Useful Knowledge[2] which had collected much information from local societies covering the period 1823-27. The Society had difficulty in selecting information largely because of the inadequate book-keeping in most societies; hence Ansell's work was based on an inadequate number of lives. His tables gave a considerably higher rate of sickness than that shown in earlier tables but even so F. G. P. Neison was to show in 1845 that, on the basis of data obtained from the government's returns for 1836-40, there was a true rate of sickness 19 per cent higher than that calculated by Ansell.

Even if sound tables had been available, based on sufficiently large samples of lives, to show contributions and benefits which would on average be safe, the membership of many small local societies might not be in any sense 'average'. When a society was established, those joining all tended to be in much the same bracket, below 35 or 40. For the first few years, other young men would join as they grew up and began to earn enough to be able to afford the contributions. But before long the original mass of members would grow old, and their periods of sickness would be increasingly frequent and expensive. Young men were reluctant to join societies whose members had a high average age, for they saw their contributions being used up to support the aged. Rather than join such a club,

[1] 10 Geo. 4, c.56, s.34.
[2] C. Ansell, *A Treatise on Friendly Societies in which the Doctrine of Interest of Money and the Doctrine of Probability are practically applied*, 1835.

there would be a strong temptation for the younger men to form a new one of their own. Only if the contributions of individual members had been carefully calculated to cover the whole of their liabilities—a rare condition indeed—could difficulties be avoided. There were very many instances of societies collapsing because they failed to attract young members to cover the deficiencies with their contributions.[1]

The need for a graduation of the size of contributions in accordance with the age at which a member joined was not understood before the development of an actuarial science. Even when the need was clearly seen by those who studied these matters, many local societies continued to charge a flat rate of contribution from all, regardless of the age of entry. Some clubs charged older entrants larger initial payments, but this could never be sufficiently large to cover in one payment the difference which should have been recovered through a graduated system of contributions related to the age of entry.

The legal complications which even registered societies encountered when they sought to protect themselves against dishonest officers were a further hindrance to the achievement of financial stability. The Select Committee of 1825 pointed out that the method of proceeding for a society was by an indictment at common law and that it would make the enforcement of the law much easier if the necessary powers were given for any two justices in petty sessions to issue an order freezing the affairs of a society and that anyone who broke such an order should be punished by summary process.[2]

As has already been noted, in the days of the Combination Acts some friendly societies with their membership confined to one trade became trade unions. Where this was not the case, societies in which the members of one trade predominated did collapse as a consequence of industrial disputes since the members fell back on their societies' funds to sustain them in their struggles. Colonel Fletcher reported from Saddleworth

[1] P.P. 1835, XXXV, First Report from the Commissioners on the Poor Laws, 1834, Appendix A, pp. 777, 783, 806, gives numerous instances of this happening in the West Riding. In Leeds, for example, where there were many societies, 'several have been broken up by young men failing to enter and keep up the funds'.

[2] P.P. 1825, IV, Report of the Select Committee on Friendly Societies, p. 21.

on 31 May 1817 that 'the weavers in several parts of the east-
ward of Manchester have meditated a turn-out or striking, and
have broken up some friendly societies, applying the money to
their maintenance during their absence from work.'[1] The same
point was made by many other observers including the members
of the Select Committee of 1825.

Undoubtedly the cause of financial difficulty which was
given most publicity by critics and moralists was the expenditure of money from the common box on drink. Local societies
used their funds quite openly for this purpose in the earlier
part of the century. In response to pressure from the Registrar,
some of the registered societies became more sophisticated as
the years went by and concealed this expenditure under more
acceptable headings in their accounts such as 'management
expenses' or 'room rent'. This custom was not, of course, confined to local societies. It was also still found to be widespread
in the affiliated orders by the Royal Commission in 1870. Those
who condemned the members of friendly societies for spending
on drink contributions calculated to cover sick and funeral
benefits were no doubt justified in the strictly financial sense in
their condemnations. On the other hand, while the working men
who joined the societies expected insurance against sickness
and death, they sought more than just this. They were also in
quest of those convivial activities and the enrichment of their
impoverished social lives which the friendly societies were
expected to afford and which the very name seemed to imply.

The great majority of local societies offered their members
three forms of social activity: club night every month, a feast
day every year—or sometimes every half-year—and the support
of the officers or members at the funeral of a deceased brother.
The funeral customs of societies will be discussed later, for it
was of course certainly not intended that they should form part
of the regular pattern of convivial activity in a society. The
basic provision of a monthly meeting at an inn along with an
annual feast was almost inevitably written into the rules of local
societies. The society of Friendly Brothers meeting at the
Duke's Head in Great Peter Street, Westminster, from 1808
might perhaps be taken as typical in this respect. According to

[1] H.O. 42/165, in Aspinall, *op. cit.*, p. 234.

the rules the members were to gather at the inn 'every fourth Tuesday throughout the year, as in the calendar, between the hours of eight and ten in the evening, from Lady-day to Michaelmas, and between the hours of seven and nine from Michaelmas to Lady-day'. Moreover in order 'to commemorate the institution of this society and to promote the unity of its members' they were to sup together in the month of August at such time and place as the stewards decided.[1]

The monthly meeting of the societies was far more than a business meeting to facilitate the collection of premiums. This was, no doubt, the main reason for gathering if the societies are thought of simply as agencies of mutual insurance. But since the convivial quality of the meetings was such a powerful attraction for members, the inevitable home for the gatherings was the working man's social centre, the inn. The landlord would provide the exclusive use of a room for the evening and in return would expect a certain amount of liquor to be purchased. In some local clubs this came out of the single monthly subscription, in others it was sometimes shown separately. Whether it was shown separately in the rules seems to have been a matter of local custom. In any event the payment of the full subscription was required of members and whether an individual was present or not his share of the cost of refreshment was collected and spent. The Articles of the Friendly Society at Breinton, dated 1807, required that every member contribute one shilling to the box and three pence to be spent adding that 'his 3d (whether present or absent) shall be spent every club night'.[2] The rules of some societies not only set out the sum which was to be spent on liquor for each member but also specify the landlord's duties in return, namely to provide a room for the meeting, to provide firing and candles 'from Michaelmas to Lady-day' and to keep the box.

There was much criticism of the meeting habits of local friendly societies from some of the clergy and others. The Vicar of Harrow published a booklet which dwelt on the allegedly evil

---

[1] *Rules and Orders to be observed by the Members of a Benefit Society called the Friendly Brothers, held at the Duke's Head, Great Peter Street, Westminster,* 1810.

[2] Quoted by F. C. Morgan, *Friendly Societies in Hertfordshire,* 1949, p. 6.

moral effects of their monthly gatherings, coming to the conclusion that such societies were 'pregnant with every possible mischief to society'.[1] These critics failed to understand how vital a role the cheerful club evenings played in attracting and holding members. After the Friendly Societies Act of 1829 some attempts were made to restrict these customs and the enforcement of this in parts of Devon was reported in 1834 as 'the cause of so many societies breaking up'.[2] Thus while plenty of cases existed where clubs spent so heavily on drink that they collapsed, attempts to restrict the merrymaking could apparently have much the same effect.

In general, the annual feast aroused less hostile comment. Here again this diversion from everyday toil was a provision which members expected of their societies, and the rules of local clubs almost invariably set out, often in some detail, the arrangements to be undertaken. It was quite customary for the day of the friendly society's feast to become a local holiday in smaller communities, both industrial and agricultural. 'Club day' was an event which came to include a procession, sometimes a religious service and often a fair, games, and amusements, as well as the feast itself.[3] The Registrar usually modified sets of rules submitted for his approval to exclude the payment of expenses from the stock of a society, but how far such a restriction was effective is dubious even in the case of the registered societies. The members of clubs usually paid a charge for their feast but this often seems not to have been intended to cover the whole cost.

Apart from the financial payment which became due on death, it was not surprising that societies which were essentially social bodies should provide for the stewards and some or all of the members to attend the funeral of a deceased colleague. Any steward or member who was required to attend a funeral but who failed to do so would normally have to pay a fine. Some

---

[1] J. W. Cunningham, *A Few Observations on Friendly Societies and their influence on Public Morals*, 1817.

[2] P.P. 1834, XXVIII, Report of the Poor Law Commission, 1834, Appendix A, p. 445.

[3] A full description of feast days in rural friendly societies may be found in Fuller, *op. cit.*, pp. 88–118; Alfred Williams, *A Wiltshire Village*, 1912, pp. 234–5, gives an understanding description of the annual club day at South Marston.

societies laid down items of dress which the club mourners were to wear while others found it sufficient to require that their members should merely appear clean and decent for the occasion. In some cases, societies purchased the symbols of mourning and appointed someone to take charge of them. The Society meeting at the house of Thomas Scott, Birtley, adopted a rule on 6 June 1812 ordering that the price of the mourning when let out was to be   'Great Pall,   5s
Little Pall,   3s
Cloaks,   4d each'.
One Sarah Peel was to have charge of these items.

Dividing societies were regarded by the Royal Commission as constituting a separate class from the ordinary local friendly societies, and by the 1870s this was a just assessment of the position. The very fact that they divided all or most of any fund they had accumulated at the end of each year, or sometimes after every two or five years, meant that they were unlikely to become as long-lasting as ordinary local clubs. Their original mutual insurance function was simply the desire of small groups of working men to subscribe to a fund in order to relieve distress among themselves in time of sickness for a stated term, usually a year, and at the end of the year to divide the balance among all the members. Those groups with a few new members added and without a few of the old members would often start a new club as soon as the fund of the old one had been divided, and repeat the process year by year. In a year of much sickness, there would be little or nothing to divide. In fact, clubs were faced with more sickness than their currently accumulating funds could meet at times so that they broke up in the course of the year and the members would have neither sick pay nor anything to divide. The absence of any permanent fund clearly made dividing societies very weak instruments of insurance.

Some early local friendly societies practised the division of part of their funds at stated intervals as an additional benefit or attraction to members to join. But the financial weakness and difficulties thus produced in societies which sought to be permanent led at times to the curtailment and abandonment of the custom. The attraction of dividing a goodly sized fund even though no division had originally been intended was too much of a temptation to members on occasions and on majority votes societies were dissolved so that the funds accumulated over the years could be shared out. When this occurred the losers were naturally the elderly members, too old to join any other society, and in greater need of the sick pay which the fund should have provided. The winners were the younger, newer members, who had paid less in contributions to the fund but generally received a share equal to that given to those who had been members for many years. Moreover, they were still young enough to join another society. In order to prevent this from happening, some societies adopted rules which weighted the votes of members if they were to decide on any dissolution in such a way as to give more votes to those who had been longest in membership. The rules of the Clothiers' Loyal and Friendly Society of Armley stated that it was not lawful to dissolve the society without the votes of $\frac{5}{8}$ths of the members, 'every one of whom shall have one vote, and for every 5 years that they shall have been in this Society they shall have as many votes, providing one member does not exceed 5 votes'. For good measure a further rule stated that 'No division whatever shall be made of the funds of this Society.'[1]

The typical local friendly society did not admit women to membership. Where a few of the 'county' societies, that is, those established and run by patrons,[2] admitted women as well as men, their rules excluded the payment of sick benefit during periods of pregnancy, for these were too frequent and would have been too expensive for societies to cover the cost involved.[3] Some societies solely for women emerged but they were very few in number. Such of them as were registered and made returns in 1872 had only 22,691 members while 17 counties apparently had no societies admitting women. While many women did, of course, work and earn wages, they were seldom the main breadwinners in their families and, quite apart from the social aspects of membership, in most working-class

---

[1] *The rules of the Clothiers' Loyal and Friendly Society held at the House of Mr. Thomas Durno, The Malt Shovel Inn, Armley, Leeds*, 1832, pp. 22–3, 25.

[2] *Infra*, p. 33.

[3] E.g. The Herefordshire Friendly Society had a mixed membership but made no payment to a mother during the month following childbirth—Morgan, *op. cit.*, p. 12.

families it would only be the principal breadwinner who would be seeking insurance against sickness. Besides, for most of the century the married woman suffered from the legal incapacity to acquire and hold earnings independently of her husband. From the moment she acquired any earnings they became the property of her husband. Eden examined the position of a number of female friendly societies and concluded that their objects could be and were 'entirely frustrated by the exercise of that legal authority with which a husband is invested. As he is entitled to receive his wife's earnings, he can not only prevent her from paying her regular subscription to the club; but if she falls sick, he is, I conceive, no less authorised by law to demand the allowance which is granted by the society, and to appropriate it to his own use.'[1] The main object of the early female societies was to provide benefit for the 'lying-in-month'. The Royal Commission was a good deal less understanding in its comments on these societies than Eden had been. The Commissioners were evidently offended by the habit the females shared with the males of meeting in alehouses and spending a fixed sum on liquor at each meeting. They commented that if the absolute prohibition of any sort of club was defensible, that of women's clubs meeting in public houses had most to be said for it.[2] In addition to following convivial practices associated with male societies, the societies for females also showed most of the other organizational and practical characteristics of societies for men. They used the same titles for their officers, seem to have chosen them in the same way, and to have given them similar duties.

II. The Beginning of the Affiliated Orders

The affiliated orders which had come to dominate the scene by the time the Royal Commission was appointed in 1870 had their traceable beginnings in groupings of local societies formed in the early years of the century. They expanded rapidly from the late 1830s and the orders which stood out were the Independent Order of Oddfellows, Manchester Unity, and the

[1] F. M. Eden, *The State of the Poor*, 1797, vol. I, p. 630.
[2] P.P. 1874, XXIII, PE. I, RCFS, 4th Report, para. 609.

Ancient Order of Foresters. The Oddfellows were the first to develop. The original lodge—as Oddfellows called their local societies—was the 'Abercrombie' and this was formed in Manchester about 1810. It took the initiative in opening other lodges in the area and by 1814 was referred to as the 'No. 1 Lodge'. Benevolent societies known as Oddfellows clubs existed in the 18th century.[1] Some of the historians of the Order have claimed the origins of Oddfellowship extend back to the ancient world.[2] The meaning of the word 'Oddfellow' has also been a matter of some speculation.[3] The early lodges of the Order in Manchester remained similar to local societies in their financial arrangements save that within a very few years they established a general funeral benefit into which all the lodges of the district paid their members' contributions for funeral benefit and on which they could draw as required to meet such costs. By 1820 the Order had spread into the West Riding and the Potteries and as the number of lodges increased, so the district organization was repeated, and the original pattern of district funeral and lodge sick funds became general.

The first corresponding general secretary of the Manchester Unity was appointed in 1816. The government of the Unity rested with the Grand Committee until 1827. This body was elected by lodges in the Manchester district only. This somewhat autocratic form of government led to difficulties with some of the new lodges outside the Manchester area, particularly with those in London which began a long line of secessions from the Manchester Unity by establishing the Improved Independent Order of Oddfellows, London Unity.[4]

[1] These 18th and early 19th century Oddfellows lodges were sometimes described as the 'free and easy' lodges. They preceded the growth of the Oddfellows as an organisation concerned with sick and funeral benefits. As late as 1817 the Loyal Northumberland County Lodge of Oddfellows adopted a set of laws for Oddfellows in Newcastle, Gateshead and Westgate which were entirely concerned with convivial activities. The only contribution was to be one penny each time a member attended a meeting. *Loyal Northumberland County Lodge of Oddfellows, Laws and Regulations*, instituted 28 April 1817, 1829.

[2] James Spry, *History of Oddfellowship: Its Origin, Tradition and Objects*, 1867.

[3] There is a discussion of this in R. W. Moffrey, *A Century of Oddfellowship*, 1910, chapter I.

[4] J. Frome Wilkinson, *Mutual Thrift*, 1891, p. 68.

A further split was threatened by the representatives of West Riding lodges gathered in Leeds, but a compromise was reached. By 1827 the form of central government which was to last for many years was established. This consisted of a Board of Directors elected by the Annual Moveable Committee, the latter being composed of delegates from all the districts. The district committees in their turn were composed of representatives from the lodges. This more democratic form of government undoubtedly did much to check the tendency of the various districts to secede and form their own unities, but a number of serious secessions were still to occur which were sometimes the result of differences of principle and policy. At the Annual Moveable Committee meeting held in Glasgow in 1838, the Manchester Unity was said to have 1,200 lodges with 90,000 members. Six years earlier the Unity had claimed to have 561 lodges with 31,000 members. The period of rapid expansion, which was to carry the I.O.O.F.M.U. to a membership of nearly 750,000 by the end of the century, had begun.

The origins of the Foresters have attracted myths and legends similar to those associated with the Oddfellows. From about 1813 the Royal Order of Foresters with its centre in Leeds began to make rapid progress and by the middle of 1834 over 350 courts, as the societies were known, had been established in the West Riding, Lancashire and Cheshire. Resentment of the 'despotic' powers claimed by the Leeds 'Perseverance' Court of the Royal Foresters over the Order led to a secessionist movement and the establishment of the Ancient Order of Foresters by a group of 297 delegates, representing the opposition, who met in Rochdale in August 1834. Within three months 294 courts transferred their allegiance to the Ancient Order and it was claimed at the first High Court meeting in Salford in 1835 that there were then 363 courts with 16,510 members. The oldest court in the A.O.F., the Court of Honour at Ashton-under-Lyne, was formed in 1814 and had been Court No. 4 of the Royal Order before the 1834 secession.[1] The period of most rapid growth of the A.O.F. and of the

[1] The main source for the early history of the Ancient Order of Foresters is 'An Historical Sketch of the Order' by T. B. Stead in the *Annual Directory of the A.O.F.*, 1891.

numerous smaller orders came in the middle years of the century.

III. *The Government and the Societies*

The attitude of some of the governing and influential groups to friendly societies was coloured at the opening of this period by fears of possible subversion of a revolutionary nature. Even among those who did not share these lively fears there was much anxiety about the possibility of the societies committing more social evil than they did good unless carefully guided and controlled. It has already been noticed that the convivial habits of the societies attracted a good deal of hostile criticism. It was undoubtedly the first of these fears which excited most political feeling.

In an era when the Combination Acts were regarded as an essential defence against revolutionary upheaval, the friendly societies seemed to offer an obvious way round the difficulties placed in the way of combination for trade union purposes. The toleration given by the law to benefit societies provided a useful shelter for trade unions which could hold their meetings under cover of the exemption from the Combination Acts afforded to the societies.[1] Governments were certainly aware of this danger and from time to time acted against trade unions calling themselves friendly societies. Perhaps the best-known case of this was the prosecution of the group of agricultural labourers from Tolpuddle, Dorset, in 1833, whose society called itself The Friendly Society of Agricultural Labourers.

Fear of the political potential of any organizations which were composed of working men was to be found in what might be called the friendly society enthusiasts among the influential classes as well as in those entirely hostile to the societies. In his pamphlet published in 1801, *Observations on Friendly Societies*, even Eden felt obliged to enter a suitable *caveat*. Association was the prevalent malady of the times and in all cases its real object needed to be ascertained and its progress watched closely by those entrusted with the government of the country.

---

[1] Aspinall, *op. cit.*, p. xxiv.

Another supporter and would-be reformer of the societies was Thomas Courtenay. In March 1819 he sought leave in the Commons to introduce a bill aimed at strengthening the societies' finances by getting them to conform to tables of contributions and benefits which were to be drawn up by two or three London actuaries. In the course of his speech he remarked that it had frequently been asserted that benefit societies had been made the pretext for meetings whose real purpose was to enable workmen to combine for illegal purposes. He believed that the measures he proposed would at least make these practices more difficult, adding that 'these combinations could not be prevented even though friendly societies which were innocent in their purposes were to lose the protection of the law.'[1] As late as 1825 the Government of the day contemplated enacting a measure which would have had the effect of suppressing the great majority of friendly societies as well as the newly-permitted trade unions. Huskisson, under pressure from shipowners and builders, decided to introduce a bill which the shipping interests had drafted, that included a provision to forbid the subscription of any funds to a trade or any other form of association unless a magistrate both approved of its objects and became its treasurer.[2]

Of all the friendly societies, the early affiliated orders caused most anxiety to some of the ruling classes since these, with their secret ritual, passwords, and widespread coverage of industrial areas appeared to be specially suited to behave as revolutionary corresponding societies. The orders did, in fact, grow in spite of their illegality in terms both of the Corresponding Societies Act[3] which rendered all societies with branches illegal and the Seditious Meetings Act[4] which prohibited certain meetings of more than 50 persons if held without notice. Even in 1848 the Select Committee of the House of Lords which had been appointed to inquire into the legislation that would be required to enable the Manchester Unity to register found that certain customs which were in use in the

[1] *Parliamentary Debates*, XXXIX, 1159–61, 25 Mar. 1819.
[2] S. and B. Webb, *History of Trade Unionism*, 1902 ed., p. 95.
[3] 39 Geo.3, c.79.
[4] 57 Geo. 3, c.19.

lodges of the Order—such as the circulation of lectures,[1] the employment of secret signs and the giving of orations after the burial service—were open to very serious objections and the Order as a whole would become highly dangerous if it should ever be turned from its legitimate objects.

Even while fears of the possible political consequences of friendly societies remained serious, members of the influential classes were active in putting forward schemes designed to improve the security of the insurance offered by the societies and to use the societies to relieve the expense and burden of the maintenance of the poor through the existing parish relief system. In 1796 Pitt had put forward proposals for a bill which would have compelled the poor to contribute to parochial sick clubs that would pay benefits to the sick and aged, the benefits being supplemented if necessary from the poor rate. These proposals were not novel and a series of rather similar schemes were also put forward in and out of Parliament over the next 30 years.[2] A scheme containing some unusually far-reaching proposals was outlined to the House of Commons in 1816 by Curwen. This was based upon his experience in Workington and Harrington collieries where for 33 years the workmen had a compulsory subscription of 6d weekly to a fund for mutual support, the employer adding one-third to the sum collected. Benefits were paid in cases of accidents, sickness or death of parents or children. The scheme was managed by a committee of workmen. On this experience Curwen proposed a national

---

[1] The objections of some clerical members of the House of Lords to these lectures was that as they had been written by an atheist—George Holyoake—they must themselves have been atheistic.

[2] Among the better-known schemes were those from P. Coloquhoun, *Treatise on Indigence*, 1806, which involved parochial benefit societies; from Jerome de Salis, *A Proposal for Improving the System of Friendly Societies*, 1815, which called for a poor assurance office run by the overseer in each parish; from a Select Committee of the Commons on the Poor Law in 1817 which urged a system of District Parochial Benefit Societies, and from Thomas Courtenay, who introduced a bill into the Commons in 1819 to set up parochial benefit societies and to compel resort to them by refusing parochial relief to those who had not become members. Courtenay explained that many persons thought this mode of providing for the wants of the poor so desirable that its operation ought not to be left to the voluntary acts of individuals. *Parliamentary Debates*, XXXIX, 1161, 25 Mar. 1819.

scheme with workmen contributing $\frac{1}{30}$th of their wages and each employer 1d weekly for each employee and 1d per head from rateable property. He calculated that this would produce £9,000,000 annually. The fund would be managed by 14,000 local committees elected by labourers, employers and persons of consequence for the relief of sickness, age, misfortune, educational needs and for all that was 'conducive to the comfort and happiness of the labouring classes'.[1]

Some of the country gentry and clergy who took an interest in social questions thought that the answer to the problem of security against sickness and death might be provided through societies controlled by themselves. An attempt was made to systematize this sort of society on a county basis, hence as a class these came to be known as county societies although many of them covered areas much smaller than geographical counties, such as the hundred or the poor law union. The earliest of this class of society to be founded was the Essex Provident in 1818. Hampshire County Society was set up in 1825 and those for Wiltshire[2] and Kent three years later. The largest of these in 1871 was the Essex Provident with 9,315 members, the second and third largest the Wiltshire and Hampshire Societies with 7,130 and 6,322 members respectively. Most of the other county societies numbered their members in hundreds rather than thousands. The rules for the management of these societies provided for two classes of members, honorary and benefit, and normally gave a majority of places on the governing committee to representatives of the honorary members. Societies of this type were mainly confined to the southern half of England. There was really no place for them in the industrialized areas and with the spread of the affiliated orders to the rural parts of the southern counties towards the end of the century, even such membership as they had achieved began to fall away. The four largest had a total of 22,921 members in

[1] *Parliamentary Debates*, XXXIV, 878–901, 18 May 1816.
[2] An extract from a cutting now in a scrapbook in the Museum of the Wiltshire Archaeological and Natural History Society at Devizes and quoted in Margaret Fuller, *op. cit.*, p. 20, summarizes neatly the aims of the founders '. . . it is only reasonable to expect Pauperism will eventually be lessened and the labouring classes be raised to that state of comparative independence, which is so essential to their moral character and necessary to the well-being of the society.'

1871 but only 18,888 by 1885.[1] The insurance these societies offered was sound and attractive but the absence of the traditional club night and the patronizing nature of the societies themselves, meant that they never became sufficiently attractive to occupy a large place in friendly society provision.

The series of acts concerned with friendly societies which were passed over the period from 1793 until 1829 were all designed with the general aims of encouraging the societies in order to relieve demands on the poor rate, while ensuring that registration with and supervision by the local magistrates would serve to check any tendency to support illegal combinations or to help trade unions. Towards the end of this first period, the legislature showed increasing signs of concern over the financial stability of the societies. All other considerations apart, if they were to be effective agents in lessening the calls on the poor rate, stability was essential. From the 1830s in this, as in other social questions, the aims foremost in the minds of those who governed changed considerably and later legislation concerning the societies reflected this.[2]

The preamble to the Act of 1793[3] suggested that the formation of societies with rules approved by the magistrates would both promote the happiness of individuals 'at the same time diminishing the public burthens'. The measure was introduced by George Rose. It declared that it should be lawful for persons to form themselves into societies of good fellowship for the purpose of raising a fund for their mutual relief in old age and sickness. No society should be deemed to be within the meaning of the act until its rules had been approved by the justices in quarter sessions. The main advantages which the act held out to societies which had their rules approved were, firstly, the security for their funds which the ability to sue and to be sued brought with it. This enabled them to protect themselves against dishonesty in treasurers or other custodians of their money. Secondly, any member who could produce a certificate of membership was not to be removable to his place of legal settlement unless he became actually chargeable. Other benefits

[1] Frome–Wilkinson, *op. cit.*, p. 169.
[2] *Infra*, pp. 63–5.
[3] 33 Geo. 3, c.54.

34

included exemption from some stamp duties and priority for a society's claim for any of its funds in the possession of a bankrupt or deceased officer. Although the Act began by appearing to make the formation of friendly societies lawful, the right of associating for mutual support had not previously been *un*lawful, nor did it become so in 1793 for any societies which did not register their rules at quarter sessions.[1] From the passing of Rose's Act dated the division of societies into two groups, those which found the advantages conferred by registration sufficient of an inducement to enrol and those which preferred not to seek the approval of quarter sessions for their rules and which therefore were unable to enjoy the legal advantages thus conferred.

At the time the measure of exemption from the laws of settlement then in force must have been a strong inducement to registration. The most important long-term advantage was the right to sue and therefore to protect a society's funds. In the eyes of the law, unregistered societies remained simply partnerships. This meant that unless all the 'partners' acted together, they could not resort to law. If one or more of the 'partnership' made off with the funds, it was hardly likely that this offending minority would join with those they had cheated to bring a case against themselves. Until the passing of Russell Gurney's Act in 1868, a member of an unregistered society could not be charged in criminal proceedings for embezzling its funds, being himself a partner.[2]

While the Savings Bank Act of 1817[3] gave registered societies the right to deposit their funds in savings banks at a favourable rate of interest, the next major legislation was the Act of 1819.[4] This measure extended to friendly societies the right previously conferred upon savings banks of investing directly with the Commissioners of the National Debt, but it was mainly concerned with the achievement of the same ends as

[1] The Select Committee on Friendly Societies of 1825 pointed this out in its Report.

[2] 31 & 32 Vict., c.116. Section I stated that 'If any person, being a member of any co-partnership etc. . . . shall steal or embezzle any such money etc. . . . of or belonging to the co-partnership . . . every such person shall be liable to be dealt with . . . as if such person had not been or was not a member of such co-partnership or one of the beneficial owners'.

[3] 57 Geo. III, c.130.

[4] 59 Geo. III, c.128.

the Act of 1793 and may be seen as a re-inforcement of both the aims and methods of that act. The preamble again explained that the purpose of the measure was to relieve the heavy burden on the poor rate of maintaining so many poor, at the same time improving the moral habits of the poorer classes by persuading them to rely on 'the fruits of their own industry'. The financial unsoundness of many societies registered under the 1793 act led to the magistrates now being required not only to approve the rules of a society but also its tables. The justices might only confirm the latter after they had been approved 'by two persons at the least, known to be professional actuaries or persons skilled in calculation'. Before agreeing to the enrolment of any new society, the justices were also directed to consider whether it was really necessary, having regard to the number of societies already in existence in the district. Competition between clubs was regarded as a cause of financial weakness which magisterial supervision might thus help to overcome.

The last friendly society legislation of the paternalist era was very largely the outcome of the investigations of the Select Committees of 1825 and 1827 which showed that the more elaborate requirements for enrolment imposed in 1819 were of little practical value. The increased complication of the requirements had led to a falling-off in the number of applications made and the legal privileges offered were too expensive at the price to be paid. The Act of 1829[1] modified the procedure for registration by requiring the rules of societies to be confirmed by the barrister appointed to certify the rules of savings banks before being submitted to quarter sessions. While the justices' certificate still remained the legal evidence of registration, the elaborate provisions for the approval of tables enacted in 1819 were dropped, and a general provision replaced them which merely required the justices to be satisfied that the tables might be adopted with safety. The adoption of the recommendation of the Select Committee of 1827 that regular returns of sickness and mortality experience be required from societies was certainly the most forward-looking provision in the Act.[2] The actual requirement was that these returns should be made to

[1] 10 Geo. IV, c.56.
[2] *Supra*, p. 19.

the local clerk of the peace who would transmit them to the central government. Thus, there was still no direct contact between the societies and the Government, and they remained within the administrative sphere of quarter-sessions.

One way of assessing the reaction of the governed to the measures taken by the state concerning friendly societies would be to study the proportion of societies which were registered at different times and which were thus prepared to pay the price required for the privileges granted. Unfortunately, it is quite impossible to obtain figures of this sort. When the Government itself tried to obtain overall figures, great difficulties were encountered. Many of the parish officers who were directed to make inquiries concerning the number of societies and members in 1813, 1814 and 1815 commented in their returns that the stewards and clerks of societies had 'refused to give any account of the number of members contained in such societies'. In some cases the basis of the reluctance to give figures may have been that the societies were really trade unions evading the Combination Acts, but much more often genuine fear and misunderstanding of the intentions of the Government would have been a likely reason for reluctance.

Quite apart from the general failure of the state to appreciate the importance of the social and convivial activities of societies to their members, the width of the gap in understanding between the government and the governed may be illustrated only too clearly from incidents in the history of friendly societies at this time. In 1819, Wilbraham Bootle asked a question in the Commons which he described as being 'of great importance to the labouring people of Lancashire'. This was, 'Would the Chancellor of the Exchequer contradict the rumour that the government was about to seize the funds of friendly societies and savings banks and apply them to the payment of the national debt?' The report had already caused the break up of a number of friendly societies. After the Chancellor had denied that the Treasury had any such intention, Brougham interjected that this was not the only time when such reports had been circulated.[1] After the Act of 1829 it was reported that nine out of the eleven friendly societies in Liskeard had broken

---

[1] *Parliamentary Debates*, XLI, 1391, 21 Dec. 1819.

up since some members feared that the Government was after their money and they did not like the management to be taken out of their own hands.[1] To the extent that legislation from the 1830s came to reflect the feeling that the Government should not try to intervene to control friendly societies through the local magistrates, it was nearer to meeting the wishes of the governed.

[1] P.P. 1834, XXVIII, Poor Law Report, 1834, Appendix A, p. 445.

Chapter Three

The emergence of the affiliated orders, 1835-75

I. Growth and distribution

'While the small bodies are decaying or sinking into neglect, the affiliated bodies are growing rapidly in strength, and extending their branches into every part of the kingdom.'[1] In this sentence the Lord's Select Committee described accurately the course of friendly society development from 1835 to the Royal Commission 1870–74. The Commissioners spoke of them as the best organized of all societies invented by working men to meet their needs and found that they deserved the first place which had come to be assigned to them.[2] The fact that for the first part of the period during which this quite remarkable growth occurred the affiliated orders had been unable to register and to take any advantage of the benefits held out to registered societies forms an interesting commentary on the attitude of contemporary working men to the state.

In 1872 there were 34 societies described as affiliated orders which had more then 1,000 members each. Their total membership amounted to 1,282,275, of which about two-thirds was

[1] P.P. 1847–8 XXVI, Report from the Select Committee of the House of Lords on the Provident Associations Fraud Prevention Bill, p. 4.

[2] P.P. 1874, XXIII, Pt. I, RCFS, 4th Report, para. 94.

represented by the Manchester Unity of Oddfellows (426,663) and the Ancient Order of Foresters (388,872). None of the other affiliated societies approached these two either in size or from the point of view of organization and development. The largest of these other orders were the Grand United Order of Oddfellows (71,000), the Order of Druids (57,000), the Loyal Order of Ancient Shepherds, Ashton Unity (46,000), the Nottingham Ancient Imperial Order of Oddfellows (40,000) and the National Independent Order of Oddfellows (35,000). The total number of affiliated societies of all sizes in existence in 1877 was 163.[1] The Royal Commission found that some of these orders possessed few reliable statistics concerning their membership, local secretaries apparently lacking the degree of business sophistication required to make returns when called for.

The many smaller societies which took the title of Oddfellow (34) or Forester (5) might perhaps be thought thereby to have been paying a considerable tribute to the standing of the two great orders which have those names. Some were the products of schismatic movements, such as the National Independent Order of Oddfellows which broke from the Manchester Unity and became independent in 1845. The Nottingham Ancient Imperial was another dissentient from the Manchester Unity. Apart from the Manchester Unity and the Ancient Order of Foresters, none of the other affiliated societies had achieved a full national coverage by the 1870s. The membership of the larger ones was concentrated overwhelmingly in Lancashire and the West Riding of Yorkshire.

The schisms that occurred within the Manchester Unity and the Ancient Order of Foresters were often due to attempts by their leaderships to make the societies more businesslike and more reliable as insurers. This was the cause of the formation of the National Independent Order of Oddfellows. The Annual Moveable Committee of 1844 asked lodges to send in returns of funds and members in order to have the data on which to base sound tables. Some lodges feared the directors were trying to

---

[1] See C. Walford, *The Insurance Cyclopaedia*, 1870–8, vol. IV, pp. 533ff. for the full list.

take over the funds or even sell the information to the government. Consequently they refused to make the returns and were suspended. The following year the Annual Moveable Committee attempted to carry out some financial reforms, a number of lodges objected and the schism of 1845 took place.[1]

Because of this increasing attention to the matter of making returns in both the Manchester Unity and the Foresters, it becomes possible to obtain continuous series of reliable annual membership figures for both of these orders from the middle of the century.[2] It is possible to build up annual series of figures showing the numbers of lodges and courts for the earlier period from the directories published by the orders. The central organizations knew from the beginning the number of dispensations they had granted for the formation of local lodges or courts from year to year and were in this respect less dependent on obtaining accurate returns from local secretaries.

From 1864 to 1870 the A.O.F. figures relate to December of the previous year, and in other years to January 1 of the year stated.

These overall figures indicate clearly the earlier growth of the Manchester Unity by comparison with the Foresters. They also serve to indicate that the growth did not show a pattern of steady increase. In the case of the Oddfellows, for instance, the annual number of new members since 1848 varied from 4 to 9 per cent, losses by death from 1 to 1.3 and of withdrawals from 3 to 5.50.[3] Apart from schisms and internal political upheavals, fluctuations in the national economy had a direct effect on the expansion of the orders. The Forester's figures for 1848 and 1849 show an actual drop in membership of 4,000 at a time when there was much unemployment and a trough in the trade cycle. There was a drop in the membership of the Oddfellows at the same time, perhaps due in part to the internal troubles of

---

[1] C. Hardwick, *A Manual for Patrons and Members of Friendly Societies*, 1859, p. 40. The total number of lodges lost to the M.U.O.F. between 1848 and 1875 formed the considerable total of 1,215 according to F. G. P. Neison, 'Some Statistics of the Affiliated Order of Friendly Societies', *J. Statistical Society*, XL, 1877, p. 58.

[2] The M.U.O.F. dismissed a dishonest Corresponding Secretary in 1848 and his refusal to hand the Unity's earlier records to his successor has resulted in the loss of much early material.

[3] Neison, *op. cit.*, p. 49.

Table 3.1.

Total membership of the Manchester Unity of Oddfellows and of the Ancient Order of Foresters, 1848-70.

Year	M.U.O.F. Members	A.O.F. Members
1848	249,261	84,472
1849	234,490	80,490
1850	224,878	80,089
1851	229,040	84,348
1852	222,194	89,875
1853	225,001	94,323
1854	231,228	100,556
1855	239,783	105,753
1856	251,008	114,020
1857	262,883	125,423
1858	276,254	135,001
1859	287,575	148,562
1860	305,241	168,576
1861	316,215	189,584
1862	335,145	207,993
1863	342,953	228,026
1864	358,556	250,703
1865	373,509	277,746
1866	387,990	301,077
1867	405,255	321,253
1868	417,422	336,791
1869	425,095	349,022
1870	434,100	361,735

Sources: *List of Lodges of the M.U.O.F.*, published annually.
Annual Directory, published by the A.O.F.

that order in the late 1840s, but also reflecting the state of the economy. When money was getting tighter for working-class households in the later 1860s resignations from the Oddfellows reflected this as they grew steadily from 1864 to 1869 and did not really begin to fall again until 1871.[1] The chief officers of the Oddfellows were certainly well aware of the effect of the

[1] E. J. Hobsbawm, *Labouring Men*, 1964, p. 135; Neison, *op. cit.*, pp. 42ff.

state of trade and the demand for labour on the affiliated orders.[1]

The Manchester Unity's most rapid decade of expansion as indicated by the foundation of lodges still in existence at the time of the Royal Commission was between 1835 and 1845 when 1,470 of the 3,074 active 30 years later were founded. These years were difficult for working men and it is worth noticing that in addition to the Manchester Unity other working-class organisations for self-help or self-defence grew rapidly at this time including the Chartists and the Primitive Methodists. The events flowing from the Poor Law Amendment Act were a significant cause of the expansion of friendly society activity.[2]

The Unity's earlier growth was centred on Lancashire and the West Riding. Although by 1895 it had lodges in virtually every county, about a half were in Lancashire and Yorkshire. The picture 30 years later had changed in that many more lodges had been established in the south and by 1876 it was growing much more vigorously there than in the north.[3] A comparison of the number of lodges in each county in 1845 and 1875 indicates that there had been a considerable decline in the industrial areas. In Lancashire there had been 737 in 1845 but by 1875 there were 507; in Yorkshire there had been 600 but 30 years later there were only 444. Other counties in which the number of lodges had declined included Stafford, Warwicks, Cheshire and Derbyshire.

There were two main reasons for this decline in the industrial areas. The first was the internal constitutional and political struggle which followed the decisions taken by the directors and the Annual Moveable Committee to require regular returns and generally to strengthen the control of the order over individual lodges. A considerable number of the older-established lodges

---

[1] *Oddfellows Magazine*, New Series, January 1859, p. 45.
The impact of cyclical unemployment on the Manchester Unity and the Foresters is discussed in P. H. J. H. Gosden, *The Friendly Societies in England, 1815–75*, 1961, App. F., pp. 237–43.
[2] *Infra*, pp. 69–71.
[3] J. M. Baernreither, *English Associations of Working Men*, 1889 ed., p. 373.
In 1876 the Unity had 136,000 members in the southern counties, 110,000 in the midlands and 166,000 in the north.

left the Manchester Unity and either joined smaller unities or formed new ones. It has already been noticed that the main strength of these other orders of Oddfellows lay in Lancashire and Yorkshire. Considering their origin or mode of expansion the independence shown by their individual lodges and the weakness of their central governments as portrayed in the Report of the Royal Commission is not surprising. The second main cause of the decline in the number of lodges in these counties was that found in many local societies; insufficient income to pay for the promised benefits with the consequent collapse of lodges through the exhaustion of their funds. The rates of contribution and of sickness benefit had been a matter for arrangement in each lodge—only the funeral fund was conducted on a district basis—and the determining factor of both rates had been very largely local custom in the older lodges. It could hardly have been otherwise since even if lodges had sought to adopt reliable tables in the early days there were none. Moreover, many of the early lodges were small and the financial unsoundness of small numbers was a recognized insurance hazard. The larger the numbers over which risks and liabilities could be averaged, the more chance there was of achieving a satisfactory result. The average number of members in Lancashire lodges was 87 in 1845, in Yorkshire it was 75. Thirty years later it was 122 in the first case and 132 in the second. By 1875 the average number of members per lodge for the whole country was 132, whereas in 1845 it was probably about 70.[1]

There were few major differences between the development of the Oddfellows of the Manchester Unity and the Foresters. Both orders experienced much the same problems and successes although the growth of the Ancient Order of Foresters came a few years later than that of the Manchester Unity. The central government of the Foresters was the weaker of the two and although this was in various ways disadvantageous yet it produced rather fewer secessions. The High Chief Ranger, the Executive Council and the annual High Court Meeting were the opposite numbers of the Grand Master, the Board of Directors and Annual Moveable Committee of the Manchester

---

[1] Gosden, *op. cit.*, App. D., pp. 231–4.

Unity. One of the most significant differences between the orders was the custom the Foresters practised of moving the seat of government every year with a tendency for the central government itself to consist of persons drawn from the locality in which it happened to be situated. The obvious advantage of this arrangement was that no group or area appeared to be able to gain permanent control and this practice may be found among other contemporary working-class organizations. The main drawback of the system was that the efficiency of the central organization suffered; it lost the benefit of the continued services of its most experienced members. It was impossible for the membership of an Executive Council which varied as much as that of the Foresters to become as well known nationally to the membership as the directors of the Manchester Unity. Consequently they tended to be entrusted with less power and authority.[1] When the younger Neison issued in 1882 the report the Order had commissioned from him on its rates of mortality and sickness, he commented on the difficulties which had arisen from the obligation to move the actual offices of the Foresters each year. His work had had to be undertaken in Sheffield, Dublin and Northampton in turn and each move involved the engagement and training of almost a new staff.[2] The Royal Commission considered that the Foresters had paid a high price for their weaker central organization in that they had achieved a financial position greatly inferior to that of the Manchester Unity. No attempt was made to enforce particular scales of contributions on individual courts before the 1870s, but the increase in the average size of courts from 45 members in 1845 to 114 in 1875 would have helped the actuarial position of many of them.

The distribution of the courts of the Foresters in the different counties followed broadly the pattern of the Manchester Unity lodges. In 1845 by far the largest number were in Yorkshire (383) and Lancashire (332). By 1875 the number of courts was showing a tendency to decline in both of these counties: in Yorkshire there were 370 and in Lancashire 357, the latter figure being higher than in 1845 but showing a fall

---

[1] P.P. 1874, XXIII, Pt. I, RCFS, 4th Report, para. 147.
[2] F. G. P. Neison, *Rates of Mortality and Sickness in the A.O.F.*, 1882, p. 9.

from the 384 courts which were affiliated to the Order in 1865. A significant difference between the two orders was the faster rate of growth shown by the Foresters in the largely agricultural southern and western counties. The courts tended to charge lower rates of subscription and benefit than did the Odd-fellows lodges, thus they were better suited to the means of working men in the predominantly rural areas where low wage rates prevailed. The exceptionally rapid progress made by the Foresters in the agricultural regions in the decade following 1858 may be seen in the figures in Table 3.2. Since individual courts still fixed their own rates of contribution and benefit, it was possible for them to admit local village societies as courts without any change in the existing scales. The high level of initiations was thus achieved at rates of payment out of all proportion to the burden entailed. The contributions demanded were in nine cases out of ten barely adequate for the youngest age eligible for admission and altogether insufficient for the older entrants.[1] Moreover, the changing situation shown in Table 3.2 certainly owed something to the rise in the money wages of labourers between 1858 and 1873.[2]

The fact that it was the better-paid working men who were first attracted to the affiliated orders was particularly true in the case of the Manchester Unity. The proportion of the membership of the Unity drawn from among such occupations as blacksmith, bricklayer, carpenter, miner, plumber, printer, stonemason, tailor and woollen and cotton manufacture was well above the proportion of males working in these occupations in 1851. On the other hand the proportion of rural labourers was far below the proportion of males employed in this way.[3] The geographical distribution of lodges and courts provides additional evidence that the orders rose and grew most readily among the better-paid workers brought together in the industrial areas.

Apart from being suited to the wages of industrial workers, another feature which the orders were able to offer them was

---

[1] F. G. P. Neison, 'Some Statistics of the Affiliated Orders of Friendly Societies', *J. Statistical Society*, XL, 1877, p. 70.
[2] J. H. Clapham, *An Economic History of Modern Britain*, vol. II, p. 286.
[3] Gosden, *op. cit.*, p. 75.

Table 3.2.

A.O.F. membership in some predominantly agricultural regions, 1858–67.

Counties	Number of Members	
	January 1858	December 1867
Surrey, Sussex, Kent Hants., Berks.	8,390	34,078
Essex, Suffolk, Norfolk.	5,587	14,342
Wilts., Dorset, Devon, Cornwall, Somerset	1,338	13,076

Source: F. G. P. Neison, 'Some Statistics of the Affiliated Orders of Friendly Societies', *J. Statistical Society*, XL, 1877, pp. 64–7.

some provision for mobility. The need for this was more likely to be appreciated by industrial workers than by those who had often not moved beyond their native rural villages. Both the Oddfellows and the Foresters developed a system of clearances by which a member who was moving could obtain a clearance certificate showing that he had met all liabilities to his existing lodge or court and present this to the lodge or court in his new district. By 1870 the Manchester Unity was granting between 600 and 1,000 clearances annually and the Foresters rather more than 1,000. The main restriction on this was that it was not open to members over 40 years of age.[1] As an alternative there was a system by which members could remain in their original lodge or court and arrange to have their contributions and benefits remitted through a local lodge in the new district.

A form of benefit which was more important in some trade unions than in the affiliated orders was travelling relief paid to members travelling or 'tramping' in search of employment. Carpenters, shoemakers, blacksmiths and tailors were well-represented in the Manchester Unity and practised the custom

[1] F. G. P. Neison, *op. cit.*, p. 78.

47

of tramping.[1] This benefit therefore made its appeal among these predominantly urban groups. The number of payments made and the total sums involved varied with the state of the employment market.[2] In the Manchester Unity a member could draw a travelling card which he presented at any lodge for his travelling allowance, lodges reclaiming the total sum thus paid out from central funds. The Foresters issued a licence and a number of cheques for presentation at courts, relief usually being 1s 3d per day. The custom of tramping had much declined by the end of the century.[3]

During the debate on Gladstone's Government Annuities Bill in the Commons in 1864, Sotherton Estcourt showed perhaps unusual understanding among members in saying that he did not believe that the working classes entered friendly societies for the sake of financial benefits so much as for companionship.[4] This was certainly well understood in the affiliated orders and in some ways they offered more in this direction than the local societies. By origin both the Oddfellows and the Foresters had developed from purely social clubs of the eighteenth century by adding to their traditional activities various financial benefits. In the process of doing this they had never abandoned their social functions. The basic requirement of a monthly gathering in an alehouse was as typical of the lodges and courts as of the local societies. The Registrar and the Commissioners complained of funds which ought to have been spent on sickness benefits being used to pay for drink in the lodges in just the same way as occurred in the independent local clubs. As individual lodges of the Manchester Unity came to be required to keep their accounts in a more orderly fashion, it became necessary to embody in 'room rent' the cost of the refreshment as well as that of the actual shelter. In this way,

[1] E. J. Hobsbawm, 'The Tramping Artisan', *Economic History Review*, 2nd series, vol. III, 1951, pp. 299–320.

[2] F. G. P. Neison, *op. cit.*, p. 79. 'The issue of these [travelling] cards fluctuates with the state of the labour market. For instance, in 1862, at the time of the great depression in the cotton manufacturing districts, the cards issued [by the M.U.O.F.] ran up to 1,378 in number. In the previous and subsequent years the numbers were as follows: 1860 406 cards, 1861 755 cards; 1862 1,378 cards, 1863 943 cards, 1864 557 cards, and in 1865 378 cards.'

[3] G. Howell, *The Conflicts of Capital and Labour*, 1890, p. 141.

[4] *Parliamentary Debates*, Third Series, CLXXIV, 238, 17 Mar. 1864.

lodge secretaries found a way of apparently reconciling the desires of their members with the requirements of the regulations. The annual feast-day was also observed as much in the orders as in the local societies and there are from time to time descriptions of what often grew into local holidays in such contemporary publications as the *Oddfellows Magazine* or the *Oddfellows Chronicle*.

Both the Oddfellows and the Foresters inherited and cultivated distinctive mystiques of 'Oddfellowship' or 'Forestry' which were developed through ritual, lectures, oaths, passwords, particular ways of shaking hands and so forth. In the case of the Manchester Unity much of the early ritual was very similar to that of contemporary Freemasonry and there is some evidence of contact between the lodges of the Oddfellows and the Masons in Manchester.[1] Passwords used for gaining admittance to lodge meetings were regularly changed to ensure that if a non-initiate should obtain knowledge of a password he would not be able to profit from it. Early passwords were often Scriptural, such as 'Judah, Strength', 'Abraham, Father of the Faithful' or 'Peter, Son of Thunder'. The first minuted resolution of the Grand Committee was 'That every Brother provide himself with an apron at his own expense' while a second was 'That each member subscribe one shilling towards purchasing funeral regalia.'[2]

The most important ceremony for the individual was his initiation. Some of the rites used during the first part of the century were intended to create a sense of awe in the novice, who was often blindfolded for the first part of the ceremony and had his bandage removed to find himself at the end of a sword obliged to beg mercy of the assembled lodge. After he had received the charge from the grand officers—duly masked as were all the other members—all would join in pledging the novice in a flowing cup, paid for by the novice himself.[3] The initiation ceremony of the Foresters included a combat until 1843. The Chief Ranger presented the candidate with two

[1] Minutes of the Grand Committees of the I.O.O.F.M.U., January, 1814 to December 1828.

[2] *Ibid.*

[3] S. T. Davies, *Oddfellowship; Its History, Constitution, Principles and Finances*, 1858, gives details of some early ceremonies.

cudgels, one of which he was to give to any brother in the room whom he then engaged in combat. At the close of the fight the Sub-Chief Ranger had to report whether the candidate's courage was such that he was found worthy of membership.[1]

At the end of life, local lodges and courts followed the same custom as many local societies and members were required to attend the funerals of deceased brethren if they lived within a certain distance. The general laws of the Manchester Unity permitted lodges to enforce attendance on those living within five miles of the lodge house if they so wished. There were also distinctive funeral prayers and prose passages which were read at the grave after the officiating clergyman had finished.

Distinctive ritual with the accompanying regalia, ceremonies, grips, passwords and so forth played a considerable part in maintaining both a sense of brotherhood and fellowship among the members and a sense of being different from other men, from those outside the brotherhood, who could not share in its mysteries. This was something which no other form of friendly society was in a position to offer and it played its part in attracting men to join an Oddfellows' lodge or a Foresters' court.

II. Financial Reforms

The friendly societies generally may be said to have passed through three stages of financial development during the century. The earliest stage involved a society in collecting from its members sufficient in any year to meet its outgoings for that year, each member paying an equal share or contribution. But it would be very difficult to operate on this basis without some sort of reserve to meet any unforeseen emergency that might arise such as an exceptionally heavy amount of sickness among members. Thus prudence seemed to dictate that contributions should be calculated with some regard to actuarial probabilities and to the need to accumulate a reserve fund. The contributions themselves were always equal among members, regardless of the age of joining their society, even although older men were unable to join as new members, yet there could be variations of as

[1] P.P. LXIX, 1890, Report of the Chief Registrar, p. 31.

much as 20 years in the ages at which different members joined up to the maximum age of 35 or 40. Since the claims for sickness benefit must inevitably be so much heavier among the older than among the younger members, those who joined late got a very good return for their money at the expense of those who joined when young.

The only way of ensuring that this equal levy system could have remained sound would have been to ensure that there was a constant succession of members maintaining approximately equal numbers in each age group. In this way the surplus arising from the contributions of the young would always be available to cover the larger sums needed to meet the sick benefits of the elderly, and as each generation of members grew old they would have been certain of being similarly paid for by the next generation and so on. Where local societies were able to maintain a balance between the different age groups, this was exactly what did happen and some of these clubs lasted a very long time. But in general if the levy system were used it could only ensure stability where some form of compulsory membership might exist so as to ensure that there would always be younger persons coming forward to contribute. There was in practice never any question of compulsory membership in this country with the exception of a few sick clubs run by employers who required their employees to join.

Thus there was a steady movement away from the levy system to the premium system of fixing contributions and benefits. This system valued contingent liabilities and reduced them to the value they represented at the time they were incurred; the present value of prospective contributions had then to be equal to the present value of the liabilities. Since it was obviously impossible to forecast the future sickness needs of any particular individual, the liabilities had to be calculated on the basis of observed averages, hence the need for reliable tables before any entirely sound system of sickness benefit insurance could be introduced in the affiliated orders. The premium or reserve system was first introduced in the Manchester Unity about the middle of the century, and it gradually came to be adopted by the other affiliated societies over the next 40 years. It was not government pressure or influence which achieved the financial stabilization of the orders, but rather it was due to the increase in the relevance and availability of actuarial knowledge and to the persistence of the leading members of the orders who themselves became convinced of the need for change and pressed their members to accept the financial reforms.

Perhaps the most important single contribution to actuarial knowledge was made by the elder Neison when he published the results of his investigations based on the data for the period 1836–40 obtained from the first returns of sickness and mortality by registered friendly societies.[1] In this work, Neison stressed the need for every society to be large enough to be likely to experience the average results anticipated in calculating tables of sickness and mortality and for each society to value its liabilities and its assets at intervals of not more than five years. The value of Neison's work lay in its pioneering nature. It was the first set of tables based on the actual sickness experience of friendly society members and was, therefore, the first to offer tables likely to prove reliable.

Five years later Henry Ratcliffe, Corresponding Secretary of the Manchester Unity, published tables and conclusions based upon his investigations of the experience of sickness and mortality among the Order's members which had been collected from lodges for the years 1846–48.[2] He later repeated his investigations on the basis of experience for the years 1856–60 and 1866–70.[3] As with Neison, the experience was classified under the three heads of rural, town and city areas; the rural lodges being those situated in places with a population of less than 5,000, the town class being places with between 5,000 and 30,000 inhabitants, and the city class being all places with more than 30,000 inhabitants. Ratcliffe analysed also the experience of the Manchester Unity by occupation.[4] The conclusions reached by Neison and Ratcliffe were very similar and the publication of their work meant that by 1850 the body of

[1] F. G. P. Neison, *Contributions to Vital Statistics: being a development of the rate of mortality and the laws of sickness from original and extensive data*, 1845.

[2] H. Ratcliffe, *Observations on the Rate of Mortality and Sickness existing among Friendly Societies*, (Manchester) 1850.

[3] H. Ratcliffe, *Observations on the Rate of Mortality and Sickness existing among Friendly Societies*, (Colchester) 1862.

[4] H. Ratcliffe, *Supplementary Report*, (Manchester) 1872.

actuarial knowledge necessary for the introduction of a sound premium system in the affiliated orders was available.

The arguments for sounder sickness insurance received a check from a somewhat unexpected source within a very few years. The quinquennial returns made by registered societies under the Friendly Societies Act for the quinquennium to 1850 were analysed by Finlaison of the National Debt Office and issued as official reports in 1853 and 1854.[1] These reports showed the sickness liabilities of Friendly Societies to be much lighter than those indicated by the calculations of Neison and Ratcliffe and those who were opposed to the introduction of contributions as large as their work had suggested was necessary were now armed with an apparently authoritative refutation of much of what the financial reformers had been urging. Apparently the reason why Finlaison produced tables showing much less sickness was because he took a definition of sickness much narrower than that for which friendly societies were accustomed to offer sick pay. He only accepted for the purpose of his calculations such sickness as was of limited duration and in need of constant medical treatment 'as contradistinguished from chronic ailment and increpitude'. Cases of slight paralysis, mental disorders, senile infirmity and blindness were 'carefully eliminated'. In his annual report, Tidd Pratt as Registrar commended the use of these tables and urged the societies to exercise more discrimination in distinguishing between real sickness and mere incapacity to labour. For friendly societies to attempt to distinguish in this manner was quite out of the question. Their members joined just as much to assure themselves of sick benefits when unable to work because of a chronic ailment as when they were unable to work because they were suffering from some acute condition requiring constant medical treatment. Twenty years later the Royal Commission described Finlaison's tables as unfortunate, pointing out that many

[1] P.P. C, 1852–3, Copy of a report and tables prepared by the Actuary of the National Debt Office on the subject of sickness and mortality among the members of Friendly Societies as shown by the quinquennial returns to 31 December 1850.

P.P. LXIII, 1854, Further report and tables by the Actuary of the National Debt Office on sickness and mortality among members of Friendly Societies, etc.

societies had in fact adopted them without discovering that they were only suitable for societies which limited their benefits to sickness as the Actuary to the National Debt Office had defined it in 1853.

The leaders of the Manchester Unity were already aware of the need for financial reform even before the actuarial studies of Neison and Ratcliffe were published. While funeral benefits were the responsibility of the district, all other financial contributions and benefits were in the control of the local lodges. The rates of contribution and of benefit were universally based on nothing more sophisticated than local custom or competition. Lodges were charging 4d, 5d and 6d weekly for a customary sickness benefit of 10 shillings weekly and £10 funeral benefit.[1] As with local societies, an unusually heavy incidence of sickness often led to the breaking-up of the lodge. In 1843, 225 lodges closed for want of funds and many more got into financial difficulties and appealed for assistance.[2] Any attempt by the leaders of the Unity to take action with a view to improving this situation was bound to encounter opposition based on constitutional and political as well as financial factors. The individual lodges were jealous of their independence and financial reform was bound to set limits to the right of lodges to charge contributions and offer benefits which could only lead to insolvency. In 1844 an attempt was made to get returns from the lodges showing their financial position and their sickness experience. While the great majority of lodges conformed, many resisted this request on the grounds that their independence was being violated, and in the year 1844–45 the board of directors suspended lodges with a total membership of 16,000.

At the 1845 meeting of the Annual Moveable Committee which was held at Glasgow a resolution was passed which took matters further by ordering every lodge to establish a separate fund for all expenses other than sickness and funeral benefits. The lodges were still to be free to fix their own contributions and benefits but the overall rate of contribution had to be ½d per week for each £1 of funeral payment and each shilling

[1] I.O.O.F.M.U., *Quarterly Report*, January 1845.
[2] *Ibid.*, July, 1844.

weekly in sick pay. These figures could not secure the solvency of the lodges, but the adoption of the proposal was an important achievement for the leadership since it established as a precedent the right of the Annual Moveable Conference of the Order to limit the financial autonomy of the individual lodge. The secessions which followed during the next few years, especially among some of the older and most independent-minded lodges of Lancashire and Yorkshire, have been described above. For a while the enforcement of the new requirements was difficult, but within a few years they were generally accepted.[1]

The next step for the leaders of the Unity to attempt was to try to secure adequate rates of contribution more closely related to the benefits and liabilities. The inadequacy of the 'guidelines' for contributions and benefits adopted in 1845 was soon illustrated by Neison who published a survey of the current financial condition of friendly societies the next year.[2] The details which he gave of the existing situation in a number of lodges emphasized the need for more drastic reform. There were six lodges in Manchester with a total of 530 members, established on an average for twelve years, whose total accumulated funds amounted to no more than £91 13s 6d which was less than one-twelfth of the initiation fees that the members had paid on joining the lodges.[3] The need for contributions to be graduated according to the age at which a member joined was emphasized by calculations showing that an annual loss of 4s 8d in the case of a member joining at the age of 20 became an annual loss of 14s 1d in the case of a member joining at 30 and an annual loss of £1 5s 6d for each member joining at 40.[4] On the basis of figures which he produced covering the whole of the Manchester Unity, Neison forecast that 'the inevitable dissolution of the Order of Oddfellowship . . . is certain'. Taking the total strength of the Unity as 400,000, he claimed that a gift of no less than £9,135,000 would be necessary to enable the Order to meet all its liabilities. For a number of

[1] C. Hardwick, *op. cit.*, p. 84.
[2] F. G. P. Neison, *Observations on Oddfellows and Friendly Societies,* 1846.
[3] *Ibid.*, p. 19.
[4] *Ibid.*, p. 27.

reasons the forecast of doom was not fulfilled. The figure of 400,000 members was a gross overestimate; the actual number was about 243,000. No allowance had been made for lapsed membership and secessions which produced a continuous reduction in the financial liabilities of the Order.[1] A friendly society was something more than an insurance company, and as a fraternity it was not unknown for a levy to be collected from all members of a lodge when the funds were exhausted. Aid was also sometimes given by another lodge or by the Unity. Furthermore, financial reform came to be accepted on an increasingly wide scale.

The Annual Moveable Committee meeting at Preston in 1853 adopted graduated scales of contributions related to the age of entry. These scales were based on the tables produced by Ratcliffe in 1850 following his examination of the life and sickness experience of the Order for 1846–48. Clearances were also more closely regulated. The advantage of being able to transfer from a lodge in one part of the country to one in another was clearly valuable to many members but the cost of the arrangement to the receiving lodge was heavy where the transferred member was well into middle age. In future, lodges were not to be required to receive transferred members over the age of 45 and entrance fees varying from 1s 6d to £1 according to age were to be imposed. The A.M.C. did not recommend that existing members of lodges should be compelled to pay the new rates of contribution but new members were to do so. Even on this limited basis many lodges did not adopt the new scales immediately, but after 1853 the constitutional struggle over financial reform within the Manchester Unity was over and the reformers had won. It would be many years before all lodges would become solvent in the actuarial sense. Twenty years later, 26 per cent of lodges were said to have a surplus of assets over liabilities while the rest had deficiencies of varying size, the largest deficiencies being in Lancashire and Yorkshire since most of the growth had

---

[1] Hardwick, *op. cit.*, p. 84, showed that from 1848–58 69,307 members left the Oddfellows, this represented an average rate of 2·6 per cent per annum which might be compared with the 26,500 deaths for the same period representing 1 per cent per annum.

occurred in those counties before the reformed rates of contribution had been introduced.[1] In 1864 the tables compiled by Ratcliffe and based on experience of the years 1856–60 were made compulsory on the whole of the Unity by the A.M.C. Seven years later the A.M.C. meeting at Bury St Edmunds ordered the valuation of the assets and liabilities of every lodge in the Order, four years before the act of 1875 was to require such valuations to be undertaken in all registered societies.[2]

Similar financial reforms were not adopted until later by the Ancient Order of Foresters, for two main reasons. Since the phase of rapid expansion in this Order came later than in the Manchester Unity, the impact of the increasing claims of a high proportion of ageing members on the funds of the courts was not appreciated so soon.[3] Secondly, the weaker central government of the Foresters already noticed made it more difficult to achieve financial reform and delayed the process. A great deal of the task of making members aware of the need for reform fell to Samuel Shawcross who became permanent secretary in 1843 and continued in office until 1899. The first attempt to move in this direction was made in 1853 when the High Court agreed to call on the courts to send in statistical returns, but these were only forthcoming in respect of about 40,000 members—less than half of the Order at the time—and nothing profitable could be done with them. Various reforms were proposed at the annual High Court meetings but none gained the support of the majority until 1864 when a resolution was passed declaring illegal the payment of liquor money for rent—'wet rent' as it was known. In the following year the High Court meeting at Plymouth took two important steps. It made compulsory the medical examination of candidates before their admission, and it sanctioned the use of a scale

---

[1] P.P. 1874, XXIII, Pt. I, R.C.F.S., 4th Report, para. 140.

[2] P.P. 1890, LXIX, Report of the Chief Registrar, pp. 24–5.

[3] The average age of members of the Oddfellows on 1st January 1876 was 36¼ while that of the Foresters was 33½ years. With the exception of Lincoln, Rutland, Cheshire and Cornwall, the Foresters were on the average of a younger age in every county. On the same date the Oddfellows had 330 members aged 80 or upwards while the Foresters had only 140. F. G. P. Neison, 'Some Statistics of the Affiliated Order of Friendly Societies', *J. Statistical Society*, XL, pp. 72–3.

of contributions and benefits proposed by Shawcross which came to be known as the 'Plymouth Tables'. No attempt was made to compel the use of these tables. Six years later, the High Court ordered that graduated scales of contribution should be used for new members but this was largely ignored by the courts and no effective steps were taken to enforce the rule until 1885 when the High Court meeting at Leeds suspended 52 courts with 5,000 members for failing to implement it.[1]

In 1873, Neison issued a report on the sickness experience of the Foresters during 1870, but he felt obliged to comment that little reliance could be placed on the figures given showing sickness experience because of the way in which the returns from the courts had been filled up.[2] Undoubtedly many local courts and societies had difficulty in finding men sufficiently versed in keeping accounts to act as their secretaries even as late in the century as this. The first comprehensive set of returns of the sickness and mortality experience of the Order was only made after 1878 when the High Court meeting at Newcastle ordered returns to be made covering the years 1871 to 1875. The permanent secretary was directed to consult with the younger Neison on the preparation of an analysis of this experience which was published in 1882.[3]

Outside of the Manchester Unity of Oddfellows and the Ancient Order of Foresters none of the affiliated orders had made significant progress towards financial reform by the time the Royal Commission examined the position.[4] The third largest order in 1875 was the Grand United Order of Oddfellows. It had been driven by the financial difficulties it had encountered in the 1850s and 1860s to give some thought to reform although this had got no further than calling for financial returns. A good many of the affiliated orders still lacked any central government capable either of gathering the

[1] *Ibid.*, pp. 32–4.

[2] F. G. P. Neison, *Report upon the Sickness Experience of the A.O.F. for the Year 1870*, 1873.

[3] F. G. P. Neison, *The Rates of Mortality and Sickness of the Ancient Order of Foresters' Friendly Society*, 1882; P.P. 1890, LXLX, Report of the Chief Registrar, p. 34.

[4] The Rational Sick and Burial Association and the Independent Order of Rechabites are excluded from this judgement. They were hardly typical affiliated orders in that their appeal was of a special and limited nature.

necessary data or of making proposals likely to correct their financial weaknesses.

III. Minority groups

The growth of the temperance movement in Victorian England led directly to the establishment in 1835 of an affiliated order, the Independent Order of Rechabites, Salford Unity. In 1870 this Order still had only about 9,000 members, yet by the end of the century it had about 140,000 and between the two World Wars had more than half a million members. The origin of the society was self-protection in that when those who had been converted to the cause of temperance joined friendly societies they had to go to public houses to pay their contributions and the temptations were so strong that they were in danger of lapsing.[1] Candidates for membership took the following pledge 'I hereby declare that I will abstain from all intoxicating liquors, except in religious ordinances or when prescribed by a physician, nor engage in the traffic of them, but in all possible ways will discountenance the use, manufacture and sale of them; and to the utmost of my power I will endeavour to spread the principles of abstinence from all intoxicating liquors.' In view of the weakness of human nature and the extent of the temptations offered by society, the Order did not expel immediately those who broke the pledge but stated that 'we deal mercifully and patiently with erring brethren, and inflict fines three times; but for the fourth offence they are expelled, and can only be re-admitted as new members.'[2] Only four years after their foundation the Rechabites separated their management and sickness funds. In 1842 a committee was established to draw up a suitable scale of contributions, and benefits for sick and funeral funds and all the tents (as the local branches were called) were obliged to accept this.[3] The Rechabites did not, however, adopt a graduated scale of contributions until 1871.

[1] J. Frome Wilkinson, *The Friendly Society Movement; Its Origin, Rise and Growth*, 1886, p. 44.

[2] Extract from a leaflet issued by the Order and quoted by J. Frome Wilkinson, *Mutual Thrift*, 1891, p. 111.

[3] *Jubilee Record of the Independent Order of Rechabites*, 1885, pp. 15–21.

Among other affiliated orders established in these years which made no general appeal to working men but still suited certain minority groups may be included the Catholic Benefit Society and the United Order of Catholic Brethren. Members of the latter were commended to recite daily the *Angelus Domini* for the welfare of the Order and the conversion of England. Expressing diametrically opposed views, the Society of Loyal Orangemen began to develop a system of friendly society benefits and contributions in some of their lodges.

Two minority groups for whom specialized societies came to be established were railwaymen and miners. It was thought that men following both of these occupations had a greater than average liability for accidents, if not for sickness, arising out of their vocation. The experience of the Midland Railway Company Friendly Society indicated that the average period of incapacity to work because of sickness or accident was about 40 per cent higher than the usual figure. Most of the larger railway companies had their own friendly societies which they required their employees, or certain classes of their employees, to join.

Some companies had more than one society attached to them. The London and North-Western Company had seven, the Great Western three.[1] The headquarters of the Great Western's societies was at Swindon where the Company employed about 7,000 persons at its workshops. Of the three societies the oldest was the Locomotive and Carriage Department Sick Fund Society established in 1844. There were three classes of membership with contributions varying from 2d to 9d, sick benefit from 4s to 12s per week and funeral allowances from £4 to £12. There were also superannuation allowances varying from 2s to 6s weekly and payable to any member aged 60 or more who had been with the Society for at least 25 years. In 1847 a Medical Fund Society was established to provide medicine and medical attendance to members and their families. The members consisted of six classes and their contributions varied according to their rate of wages. The third society was the Enginemen and

[1] P. W. Kingsford, *Victorian Railwaymen: The Emergence and Growth of Railway Labour 1830–70*, 1970, Appendix I prints a list of all those railway friendly societies existing in 1871. 46 are shown as 'railway company' societies and 14 as 'railwaymen's' societies.

Firemen's Mutual Assurance, Sick and Superannuation Society, which was confined as its name implied to footplatemen, the most highly-paid group of the Company's workmen. The weekly contributions were 1s 6d first class or 1s second class, the corresponding sick-pay rates being 15s and 12s 6d. The superannuation allowances were 12s for the first class and 7s 6d second class payable to members aged 60 and over who had been members of the society for at least ten years. The superannuation allowance was payable on permanent disablement of a member as on retirement at the age of 60 or above.[1] Superannuation provision became more widespread in the railway company societies towards the end of the century.

The companies sponsored friendly societies for their employees as 'a relief from the burden of maintaining servants disqualified by age or accident, or contributing to the support of families of persons killed in their service'.[2] The aim of the subsidies was to cover part of the accident risk while the employees' contributions covered the rest. The Royal Commission criticized this group of societies in 1874 as financially unsound. There was a false confidence among members that benefits were underwritten by the subsidizing companies and that if resources were inadequate the companies would make good what they had more or less directly joined in promising. 'Any reliance of this kind tends at best to laxity of management by the members.' Moreover even the current subsidies were never incurred as legal obligations by the companies and might be cut off. The subsidies were usually fixed annual payments and even if enough to supplement contributions when first agreed, subsequent growth in membership upset the calculations and the fixed subsidies became inadequate as means of fulfilling their original purpose; 'all parties discover at length that they have been misled and dissatisfaction or worse results too probably follow.'[3]

The other disadvantage of railway company friendly societies was their compulsory, or semi-compulsory, nature. The Royal

---

[1] Baernreither, *op. cit.*, pp. 206–17.
[2] Railway Clearing House, Provisional Committee Report, 1850, quoted by Kingsford, *op. cit.*
[3] P.P. 1874, XXIII, Pt. I, RCFS, 4th Report, para. 291.

Commission pointed out that any employer who obliged his workmen to join a society took upon himself a grave moral responsibility for the actuarial soundness of that society.[1] Furthermore, if a man who was already a member of a society went to work for the railway he would have to abandon his society unless he felt he could afford to pay two contributions at the same time. If a man over 40 left or was dismissed by his company, he would forfeit the benefits his contributions had earned and would be too old to join another society. In his evidence before the Royal Commission on Labour in 1892, the former Chief Registrar, Ludlow, cited compulsory membership of railway societies as one of the causes of friction between employer and employee, stating that 'the men chafe very much under that obligation. . . .'[2]

The obligation to join pit clubs run by the employing company was a source of constant complaint among coal miners who regarded such clubs as little more than devices for withholding part of a man's pay. In the areas where they existed on any scale as late as 1870 such as South Lancashire, Staffordshire and Worcestershire, the Assistant Commissioners found them to be very unpopular.[3] The pressure exerted by miners' unions and the Truck Act of 1861 helped to put an end to the pit clubs and to clear the way for the development of Miners' Permanent Relief Societies. The first of these to be established was the Northumberland and Durham Permanent Relief Fund in 1862, but their main period of growth was in the 1870s and 1880s.[4]

A minority group who disliked 'the nonsense and mixed company of the club nights' and who looked 'for an investment of their savings on purely business principles' had their needs met by the growth of ordinary large societies—sometimes called the centralized class. The largest society of this type in 1870 was the Hearts of Oak which had been founded in 1842. The other principal societies of the same class were the Royal Oak, the United Patriots, the London Friendly and the Royal

[1] *Ibid.*, para. 292.
[2] P.P. 1894–4, XXXIX, Royal Commission on Labour, Minutes of Evidence, QQ. 1758–61.
[3] P.P. 1874, XXIII, Pt. II, Reports of Assistant Commissioners, pp. 89, 172–4.
[4] *Infra*, p. 110–11.

Standard. These were really offices for life and sickness insurance in which there was no personal connection or acquaintance between members. They were completely centralized; the members sent their contributions in by post and received their benefits by the same means. The control of these societies was in practice in the hands of a management committee. With their scattered and impersonal memberships the annual general meeting of members could be no more than a formality. The membership consisted largely of tradesmen, shopkeepers and clerks who valued respectability, a word which was widely used in the early rules of the Hearts of Oak. Presumably in the same spirit the rules also dealt with immigrants by stating that 'no Irishman shall be allowed to become a member of this society unless recommended by one or more members, nor after such recommendation unless that person be known to be a respectable and good mechanic'.[1] In any case, the contributions and benefits of these societies were higher than those customary in societies which appealed to most working men, and an unusually large number of occupations were generally excluded. In the case of the Hearts of Oak the excluded occupations varied from cigar-makers and confectioners to gamekeepers and brewers' draymen with the umbrella phrase 'any other occupation which the committee may conceive dangerous or injurious to health'.[2] Although founded in 1842, rapid growth did not begin in the Hearts of Oak until the 1860s. In 1865 it had 10,571 members, in 1870 21,484 and in 1875 64,421. Over the same period the annual income had risen from £20,000 to £117,000 and accumulated funds from £40,000 to £179,000.

V. Legislation and the Registrar of Friendly Societies

From the 1830s the attitude of the state and of the governing classes generally towards friendly societies changed markedly. This was part of the widespread development of new political and social attitudes. One expression of this was the new approach to the poor law problem in 1834. Increasing stress

---

[1] Frome, Wilkinson, *op. cit.*, p. 115.

[2] Baernreither, *op. cit.*, p. 199; for an account of the early growth of the Hearts of Oak, W. G. Bunn, *History of the Hearts of Oak Benefit Society*, 1879.

came to be placed upon the need to encourage independence and self-help, the need to persuade the societies and their members to stand on their own feet, not to expect the state or the local authorities to prop them up. One of the earliest and one of the most succinct descriptions of what came to be the prevailing attitude of the state to the friendly societies was that written by Edwin Chadwick which appeared in 1828: in dealing with the problem of poverty it was the duty of the government to enable the community to defend itself at least expense against the social consequences arising from sickness and death. The Government could best do this by collecting data concerning sickness and death. This was a task which the Government itself must undertake since it was alone in being in a position to secure the necessary information. The higher classes had shown a strong and misguided desire to help the local poor in their neighbourhoods with inconsiderate charities and the profuse expenditure of the poor's rates, which taken together 'have formed the most potent means of retarding the improvement of the labouring population; and it seems to us that the wealthy have yet to learn what are the means by which they may render the best services; which means, we conceive, will be found to be in acting with the labouring classes rather than for them: in enabling them to act for themselves, by provident institutions, securely based on sound knowledge of the nature of that which we have treated'.[1]

The view that the state should go no further than help societies through requiring returns, collecting and publishing such data as was collected became widely accepted. The Royal Commission concluded that it would be wrong for the Government to oblige societies to use specific tables and it rejected a suggestion that minimum contributions be fixed for certain benefits.[2] It was felt that such intervention would have been unjustifiable, that it might have involved the state in some moral responsibility if a society which was acting on the instructions of the Government experienced a bout of sickness far in excess of the national averages and as a consequence ran out of funds.

---

[1] E. Chadwick, 'An Essay on the Means of Insurance against the Casualties of Sickness, Decrepitude and Mortality', *Westminster Review*, XVIII, April 1828.
[2] P.P. 1874, XXIII, Pt. I, RCFS, 4th Report, para. 57.

The benevolent efforts of some old-fashioned rural gentry and clergy who, prompted by patriarchal benevolence, still intervened to lend their support to some societies in country areas were strongly criticized in the Report of the Assistant Commissioner for Wales and the Border Counties. The Report spoke of influential gentlemen and clergymen who patronized and endorsed ricketty schemes 'with no more sense of the responsibility they were incurring than if the proposed society had been one for soup to the poor under exceptional pressure, or flannel petticoats during a sharp winter'. Writing twenty years later, Frome Wilkinson expressed a similar view when he commented that it was 'scarcely to be believed' that when the government had imposed the certifying by authority of safe tables before allowing registration, no such tables in fact existed.[1]

The first legislation which reflected the new ideas following the paternalist era was the Act of 1834.[2] This made a number of significant changes in the arrangements for registration. It repealed the provisions of earlier acts requiring tables of contributions and of benefits to be submitted to the authorities, that is, the justices. The requirement that the rules of a society seeking registration had to be submitted to quarter sessions and be confirmed by the justices was also repealed and replaced by an arrangement under which the secretary of a society was to send the rules directly to the barrister appointed to certify the rules of savings banks. He was to certify the rules, provided that they did not contravene the law, and send a copy to the clerk of the peace of the county to be filed with the Rolls of the Sessions—the justices being required 'to allow the same'. The returns of sickness and mortality, first demanded by the act of 1829, were to be sent directly to the barrister certifying the rules and not to the clerk of the peace. The change from local to central administration gave registered societies a greater measure of freedom. The temptation which some bodies of magistrates had felt to meddle was removed while certification of the rules of societies by the centrally-appointed barrister proved to be much less haphazard than local registration had

---

[1] Frome Wilkinson, *op. cit.*, p. 82.
[2] 4 & 5 Wm. IV, c.40.

been. The scope of action of registered societies was also much enlarged in 1834 to 'any other purpose which is not illegal'.

The legislative developments of 1834 were taken further by the Act of 1846.[1] The barrister who certified the rules of societies was given the title of 'Registrar of Friendly Societies' and was to be appointed by the National Debt Commissioners. Instead of forwarding copies of certified rules to local clerks of the peace for filing, he was to file them himself and was to be paid a net salary of £1,000 per annum in place of the fees which he had charged applicants for registration hitherto. Among the purposes for which friendly societies could now be established was that of purchasing food, firing, clothes or other necessaries, the tools or implements of their trade or calling, and to make frugal investments allowing members to take part of the profits arising on the sale of these items in the form of dividends on their shares. This provision opened up registration to cooperative societies and enabled them to acquire a legal status. The Rochdale Pioneers took advantage of this clause and became a registered friendly society at this time. This act also took the first step towards enabling the affiliated orders to register by declaring that the provisions of the Corresponding Societies' act[2] and the Seditious Meetings act[3]— which taken together rendered societies with branches illegal and prohibited certain meetings of more than 50 persons— should not apply to registered friendly societies. The orders were still unable to register for a number of other reasons, partly because their objects went beyond those accepted under current legislation.[4]

The dangers from lack of legal protection which could overtake even the largest societies were illustrated by events in the Manchester Unity in 1848. No less a person than the Corresponding Secretary of the Unity, W. Ratcliffe (brother of Henry Ratcliffe) embezzled £4,000 entrusted to his care. He declined

[1] 9 & 10 Vict. c.27.
[2] 39 Geo. III, c.79.
[3] 57 Geo. III, c.19.
[4] Other reasons were (1) the procedure for dealing with disputes within the orders was not acceptable (2) the annual moveable meetings of the Oddfellows and Foresters could not be considered as general meetings called annually in the county where the society was established.

to resign from office or even to hand over the records and the premises of the Unity's headquarters and the offices had to be taken by storm on 9 March 1848 when Ratcliffe was taken off to prison.[1] He was tried at Liverpool assizes but was acquitted on the grounds that the Manchester Unity was both a mere partnership and an illegal organization. The blow to the Order was enough to lead to a campaign to bring about a change in the law to permit registration. The *Oddfellows Chronicle* called on members to make a united and determined effort to achieve this; 'full and cordial assistance to those whom you have placed in power, before long will place your property within the pale of legal protection, and no more plunderers of the Order will escape with impunity'.[2] The directors of the Order asked for a hearing before a Select Committee of the Lords then sitting with a view to presenting the case for granting legal protection. Following the reports from this committee and from a Select Committee of the Commons[3] a new Act was passed in 1850[4] which consolidated existing legislation and permitted the registration of societies with branches, thus finally enabling the affiliated orders to claim some protection from the law. Societies were to make annual returns to the Registrar who was to lay before Parliament abstracts of these annual and quinquennial returns. The interest payable to friendly societies on funds they placed with the National Debt Commissioners was reduced to 3 per cent since it was considered that there were no grounds for offering a subsidy in the form of a rate of interest more favourable than that obtainable on Consols. However, societies registered before 1844 were still able to place their funds at the concessionary rate of interest. The Ancient Order of Foresters registered its general rules in 1850 and the

---

[1] *Oddfellows Chronicle*, March, 1848.

[2] *Ibid.*, April, 1848.

[3] P.P. 1847–8, XXVI, Report from the Select Committee of the House of Lords on the Provident Associations Fraud Prevention Bill.

P.P. 1849, XIV, Report from the Select Committee of the House of Commons on the Friendly Societies Bill.

The Select Committee of the Lords put forward a bill proposing numerous restrictions on the orders as the price of registration. The Select Committee of the Commons, chaired by Sotheron-Estcourt, recommended the dropping of these restrictions and produced the bill that was enacted in 1850.

[4] 13 & 14 Vict. c.115.

Manchester Unity the following year. Individual courts and lodges had to register separately. Most of the other orders did not register at this time, largely because the law as interpreted by the Registrar would only grant registration to each branch as an entirely separate society.

The Act was only considered as a temporary measure and was renewed annually until a permanent measure was passed in 1855[1] following a further review by another Select Committee in 1854. All fees for registration were now abolished and the purposes for which friendly societies might be formed were redefined so as to drop the limitation of risks to those which 'could be calculated by way of average', and the final wide phrase was included of 'any purpose which shall be authorized by one of Her Majesty's Principal Secretaries of State'. It was also provided that any friendly society might simply deposit its rules if it so wished and thereby gain recognition as a legal body with the right to sue and of settling disputes in the form provided by its rules. Finally this act began the long series of valuable reports on friendly societies from the Registrar by requiring him to lay an annual report before Parliament in addition to the abstracts of returns.

The position established by the Act of 1855 remained unchanged for twenty years and as the law then stood the main advantages conferred by registration were that registered societies could hold property in the name of trustees; they could sue and be sued; they could proceed against fraudulent, and had a first claim on the estates of deceased officers; they could enforce rules for the settlement of disputes among members by arbitration; they could invest funds with the National Debt Commissioners; could be dissolved without difficulty or expense, and enjoyed some exemption from stamp duties. The only privileges which amounted to very much were those of being able to sue and protection against defaulting officials. This was shown by a comparison with the position in Scotland where the existence of a public prosecutor largely protected the unregistered against fraud and the common law afforded them greater facilities for legal proceedings, so that the proportion of unregistered societies was much higher in that

[1] 18 & 19 Vict. c.63.

country than in England—in fact, 84 per cent. On the other hand the restrictions imposed on registered societies were considerable. Not only were they unable to make provision in their rules to spend any part of their funds on social activities, but their field of investment was greatly narrowed, and the requirement of regular returns and the need to register any amendments to the rules all served as further disincentives to registration. It could be argued that even after 1855 the state had not made registration very attractive.[1]

While no other major legislation specifically concerned with friendly societies was enacted until 1875 after the Report of the Royal Commission, it is impossible to ignore the impact of the Poor Law legislation. The principle of less eligibility, the imposition of the workhouse test and the successful conversion of pauper relief into something conveying an impression of horror and revulsion in the minds of most people ensured that working men's associations would avoid all contact with the Poor Law. Baernreither observed that it was a very marked feature in the educated working man to regard going into the workhouse as a disgrace.[2] It was mostly the better-off working men who formed the orders and looked to them for independent support during periods of sickness and incapacity, however protracted, and their leaders put this view vigorously. Charles Hardwick, Grand Master of the Manchester Unity, emphasized that it was no part of the task of friendly societies 'to form a stepping stone, to aid the industrious and prudent to pass from the active and manly independence of their days of vigorous labour to the degraded pauperism of the workhouse.'[3] The rapid growth of friendly societies among the 'soundhearted' was the 'honourable substitute for the parish relief of the semi-slave by Act of Parliament'.[4]

The statistics show a very rapid growth in the size of the friendly society movement in the decade following the Poor Law Amendment Act of 1834. The figures for the foundation of

[1] Charles Cameron, 'What Legislation should follow upon the Report of the Commission on Friendly Societies?' *Trans. of the National Association for the Promotion of Social Science*, 1874, pp. 794–7.

[2] Baernreither, *op. cit.*, p. 350.

[3] Hardwick, *op. cit.*, p. 63.

[4] *Ibid.*, p. 32.

lodges in the Manchester Unity of Oddfellows shown in Table 3.3 are particularly impressive.[1] The Poor Law Commissioners

Table 3.3.

Decade in which I.O.O.F.M.U. lodges active in 1875 were founded.

Decade	Number of lodges founded
1825–35	455
1835–45	1,470
1845–55	297
1855–65	358
1865–75	354

Source: *A List of the lodges comprising the I.O.O.F. (M.U.), 1875.*

claimed that one of their aims was to encourage men to join the societies and they believed that the administration of the new act was leading to an increase in both their number and size. In 1836 Chadwick, Secretary to the Commissioners, had his *Essay on the Means of Insurance* republished in booklet form and explained that he was doing so because of the increase in friendly societies created by the administration of the Poor Law Amendment Act. Tidd Pratt, the barrister appointed to certify the rules of friendly societies, reported a large increase in the number of new societies seeking registration after 1834.[2] In their reports, Assistant Commissioners of the Poor Law Commission often attributed the rapid growth in friendly societies in their districts to the influence of the amended Poor Law. The Commissioners made no secret of their belief that the more strictly poor relief was administered, the more helpful the friendly societies would find it since working men would become increasingly eager to provide for themselves.[3]

[1] Gosden, *op. cit.*, pp. 207–9, for a fuller discussion of the impact of the Poor Law Amendment Act on the foundation of friendly societies.

[2] P.P. 1837–38, XXVIII, Poor Law Commission, 4th Annual Report, p. 247.

[3] P.P. 1835, XXXV, Poor Law Commission, 1st Annual Report, p. 31; W. Chance, *Our Treatment of the Poor*, 1899, chapter III, contains an interesting discussion of the relationship between the reformed Poor Law and friendly societies.

Similar views were put forward in their final report by the members of the Royal Commission on Friendly Societies 40 years later. The chairman of the Commission instructed the Assistant Commissioners to examine carefully in their districts the bearing of the friendly societies 'upon the self-maintenance of the people and the administration of the Poor laws'. The Commission concluded that the policy of total separation between the two, followed since 1834, was right. The societies themselves objected very strongly to the suggestion of any connection with poor relief. It was argued from time to time that the guardians should discount to some extent sick pay from friendly societies in calculating relief, but the Royal Commission deprecated the suggestion, arguing that it would merely encourage men to insure for less than their real needs with a friendly society and to rely on the Poor Law to make up the minimum sum needed for support. In some respects the Friendly Societies Commission would have gone further than had the Poor Law authorities. Outdoor relief was commonly granted to those too old to work and the Commissioners commented that if this could no longer be counted on with comparative certainty, a great stimulus would be given to exertions towards making some provision for old age, 'the workhouse test would invest providence with new and hitherto unknown attractions'.[1]

From 1829, every enactment concerning friendly societies modified in some sense the duties of John Tidd Pratt who became the first Registrar. In 1828 he was appointed by the National Debt Commissioners to examine and certify the rules of savings banks; these had hitherto been submitted for approval to quarter sessions. The next year he was given the task of examining and certifying the rules of friendly societies. During the 1830s, further duties were added, including the examining and certifying of loan societies, then, similar functions in the case of benefit building societies and a little later, similar duties in respect of societies for the pursuit of literature, science and the fine arts where Tidd Pratt's certificate conferred exemption from payment of rates. The number of functions attached to this office continued to accumulate and in

[1] P.P. 1874, XXIII, Pt. I, RCFS, 4th Report, paras. 828, 833.

1846 it was enacted that the Registrar of Friendly Societies in England should be paid by salary instead of fees.[1] The Act of 1846 made provision for the payment of the salaries of clerks, office expenses and so forth for the actual accumulation of work and of documents had made it essential for a regular department to be established. Some 30,000 sets of rules and amendments alone had to be registered and catalogued by the Registrar at this time.[2]

The expansion of Tidd Pratt's duties and influence up to his death in 1870 was considerable. It was due partly to legislative changes and partly to his personality and influence. The Royal Commission described him as 'minister of self-help to the whole of the industrious classes' and pointed out that whether a man joined a savings bank, a friendly society or a trade union, shopped at a cooperative store or bought his house through a building society, the Registrar's certificate would follow him.[3] Tidd Pratt was short in stature, had an animated manner and impressed those who encountered him as a man of strong convictions. For a society to be 'certified by Tidd Pratt' was in the eyes of many the hallmark of respectability, while his name was said to have been invoked as an object of terror to societies suspected of evil designs; 'if you do this, you will have Tidd Pratt upon you'.[4] He inveighed constantly against the evils of compulsory payments for drink on club nights and he devoted much energy to trying to get societies to become more reliable insurers. It was with this aim in view that he wrote such works as *Suggestions for the Establishment of Friendly Societies* (1855) and *Instructions for the Establishment of Friendly Societies* (1860). The statutory annual reports of the Registrar along with their appendices which first appeared in 1856 contained a great deal of well-meant advice. It was unfortunate that the one group of friendly societies for which Tidd Pratt had no time at all were the affiliated orders.[5] Even after 1850, the Registrar seemed intent on putting as many obstacles as possible in the way of registration by the orders. He was prepared to register the

[1] 9 & 10 Vict. c.27. s.10.
[2] E. W. Brabrook, *Provident Societies and Industrial Welfare*, 1898, p. 15.
[3] P.P. 1874, XXIII, Pt. I, RCFS, 4th Report, App. I.
[4] Brabrook, *op. cit.*, p. 12.
[5] Frome Wilkinson, *op. cit.*, p. 104.

general rules of an order but refused to recognize any registration of a branch except as a separate society, an independent unit, free of all central control, able to dissolve itself when it pleased. Thus, by the end of 1858 only 1,673 out of 3,198 M.U.O.F. lodges had registered and only 926 out of 1,876 A.O.F. courts had done so. He was prepared to strain the law to favour patronized county and large ordinary societies, but he undoubtedly regarded the affiliated orders as dangerous combinations. He was said to think it his duty to treat members of the affiliated orders 'much in the light as the master of a union workhouse, a militia drill-sergeant, and the governor of a convict prison do the specimens of humanity committed to their charge'.[1]

The extent of Tidd Pratt's activities was such that his death raised the whole question of the future of the office and of the relationship of the state with the organizations which it registered. The Gladstone Cabinet, much influenced by the economical ideas of Robert Lowe who was Chancellor of the Exchequer, introduced a bill to abolish the office and to enable societies to operate within the framework of joint stock company legislation, registering with the Board of Trade, disputed issues being adjudicated by county courts.[2] This proposal aroused a great deal of opposition from friendly societies, cooperatives and trade unions and the outcome was the

---

[1] Hardwick, *op. cit.*, p. 69.

[2] N. C. Masterman, *John Malcolm Ludlow*, 1963, pp. 219–20, sets out the sequence of events leading to the appointment of the Royal Commission following the version given in Ludlow's unpublished autobiography. On the death of Tidd Pratt, Tom Hughes, an M.P. who claimed to represent working class interests, acted through Alfred Nutson, Secretary to Henry Bruce (the Home Secretary) to secure the appointment of Ludlow as Registrar. Bruce appeared to agree to Ludlow's appointment. Then it was found that the right to nominate lay in fact with the Chancellor of the Exchequer, Robert Lowe, who was a notable advocate of the extreme *laissez-faire* economics and stood for the greatest economy in government. For some while he had been the principal target for Ludlow, the Christian Socialist, and his friends. According to Ludlow, Lowe 'finding it difficult to appoint anyone else in the face of the expressed views of several of his colleagues hit upon the idea of suppressing the registrarship altogether'. Ludlow believed that he had thus been largely responsible for rousing Lowe's active opposition which in its turn produced a strong enough reaction to have the commission set up. In this way Ludlow considered himself largely responsible both for the commission and the legislation which followed in 1875.

appointment of the Royal Commission on Friendly and Benefit Building Societies. The main topics for inquiry were listed in its warrant as (1) the operation of existing legislation, (2) the organization and condition of the societies established under this legislation, (3) the office and duties of the Registrar of Friendly Societies.

Sir Stafford Northcote was chairman of the Commission and the secretary was J. M. Ludlow. Assistant Commissioners were appointed to carry out detailed inquiries in different parts of the country and over the next few years a great deal of evidence was taken orally and in writing which makes the reports of the commission the most valuable single source of information on the friendly societies in the 19th century.[1] The known membership of friendly societies making a return in 1872 was 1,857,896 (comparable figures for trade unions being 217,128 and for cooperatives 301,157)[2] but on the basis of the evidence before it the commission concluded that there were probably 4,000,000 members of friendly societies and about 8,000,000 persons interested in them as beneficiaries. These members were distributed over 32,000 societies, registered and unregistered, possessing funds of about £11,000,000. It was one of the main achievements of the commissioners to indicate the actual extent of the friendly society movement.

Their recommendations were later reflected in a new act passed in 1875. They were concerned with the management of registered friendly societies and with their relationship with the Registrar. The guiding aim of the Commissioners was to make these societies more reliable as insurers and to achieve this by

[1] The First Report of the Commission (P.P., 1871, XXV) was devoted entirely to questions and answers from witnesses.

The Second Report (P.P. 1872, XXVI) contained three parts, the first the material on building societies, the second more evidence on friendly societies and the third a comprehensive index.

The Third Report (P.P. 1873, XXII) contained the examinations of more witnesses on friendly societies.

The Fourth Report (P.P. 1874, XXIII, Pt. I) contained the Commissioners own report along with appendices covering the historical development of societies and their relation to the State and the Poor Law etc.

The Reports of Assistant Commissioners (P.P. 1874, XXIII, Pt. II) included a great deal of valuable local material.

[2] P.P. 1874, XXIII, Pt. I, RCFS, 4th Report, App. I.

getting them to manage their financial affairs more efficiently. Every society should have its accounts audited annually; annual and quinquennial returns should be required; societies should be valued quinquennially; actuarial staff should be appointed to the office of the Registrar and tables of contributions and benefits be prepared and issued (but their use should not be made compulsory), and the Registrar should be empowered to dissolve a society or to vary its tables on application by a number of members of a society. The enactment of many of these recommendations in the legislation of 1875 with its emphasis on the insurance function of friendly societies above all else, served to indicate the paramount consideration of the last quarter of the century.

Far from suggesting its abolition, the Royal Commission proposed that the Registry of Friendly Societies should be extended by having local machinery in order to enforce the decisions taken centrally and to try to improve the lamentably small proportion of registered societies which in fact sent in their returns. Local 'Deputy Registrars' should collect returns, hold copies of the rules of societies in their districts and act as local representatives of the Chief Registrar. These proposals for the future development of the office of Registrar were the work of Ludlow and he developed them as his answer to the vital question which he posed in a paper for the Commission.[1] 'How is one man in London to keep nearly 22,000 bodies of men in all parts of England, in the most remote villages, in the most crowded cities, bodies composed to an enormous extent of the ignorant and prejudiced, to a large extent of the ignorant and self-willed, to some extent it is to be feared of the dishonest and malevolent, up to any conceivable standard, however low it be fixed?' Although not all of these suggestions were adopted, the office of Chief Registrar was established and the Registry was reorganized. Assistant Registrars were appointed for Scotland and Ireland, subordinate to the Chief Registrar.[2] Ludlow became the first Chief Registrar in 1875 and held the post until retirement at the age of 70 in 1891. A barrister, he had acquired

---

[1] 'Suggestions by the Secretary', is among some unpublished papers of J. M. Ludlow in the Goldsmiths' Library of the University of London.
[2] *See overleaf.*

a considerable repute as a Christian Socialist and friend of both Charles Kingsley and F. D. Maurice; his considerable personality played a major role in the development of the office of Chief Registrar.

[2] Hitherto the Registrar of Friendly Societies for Scotland and the Registrar of Friendly Societies for Ireland had been independent of the Registrar for England and Wales in London. In its Second Report of 1872 the Royal Commission stated that 'A painful part of our duty has been the investigation into the office and duties of the Registrar of Friendly Societies for Scotland. In Mr. A. Carnegy Ritchie we found an aged gentleman of courteous manners and evidently benevolent character, who threw his office open to the inquiries of our Assistant Commissioner with entire unreserve. But it would be idle to attempt in any way to gloss over the fact that Mr. Ritchie is now perfectly incompetent for the fulfilment of his duties' (para. 7). The Register itself was a mere waste-book of the most insufficient description, and most wretchedly kept. . . . It is in such a state that the law cannot possibly be carried out.' (Appendix no. 1). The position in Ireland was comparable. The Registrar 'scarcely ever attends at the office' (para. 9). In view of these findings the recommendation for a reorganized and centralized Registry for the United Kingdom was not surprising.

Chapter Four
Friendly Societies after 1875

I. Registration and the Friendly Societies' Acts

The question of what legislation should follow the Report of the Royal Commission was discussed at some length by the National Association for the Promotion of Social Science at its meeting in 1874. All shades of opinion were agreed on the importance of the matter, but some of the views expressed differed considerably from those of the commissioners. Registration already seemed to many friendly societies not to be worth the trouble it involved. In a paper he read on this subject, Charles Cameron claimed that to make the conditions imposed on registered societies even more stringent would worsen the situation and lead to even fewer being registered unless registration were made compulsory. There was a good deal of support for compulsory registration in the ensuing discussion. E. W. Brabrook, then Assistant Registrar of Friendly Societies, put the contrary view and held that registration should be universal but not compulsory. He hoped that this end could be achieved by wise legislation. In practice it would be impossible to enforce compulsory registration by means of legal sanctions.[1]

Lyulph Stanley, who had been an assistant commissioner to the Royal Commission, also doubted the value of state compulsion. Even if the Registrar's Office were given authority to insert model rules in the laws of all societies, the result would be that the printed rules would be merely for show and not for use. If any attempt were made to enforce them, the societies would be dissolved. No effective steps could be taken in such cases to enforce the law, 'any extensive attempt to do so would be odious, and would result in an agitation which would probably repeal the law'. Stanley believed that the two essential requisites for the success of a society were efficient management and adequate contributions in proportion to benefits, the first being more important than the second. Wise self-government was essential and it was this which should be encouraged. The jealousy and suspicion of government interference which were widespread 'even among the superior artizans and mechanics' should make legislators beware of increasing the stringency of the requirements for registration for fear of checking the existing tendency among many leading societies to seek 'the protection and discipline of the Friendly Societies' Acts'.[2]

The idea that registration should be encouraged but not be made compulsory had run through the recommendations of the Royal Commission and was to shape the Friendly Societies Act of 1875. It was hardly surprising, therefore, that J. M. Ludlow, having been Secretary to the Royal Commission and soon to become Chief Registrar, should have supported this attitude before the 1874 meeting of the National Association for the Promotion of Social Science. Ludlow examined the principal forms of state aid to registered friendly societies and listed eight:

1 Advice, both in special cases and more generally
2 Legal security

---

[1] Charles Cameron, 'What Legislation should follow upon the Report of the Commission on Friendly Societies' and subsequent discussion, *Trans. of the National Association for the Promotion of Social Science*, 1874, pp. 794-7, 824-5.
[2] Lyulph Stanley, *ibid.*, pp. 805-7.

3 Special remedies against wrong-doing
4 Special remedies in disputes
5 Aid in management
6 Privileges against individuals
7 Fiscal exemptions
8 Direct pecuniary aid

He explained that for himself, being someone who had 'never belonged to the mere *laissez faire* school', in general expediency and degree should determine the aid to be offered. He was only entirely opposed to the granting of privileges against individuals. These were really extreme instances of the aid afforded by special remedies against wrong-doing, since every such special remedy was virtually a privilege against someone. An instance of this could be found in the priority still given to friendly societies over other creditors against the estates of their deceased officers and the priority formerly granted to them against the estates of such officers when bankrupt which the societies were claiming should be restored. This was entirely indefensible since it could not be more criminal to embezzle the money of several persons than of one. If the purposes for which the money had been collected had to be taken into account, then the remedy of any single rich individual, widow or orphan against a dishonest trustee should be just the same as that of any sick fund or widows' and orphans' fund. This granting to a certain class of organizations of privileges against individuals was alone absolutely condemnable. Even direct subsidies by the state to friendly societies might be worth granting if these would bring more than equivalent benefits in return to the community. Moreover, a subsidy could be accurately gauged and its results set out clearly in a profit and loss account.[1]

On such controversial issues as the compulsory registration of societies, the Friendly Societies Act[2] followed the recommendations of the Royal Commission. As it happened, the

---

[1] J. M. Ludlow, 'On the different modes of State Aid to Private Undertakings, and in particular to Friendly and other Societies', *Trans of the National Association for the Promotion of Social Science*, 1874, pp. 811–23.

[2] 38 and 39 Vict., c.60.

general election of 1874 led to the chairman of the Royal Commission, Sir Stafford Northcote, becoming Chancellor of the Exchequer and taking charge of subsequent legislation in the House of Commons. In a confidential minute of 20 December 1874 he set out his aims in this legislation. The bill would aim at two objects; the giving of information which would be of use to managers of societies in framing proper rules and requiring societies to give such information to the public as would enable intelligent persons to judge for themselves the position of a society. Subject to those two conditions, 'it is the general intention of the bill to leave the managers of societies as free as possible to follow any course they please with regard to their constitution and management'.[1] The preparation of the bill afforded an opportunity not merely to make certain reforms but to bring together all friendly society legislation into a single comprehensive measure. The purposes for which friendly societies might be formed and registered were widened slightly to include fire insurance of up to £15 of the tools of trade of members. Two important changes were made in the classes of society that could register. Whereas each branch of an affiliated order had needed to register separately hitherto, affiliated orders could now register centrally as such. The purpose of this was to strengthen the position of the central government of an order with regard to its branches and in this way to improve the reliability of many of the orders as insurers. The second change was that dividing societies were now permitted to register if they wished, whereas previously they had been excluded from the register. On the other hand the system which had existed under previous legislation whereby societies whose rules failed to fulfil the requirements for registration might 'deposit' them and thereby gain the right to legal action for fraud or misappropriation of funds was ended and no 'deposit' of rules was permitted.

Once a society was registered, the new Act followed the recommendations of the Royal Commission in requiring it to have its accounts audited annually, either by a public auditor or by one of its own choice. It was to forward annual returns of

[1] Andrew Lang, *Life Letters and Diaries of Sir Stafford Northcote, First Earl of Iddesleigh*, 1890, vol. II, p. 45.

receipts and expenditure to the office of the Registrar. Quinquennial returns of sickness and mortality were also required along with quinquennial valuations of assets and liabilities. Failure to carry out these provisions became a punishable offence. Disputes within societies were to be settled in accordance with each society's rules; appeals might be made to the Registry, which was empowered to require the attendance of witnesses and the production of all documents relevant to the matter of contention. Societies which failed to make the returns required or to furnish any information called for by the Registry were liable to penalties in a court of summary jurisdiction. The aim of these provisions was not so much to secure state supervision as such but to ensure full publicity for the affairs of societies, with a view to enabling and encouraging members to satisfy themselves as to the soundness of the management of their clubs and the reliability of the insurances offered. Every registered society was bound to allow any member or other person having an interest in its funds to inspect its books and to supply him with a copy of the last annual return.

The replacement of the existing Registrar by a Chief Registrar and an Assistant Registrar for England and Wales as well as Assistant Registrars for Scotland and Ireland has been referred to above.[1] The Chief Registrar was to be a barrister of not less than twelve years' standing and an actuary was attached to the Registry. The Act did not go so far as the Royal Commission had recommended in strengthening the Registry. The Commission had recommended that local machinery should be created under central control in order to enforce the requirements of registration in the localities.[2] Ludlow came to believe that the failure to create this local machinery was the main weakness of the Act. He described the Registry as 'simply a head without limbs'. What was wanted was 'officers under the control of the central office, spread over the country in sufficient numbers to be able to look after the working of societies in their districts, were it only for the purpose of getting in returns and valuations'.[3] His successor, E. W. Brabrook, was of the same opinion. As late as 1892 he pointed out that the valuable recommendation for district registries had never been enacted by the Government since it feared these would prove to be both expensive and cumbersome.[1]

Administratively, a new register had to be made in order to bring the system established by the Act into operation. This ran to 74 volumes for England and Wales in 1875 and consisted of detached half-sheets, one for each society, so that as soon as a society became extinct, its entry could be removed to a register of extinct societies. As a precaution against the confusion arising from similarity of names, alphabetical lists were maintained in the three centres of London, Edinburgh and Dublin. Lists of new applications were exchanged weekly between the centres and revised lists of all registered societies every month.[2] Many of the societies already registered had the impression that they needed to re-register under the new legislation while others thought they could take themselves off the Register if some of the new provisions did not suit them. The Chief Registrar and his staff spent a good deal of time dispelling these impressions. Much of the time and effort of the Registry in years to come was to be spent in trying to extract the required returns from societies and the comment of the Chief Registrar in his first annual report was indicative of things to come when he wrote that 'nothing has been more difficult than to convince a vast number of societies that under S14 (5), their annual returns must be in the prescribed form, and that it will no longer suffice to send up to the Registry office anything which the society chooses to call its last annual report'. But on the whole, the Act appeared to have been not unwillingly received by the bulk of the societies.[3]

The Act formally recognized the affiliated orders as 'registrable units' thereby seeking to remove the difficulties which arose from the Act of 1855 as interpreted by Tidd Pratt who required each branch of the orders to register as an independent society, with absolute power so to alter its rules and to change

[1] P.P. 1893–4, XXXIX, Royal Commission on Labour, Minutes of Evidence, QQ. 1603–4.
[2] P.P. 1876, LXIX, Report of the Chief Registrar for 1875, p. 13.
[3] *Ibid.*, p. 16.

its name as to enable it to end all connection with its order. While the new act was intended to favour especially the affiliated orders, the transition for their lodges and courts from registration as a separate society to registration as a branch was more complicated and expensive than it need have been. The existing registration could in such cases now be cancelled and the lodges or courts were then free to re-register as branches of an order. The procedure laid down required advertisements to be inserted by each branch in *The London Gazette* and in local newspapers announcing the intention to cancel the existing registration. Rules often needed to be redrafted and reprinted to conform with the new position before registration could be accepted. The expense of advertising for the conversion of branches would have amounted to about £40,000 for the Manchester Unity and the Foresters.[1] The Chief Registrar believed that it was not simply the financial and technical difficulties which caused the trouble but that in many existing courts and lodges the feeling in favour of a real unity was weaker than had been supposed, so that the cost of advertising, printing new rules and so forth were used as excuses by members of the orders in some localities for their failure to follow the calls made by the executives for them to re-register their local branches as branches within the meaning of the Act.[2]

The Government was persuaded to pass an amending act in 1876[3] in the face of the complaints from the orders. This provided that if three-quarters of the members of a society present at a meeting voted to become a branch, the Chief Registrar could register it as a branch and cancel its existing registration as a society without any need for advertisements. The measure went some way to meeting the complaints of the orders but the business of calling special meetings at which not fewer than three-quarters of the members attended and voted for the necessary resolution and made the required amendments to the rules continued to slow down the process of re-registration as branches. Even so a very large part of the business of the Registry during the five years following 1875 was concerned

---

[1] Frome Wilkinson, *op. cit.*, p. 146.
[2] P.P. 1876, Report of the Chief Registrar for 1875, p. 18.
[3] 39 & 40 Vict., c.32.

with the re-registration as branches of bodies previously registered as societies; about 6,000 had been dealt with by 1880. In addition to these more than 1,800 branches had been registered for the first time so that about a half of the registered bodies in existence were registered as branches. In commenting on this position, Ludlow said that the fact that over 6,000 bodies had renounced a position of legal independence for one of legal subordination showed 'the strength of the federal principle amongst our industrious classes. That their confidence in that principle is justified appears, moreover, by the progress which is visible in almost all the affiliated bodies'.[1] In retrospect these developments appear to have been indicative of the increasing rate at which the orders themselves were growing into and emphasizing increasingly their role as national mutual insurance organizations. The accompanying graph illustrates the actual rate of conversions from societies to branches from 1876 to 1890. The total number of conversions during the 15 years amounted to 10,304 but even in 1890 a large number remained unconverted in some of the smaller orders, such as the Grand United Order of Odd Fellows.[2]

The powers of the Chief Registrar after 1875 were wider than those of his predecessor but they remained very strictly confined. He might cancel a society's registration if satisfied that it had been obtained by fraud or by mistake, or if the society had wilfully violated the act or ceased to exist. The lesser penalty of suspension for a period of up to three months could be imposed in place of cancellation. A society could, of course, appeal to the courts against any penalty if it wished. If approached by a certain proportion[3] of the membership of a society the Chief Registrar could, with the consent of the Treasury, either appoint inspectors to examine the affairs of the society, or call a special meeting at which the issues could be discussed.[4] In the case of societies with branches the consent of the central body was also required before any inquiry could be held. In certain

---

[1] P.P. 1881, LXXXIV, Report of the Chief Registrar for 1880, p. 4.
[2] P.P. 1890–1, LXXIX, Report of the Chief Registrar for 1890, p. 19.
[3] Normally at least ⅕th of the members, or 100 members in the case of a society with 1,000 to 10,000 members, or 500 members in the case of a society with more than 10,000 members.
[4] 38 & 39 Vict., c.60, s.23.

CONVERSIONS OF REGISTERED SOCIETIES
INTO BRANCHES 1876–1890

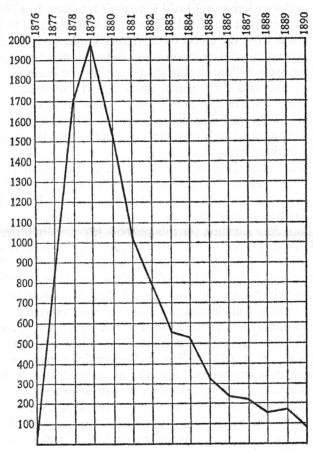

circumstances the Chief Registrar was also empowered to order the dissolution of a society on the application of a minority of its members if its financial condition appeared to warrant it.[1]

These powers were in fact used very cautiously by both Ludlow and his successor, Brabrook. By 1890, twelve inspections and twelve special meetings had been held.[2] The most

[1] *Ibid.*, s.25.
[2] P.P. 1890–1, LXXIX, Report of the Chief Registrar for 1890, p. 21.

notable of these had been concerned with collecting societies, but some of the subsequent reports indicated that some ordinary friendly societies could still have their troubles. In 1881 the inspector reported that the books of a society appeared to have been stolen from the club box. A trustee could supply neither the books nor any information about the accounts. None of the members were willing or able to account for the disappearance of the books and the balance unaccounted for amounted to £537. New officers had now been appointed. 'The inspector thought it only justice to the members to state that they were principally agricultural labourers and quite incapable of managing or checking accounts.'[1]

Although the Registry had not been well organized to enforce the making of valuations and returns, the right to suspend societies which violated the Act was used 785 times between 1875 and 1890 as a means of enforcing the obligation of valuation. As a sanction for this purpose it generally proved to be effective.[2] Prosecutions were undertaken for failure to make returns and valuations, for illegal dissolutions and for illegal investments. These had at first been conducted by local solicitors hired for each case, but this had proved to be both expensive and inefficient. Many solicitors were swayed by local considerations and they were not familiar with friendly society legislation, so prosecutions had been placed in the hands of the Chief Clerk.[3] In 1889, a Treasury committee examined the administration and internal organization of the Registry and as a result a Law Clerk was added to the staff who then took over prosecutions from the Chief Clerk. The Registry itself was reorganized in three branches after 1899, headed by the Assistant Registrar, the Actuary and the Chief Clerk. The office now comprised:[4]

Chief Registrar (with law clerk)
Assistant Registrar for England and Wales
Actuary (with one clerk and a variable copying staff)
Chief Clerk

[1] P.P. 1882, LXVI, Report of the Chief Registrar for 1881, p. 25.
[2] P.P. 1890–1, LXXIX, Report of the Chief Registrar for 1890, p. 20.
[3] *Ibid.*, p. 21.
[4] *Ibid.*, pp. 3 and 6.

A Senior Clerk
Three Clerks
Four Second Division Clerks
One Messenger
A number of Copyists

The Chief Registrar found himself in one sense a spokesman inside the administration for what might be described as the friendly society interest. This was of some importance in connection with the continuing uneasy reationships between the societies and the Poor Law authorities to which reference has been made above. Difficulties arose under the Divided Parishes and Poor Law Amendment Act of 1876.[1] Section 23 provided that where the guardians incurred expenses in the case of pauper lunatics in their care who were entitled to benefits from friendly societies, they might claim these benefits from the societies. The consequence of this was to deprive the lunatic pauper's wife and dependents of the benefits they would otherwise have received from the unfortunate member's society and making them dependent on poor relief. After three years of agitation by the friendly societies, the Act of 1876 was amended so that it should no longer apply where a pauper or pauper lunatic had a wife or dependents but that in such cases the benefits should go to the wife or dependents. Where the pauper had no dependents, the guardians could only make a claim if their relief were given on loan and if they had given 30 days notice to the society.[2]

Quite naturally, societies had no interest in paying benefit to the guardians where there was no wife and no dependents, so they drew their rules to exclude benefit in such cases. The Oddfellows, for instance, had a rule which stated that 'If a member is in a workhouse or lunatic asylum at the charge of any parochial board, no sick pay shall be allowed unless he has a wife or children, or some other relative dependent upon him for support when the amount due shall be paid for their relief and maintenance.' (Rule 63). The guardians of the Caistor Union in Lincolnshire challenged the validity of this rule which seemed to be deliberately drawn 'in order to repeal the Act' as their

[1] 39 & 40 Vict., c.61.
[2] 42 & 43 Vict., c.12.

Counsel put it.[1] The matter arose when the Caistor guardians sued the secretary of the Heart of Honesty Lodge, I.O.O.F.M.U. for £15 18s 6d expended on a pauper lunatic Oddfellow inmate. The magistrates at Market Rasen dismissed the case and it was taken on appeal to the High Court. In his judgement, the Lord Chief Justice upheld the decision of the magistrates. The words of the statute of 1879 and of the 63rd rule were perfectly consistent with each other; the former did not over-rule the latter. 'On the contrary the 63rd rule expressly disentitles him (the pauper lunatic Oddfellow) under the circumstances found in the case to receive that sum of money which it is said ought to be paid. The words of the Act of Parliament and the words of the rule are perfectly consistent, and under the words of the Act of Parliament and the words of the rule it appears to me that the magistrates have decided perfectly rightly, and this appeal must be dismissed with costs.'[2] The decision was greeted with satisfaction and relief by the friendly societies whose members did not expect their subscriptions to be used to relieve the poor rate.

Whenever assistance from public funds in old age or sickness is made subject to any sort of means test it must always lead to a situation in which the 'thrifty' seem to do less well than the 'unthrifty' who have never attempted to make provision for the future. The organizers and promoters of thrift schemes are bound to feel themselves in conflict to some extent with the public relief system.[3] In spite of the welcome Act of 1879 and the judiciary's favourable interpretation of it, officers of the friendly societies resented the systems used by boards of guardians in distributing aid to the chronically sick and aged. Where an applicant had paid into a society and become entitled to a small weekly benefit perhaps at the reduced rate of a quarter or a half of the normal rate of sick pay, his weekly public relief would usually have that sum deducted from it, while his neighbour, 'who had been utterly neglectful of his

---

[1] J. Diprose and J. Gammon, *Reports of Law Cases affecting Friendly Societies*, 1897, p. 380.

[2] *Ibid.*, pp. 359–82. Guardians of Caistor Union v. Cleaver, Queen's Bench Division, 30th November 1891, before the Lord Chief Justice and Mathew J.

[3] W. Chance, *Our Treatment of the Poor*, 1899, pp. 123–44, discusses the position at the very end of the 19th century.

economic duty' would receive full relief from the poor rates. It was argued that this encouraged improvidence and harmed the cause of thrift and self-help. On the other hand, there were those who blamed the weaknesses of the friendly societies themselves for the number compelled to resort to poor relief. Some Members of Parliament took this view and from time to time called for returns of the numbers of those who had been members of friendly societies and were now paupers in workhouses. A return of 1881 showed that there were then 11,304 adult male indoor paupers who had been members of societies. Of these some 7,391 had failed to keep up their contributions while the societies to which the remainder had belonged had broken up for one reason or another.[1]

Apart from the inevitable friction with the Poor Law, the favourable legislative position accorded to the affiliated orders in 1875 and 1876 remained substantially unchanged for the remainder of the century. The Friendly Societies Act of 1887[2] removed certain limitations on the acquisition of land by friendly societies and strengthened the position of the leaders of the orders by requiring a seceding branch to produce a certificate of secession before it could be registered as a separate society. The Friendly Societies Act of 1896[3] was a consolidating measure so far as friendly societies themselves were concerned, but collecting or burial societies were for the first time dealt with differently in a separate act; the Collecting and Industrial Assurance Companies Act.[4] In 1896, there were 43 registered collecting societies with 3,875,215 members or 90,121 per society on average. Other friendly societies or branches of orders had an average of 181 members.[5] It was held that friendly societies proper had all the elements of self-government and could, in general, be left to work out their own salvation with such assistance facilities and remedies as the Friendly Societies Acts provided for them. By contrast persons insured in collecting societies needed much stronger measures

---

[1] P.P. 1881, LXXLX, Return on 31st March 1881 of those who had been members of benefit societies and were now paupers in workhouses.
[2] 50 & 51 Vict., c.56.
[3] 59 & 60 Vict., c.25.
[4] 59 & 60 Vict., c.26. This measure is discussed more fully in the next chapter.
[5] P.P. 1897, LXXXII, Report of the Chief Registrar for 1896, p. 2.

of protection since these were akin to industrial insurance companies and the managers were not really responsible to the members. Indeed, the Chief Registrar contrasted the aims of the two forms of organization quite tersely by stating that the friendly societies were conducted for the benefit of their members while the collecting societies were promoted and conducted for the benefit of their managers.[1]

The main legal privileges which registered friendly societies enjoyed during the latter part of the nineteenth century had come to include:

(1) the right to hold land and other property in the names of trustees
(2) while the only remedy open to an unregistered society against fraud was confined to larceny or embezzlement, a registered society had a remedy on summary conviction whenever any person:
  (a) obtained possession of any of its property, by false representation or imposition
  (b) having possession of any of its property, withheld or misapplied it
  (c) wilfully applied any part of such property to purposes other than those expressed by the rules
(3) priority for any claim a friendly society might have on the assets of its officers if they became bankrupt
(4) removal of untraceable or lunatic trustees by simple direction of the Chief Registrar instead of by application to the high court.
(5) freedom from stamp duties
(6) ability for members of societies to insure the lives of their wives and children without having an insurable interest in their lives.
(7) the right for members of societies to dispose of sums up to £100 payable on their death by the society by written nomination without a will; where there was no nomination, the society's trustees might distribute without letters of administration.[2]

[1] *Ibid.*, p. 3.
[2] P.P. 1905, LXXV, Report of the Chief Registrar, Appendix A, p. 48.

II. Financial position of the societies

The growth of registered friendly societies (excluding the collecting societies) during the latter part of the nineteenth century may be seen from the following table. It should, perhaps, be added that these figures may not represent the rate of

Table 4.1.

Growth of registered friendly societies under the Act of 1875[1]

Date	Number of Members	Funds £	Funds per Member £
1877	2,750,000	12,700,000	4–13–0
1887	3,600,000	20,000,000	5–11–0
1897	4,800,000	30,500,000	6– 7–0
1904	5,600,000	41,000,000	7– 6–0

growth in total friendly society membership since some societies already in existence before 1877 may have moved on to the register after an earlier period as unregistered societies, but the overall picture of considerable growth of both membership and funds per member seems to be a fair representation. The Chief Registrar was asked by the Royal Commission on Labour in 1892 to estimate what proportion of the industrial classes in the country were insured against sickness through friendly societies or through subscribing for friendly society benefit offered by some trade unions. He replied that if the total number of the male industrial population was in the region of 7,000,000 then against that there were 3,860,000 members of registered friendly societies (excluding collecting societies) and probably about 3,000,000 members of unregistered societies. There was, no doubt, some overlapping membership but there were also men not in societies who contributed to trade unions for these benefits. The Chief Registrar concluded that 'It

[1] Randolph G. Smith, 'Progress and position of Friendly Societies', *Transactions of the Insurance and Actuarial Society of Glasgow*, Series 6, No. 7, 1908.

would look as if there was really merely a kind of residuum left of those who are in uncertain work or otherwise, and are not able to insure in some shape or another.'[1]

There was a great improvement in the collection of financial and actuarial material concerning registered societies after 1875. There was still considerable difficulty in getting returns from secretaries of some local societies or branches of the affiliated orders where the secretaries themselves were not men accustomed to dealing with official forms or regulations. At the same time it was not really clear exactly what proportion of local bodies did disregard their obligation to make returns since the register itself dated back to the 1830s and contained a mixture of the living and the dead.[2] The Registry made considerable efforts to improve the flow of returns and the Chief Registrar provided these figures in 1892 relating to the previous year:[3]

independent societies (a) receipts £2,117,000
                 (b) (i) benefits paid £1,596,000
                      (ii) expenses £195,000
                      (iii) balance invested £326,000
affiliated orders   (a) receipts £3,555,000
                 (b) (i) benefits £2,681,000
                      (ii) expenses £449,000
                      (iii) invested £425,000

The greater effort to collect financial statistics after 1875 made it possible to build up a fairly comprehensive picture of the way in which societies invested their funds. The details given in the annual returns for 1877 form the basis for the accompanying table. It may be seen that by far the largest single class of investments were real securities including mortgages. Next in order but a long way behind were investments with the National Debt Commissioners and with Trustee Savings Banks. There were very great variations between counties. Many of those near London appeared to prefer the

[1] P.P. 1893–4, XXXIX, Royal Commission on Labour, Minutes of Evidence, Q. 1331.
[2] J. Frome Wilkinson, 'Friendly Society Finance', *The Economic Journal*, vol. II, p. 722.
[3] P.P. 1893–4, XXXIX, Royal Commission on Labour, Minutes of Evidence, QQ. 1319 and 1321.

National Debt Commissioners to the Trustee Savings Banks. The sums invested with the National Debt Commissioners varied from nil in some counties to 50.45 per cent of total investments in Devon. It should be remembered that the deposit of funds with commercial bankers, cooperative societies and so forth was illegal. The Chief Registrar pointed out in his report for 1878 that 'the failure of Messrs. Fenton's Bank at Rochdale is an object lesson to the societies since some wrongfully had money in it and lost it.'[1] Between 1877 and 1899 the proportion of investments in government securities and savings banks decreased from 42% to 22% of the whole while investment in land, buildings and mortgages increased from 30% to 52%. This seems to have been due in part to a larger share of the total sums for investment being in the hands of the affiliated orders rather than in those of the local societies.[2] It may also have reflected the better returns available on mortgages than on government funds at the end of the century.

The rate of interest earned on funds invested obviously had a considerable impact on the solvency of societies as shown by valuations. The rate used in valuing societies was most often 3 per cent, but sometimes 4 and even 5 per cent were assumed by the valuer who could use whatever rate he decided so far as the Registry was concerned. The rates actually earned—as distinct from the rates assumed—varied greatly, from little more than 1 to over 6 per cent. The Chief Registrar, Brabrook, could only suggest that where a society showed a very poor return, a large proportion of its funds must be uninvested for some reason. He admitted in 1892 that the rates shown in

---

[1] P.P. 1878–9, LXV, Report of the Chief Registrar for 1878, p. 13.

The trustees of a registered society were, subject to the society's rules, to invest its funds:
with the consent of committee or members
in any savings bank, to any extent
or in the public funds
or on loan to any member upon his policy of assurance
or by granting loans to members out of a separate loan fund
or with the National Debt Commissioners
or in the purchase of land.
Investments might not be made on personal security (38 & 39 Vict. c.60, s.16 and s.18).

[2] Randolph G. Smith, *op. cit.*

Table 4.2.

Table showing for each county the proportion of assets of friendly societies invested in the stated forms of security. The details are taken from annual returns for 1877. They do not include collecting societies and are given as percentages correct to 2 places of decimals.

	Trustee Saving Banks	Post Office Savings Bank	Public Funds, Government Securities	National Debt Cssrs.	Land, offices and buildings	Mortgages and other real securities	Railway and other debentures	Local Securities	Building Societies	Stocks and Shares	Illegal investments e.g. on personal security	Furniture, regalia, not specified etc.	Cash
Bedford	18·11	9·92	3·47	·85	6·79	45·03	1·71	—	1·05	·26	7·81	·35	4·65
Berks	32·33	9·39	7·33	3·14	2·79	16·54	17·70	3·56	—	2·22	·59	·55	3·86
Bucks	10·03	11·15	10·88	30·94	8·28	23·77	—	—	·69	·15	·49	·30	3·32
Cambs	20·51	16·07	3·32	1·67	2·56	44·53	·46	·39	·13	·43	5·23	·32	4·38
Cheshire	25·06	6·04	2·15	4·70	5·19	26·26	1·67	14·94	1·00	5·68	2·63	1·09	3·59
Cornwall	39·20	9·25	4·70	9·77	·46	23·04	2·02	4·92	—	·98	1·93	·31	3·42
Cumberland	19·58	2·05	·42	2·10	9·58	19·05	7·89	11·42	8·16	8·99	6·79	·58	3·39
Derby	20·26	5·05	·98	1·82	8·50	29·34	10·74	9·86	1·27	1·46	4·12	1·52	5·08
Devon	20·28	2·30	1·20	50·45	1·23	9·09	1·79	8·53	·26	·15	1·90	·70	2·12
Dorset	23·23	5·90	14·50	7·95	·47	13·59	13·12	1·98	—	—	13·37	2·95	2·94
Durham	16·13	16·63	1·09	·08	4·05	33·01	4·69	3·68	4·26	2·24	6·42	1·17	6·54

Glos	27·58	9·05	2·65	9·59	2·85	28·48	3·28	6·74	—	1·07	4·51	·34	3·86
Hants	8·77	9·74	8·29	35·22	2·11	24·05	·68	1·33	·54	·74	3·70	2·25	2·58
Hereford	17·35	2·00	2·20	13·07	2·52	23·84	—	27·04	—	—	4·92	3·82	3·24
Herts	1·92	8·72	19·27	45·44	5·13	9·44	3·39	—	—	2·15	2·08	·32	2·14
Hunts	4·60	13·38	5·94	—	5·79	50·75	—	—	·25	—	15·04	·28	3·97
Kent	7·52	15·18	17·66	26·61	·76	15·60	1·87	4·10	1·08	2·31	3·66	·22	3·43
Lancs	16·65	2·38	1·20	·75	9·69	21·40	1·62	26·10	5·04	6·13	3·16	1·42	4·46
Leics	11·47	9·54	3·36	2·31	13·92	34·36	3·59	6·14	·66	4·11	5·07	·97	4·50
Lincs	15·85	4·10	·49	·53	7·84	58·15	·24	—	·48	·34	4·79	2·81	4·38
Middlesex	6·09	3·29	13·35	44·33	2·34	7·46	7·08	6·05	—	4·94	2·19	·88	2·00
Monmouth	4·11	14·47	·56	·08	13·60	28·32	15·12	·09	2·15	3·58	10·42	2·01	5·49
Norfolk	14·36	9·91	7·30	7·10	1·84	42·82	·38	5·00	—	—	7·95	·40	2·94
Northants	17·37	7·38	·98	2·62	14·79	37·72	·09	·51	—	1·96	12·10	1·27	3·21
Northumberland	32·82	9·94	2·23	1·57	6·60	20·33	·37	8·45	6·35	·02	2·52	3·07	5·73
Notts	9·30	3·62	·72	—	9·83	45·89	1·73	13·76	·04	1·93	9·14	1·20	2·84
Oxford	26·07	15·94	7·52	9·08	2·00	28·61	—	1·59	—	2·72	1·52	·50	4·45
Rutland	42·45	4·16	4·01	32·33	1·11	10·83	—	—	—	—	·44	—	4·67
Salop	17·17	9·67	4·51	6·22	5·78	30·10	3·59	8·16	·21	1·77	7·50	1·94	3·38
Somerset	14·57	14·84	4·09	35·82	·44	20·93	·18	·78	·12	1·07	2·49	·90	3·77
Staffs	8·46	11·59	1·34	4·54	3·04	47·58	1·56	7·58	1·32	2·18	5·21	1·62	3·98
Suffolk	11·97	7·85	3·34	24·19	2·58	31·38	2·90	4·06	·08	1·64	2·41	5·16	2·44
Surrey	8·88	16·76	28·38	11·19	·48	12·09	·09	2·06	·55	11·59	3·76	·39	3·78
Sussex	13·78	10·20	4·85	3·67	·30	30·63	4·54	24·69	·44	·92	1·43	1·22	3·33
Warwicks	8·85	7·58	2·67	7·74	1·48	24·70	3·04	35·95	·04	7·13	3·47	·34	2·01
Westmorland	4·01	3·16	4·62	—	7·53	34·05	9·23	16·25	—	10·98	8·13	·13	1·91
Wilts	27·42	4·90	7·32	13·17	1·95	26·95	·26	7·67	—	·48	5·78	·52	3·58
Worcs	7·04	16·21	3·18	8·16	7·79	35·98	1·26	9·00	·03	3·28	3·35	·51	4·21
Yorkshire	17·86	2·12	2·40	·72	9·96	24·36	2·86	17·23	6·77	6·26	4·74	1·26	3·46
National	13·65	7·18	6·08	15·07	4·94	25·13	3·20	10·85	1·69	3·52	4·09	1·21	3·39

valuation varied from 50 to 100 per cent more than the actual realized. When questioned on this point before the Royal Commission on Labour, he explained that it would be the duty of the valuer (who was appointed by the society itself) to point to the need to arrange the society's affairs so as to earn as much interest as his valuation assumed would be earned. 'The valuation speaks of the case wholly in the future. Whatever the amount of interest realized in the past, the valuation is a true one if the rate of interest it assumes is realized in the future.'

The Chief Registrar had no legal authority to intervene in this matter, however serious the possible consequences.[1] The previous Chief Registrar, Ludlow, was asked by Jesse Collings, one of the Commissioners, whether the fact that a society was registered at the government registry was not likely to give false confidence to an ill-informed labourer. He replied that during his period at the Friendly Societies Office 'we never wearied in taking every opportunity we could of warning people that the fact of registration was no guarantee of solvency. In every possible shape and on every possible occasion we have set that forth, and we could not do more than that.'[2]

Registered societies were obliged to have their assets and liabilities valued at least every five years and to send to the Registry a report on the results of the valuation along with a return 'containing such information with respect to the benefits assured and contributions receivable by the society and of its funds and effects, debts and credits' as the Chief Registrar might require.[3] The collection and publication of this data served, of course, to indicate the extent to which the assets of many societies were inadequate in terms of the liabilities they had undertaken. But, perhaps more significantly, the data showed that during the latter part of the century there was a steady improvement in the financial strength and reliability of friendly societies generally and particularly of the affiliated orders. Table 4.3 shows the extent of this, the position being summarised in column (6).

[1] P.P. 1893–4, XXXIX, Royal Commission on Labour, Minutes of Evidence, QQ. 1445–53.
[2] *Ibid.*, Q.1901.
[3] 38 & 39 Vict., c.60, s.14.

Table 4.3.

A summary of the aggregate results of the valuations of friendly
societies forming the affiliated orders, 1876–1900.[1]

Date (1)	Number of Valuations (2)	Total assets (3)	Total liabilities (4)	Net deficiency (5)	Ratio of assets to liabilities (6)
		£	£	£	£
1876–80	12,953	49,106,101	57,004,077	7,897,976	17s 3d
1881–85	13,727	57,879,857	66,581,579	8,701,722	17s 5d
1886–90	13,706	63,472,035	72,465,644	8,993,609	17s 6d
1891–95	11,406	47,885,109	52,962,089	5,076,980	18s 1d
1896–1900	14,657	87,661,860	94,867,139	7,205,279	18s 6d

While he was Assistant Registrar, Brabrook, in his Introduction to a new edition of Tidd Pratt's *Law of Friendly Societies*,
cautioned critics against forming hasty conclusions adverse to
the societies on the grounds that valuations revealed deficiencies. He felt it would have been strange if it had been otherwise when 'scientific tests' were applied to contracts which had
been in existence for many years without any actuarial basis.
But contracts made by friendly societies with their members
were elastic and the terms could always be corrected if the error
were found in time. Words such as 'insolvency' and 'rottenness'
to describe societies were quite out of place. By comparison
with friendly societies in general, none were 'managed with
greater rectitude, and few with equal success'.

One problem which grew in importance and which was not to
be dealt with until the 20th century was that of elderly members
who received as sick pay what were really weekly old age
annuities. In these cases the sick pay covered the loss of earning
powers arising from the disability of old age and which had
never been paid for. Friendly society benefits were never intended to do more than secure contributors against loss of
earnings caused by sickness during normal working life. The
period after working life needed to be separately insured for.
Since it hardly ever was, an increasing strain fell upon sick

[1] Smith, *op. cit.*, and relevant reports from the Chief Registrar.

funds which they were never intended to bear. In the older lodges and courts this became a prime cause of deficiencies.[1]

III. *The affiliated orders*

At the time when the Royal Commission reported it looked to some observers as though the affiliated orders might by the end of the century occupy nearly all the ground which the various permanent societies then held. This was the form of society for which the Commissioners held the highest hopes of future improvement. The law should favour them and use their machinery for the improvement of friendly societies. The main need was to strengthen the tie between the branches and the executive of an order, the enforcement of an order's general laws and put an end to secession by individual lodges and courts. In this way the executives—who in general saw the need for financial and organizational reform—would be able to cause these reforms to be carried out rapidly and to be enforced thoroughly.[2]

Whereas previous legislation had tended to strengthen the feeling of independence in the branches of the orders by causing each to register as an independent society, the Acts of 1875 and 1876 operated in the contrary manner. The criterion for registration as a society with branches was now to be regular contributions by the members to a central fund. The weakness of the authority of the central organizations in the orders hitherto can be judged by the fact that it was this requirement of the new legislation which led to the creation of such a central fund in most cases. Before 1875 the local branches generally made no contribution whatever to the central funds of their orders, the whole of the central expenses being met generally from the sale of regalia and the like which every branch was required to purchase from the central body.

---

[1] J. Frome Wilkinson, 'Some illustrations of Friendly Society Finance', *Jnl of Statistical Society*, LVIII, 1895, pp. 319–20.

The difficulties raised by the problems of insurance for old age are discussed below in chapter 9.

[2] Lyulph Stanley, 'What Legislation should follow upon the Report of the Commission on Friendly Societies?' *Trans. of the National Association for the Promotion of Social Science*, 1874, p. 808.

The Manchester Unity of Oddfellows and the Ancient Order of Foresters, as well as many of the smaller orders, now arranged for a contribution of a halfpenny or a penny per member per annum to a fund for assisting distressed branches, the hope behind this being that eventually the orders might be able to guarantee the solvency of their branches. By the end of the century, this was still not the position. So far as sick pay and contributions were concerned, every branch remained financially distinct and independent. Financially distressed branches still had no legal claim on the central fund of their order and whatever relief was given from that fund was a matter of discretion for the executive of the order. Even so, the mere creation of a central fund to which all members contributed led to a great advance in the direction of centralization.[1] The advice and guidance of the leaders was more readily heeded. They became more influential and better able to guide their local branches towards implementing the rules which most of the orders adopted requiring branches to have adequate rates of contribution for the benefits they insured.

Some important judgements in the law courts served to reinforce the centralizing tendencies in the legislation of 1875. The executives of the orders gradually came to claim the right to direct the application of surplus funds in a branch. They were strengthened in this by two cases involving the Manchester Unity. Cox v. James and Avery v. Andrews established that an order could by injunction restrain its branches from dividing a surplus among the members in violation of the general rules of the order and that such injunctions would be enforced by imprisonment if disobeyed, as the trustees of the Loyal Brunswick Lodge of the Manchester Unity discovered to their cost in 1882.[2]

The judgement in the case of Schofield v. Vause established that lodges and courts which had not registered as branches under the Act of 1875 but which had remained on the register

[1] P.P. 1893–4, XXXIX, Royal Commission on Labour, Minutes of Evidence, Brabrook, Q. 1266.

[2] The trustees were committed to prison by Justice Kay in the Chancery Division on 10 February 1882, for dividing the sum of £2,000 among members, thereby contravening the general laws of the Manchester Unity and breaking an injunction granted to the Board of Directors.

as independent societies were nevertheless subject to the general rules of the orders to which they belonged and could not secede from that order if the general rules did not permit this. The Directors of the Manchester Unity sought an injunction to restrain the trustees and officers of the Loyal Caledonian Lodge, Bolton, from carrying on the business of the lodge as a separate society. The lodge had been founded in 1830. It had been registered in 1873 under the Act of 1855 and declined to re-register as a branch under the Act of 1875 on being ordered to do so by the Unity. The lodge resolved instead to break with the order and to become an independent society. The court granted the Directors an injunction to restrain the trustees and officers of the lodge in November 1885 and this decision was confirmed by the Court of Appeal the next year. It was held that when a member joined a lodge he also became a member of the Unity of which the lodge formed a part and the tie between the two could only be ended in accordance with such rules as the Unity might determine.[1]

The greatly increased power of the executives of the affiliated orders led to the general adoption of more businesslike arrangements for insurance. The increasing standardization of benefits and contributions, the requirements of regular audits and returns, all tended to put an end to the practice of paying for lodge liquor out of ordinary contributions. Convivial activities continued and the sense of brotherhood was very actively cultivated by the orders, but the overwhelming importance of the insurance element could no longer be doubted by the end of the century.

A contemporary foreign observer remarked in 1883 that forms of ritual and mystery 'have now only a subordinate importance'. The passwords, eccentric devices, symbols and emblems presented 'a strange contrast to the thoroughly practical and sober objects of insurance against sickness and accident'.[2] The Chief Registrar commented on the more business-like attitude to be found in the orders when he repeated that whilst only 46 per cent of the ordinary societies made their returns of sickness and mortality regularly, 68 per

---

[1] Diprose and Gammon, *op. cit.*, pp. 437–509.
[2] Baernreither, *op. cit.*, p. 221.

cent of branches of the orders did so. This he described as 'an instance of the superior development of the orders'.[1]

The improvement in the financial reliability of the affiliated orders became increasingly evident. A crude measurement of the total funds of the lodges of the Manchester Unity of Oddfellows showed an increase of 15 per cent between 1884 and 1889 and a further increase of 18 per cent during the next five years. In the case of the funds of the courts of the Foresters, there was an increase of 19 per cent in the first five year period and a similar increase in the second.[2] These two orders were undoubtedly financial leaders of their class. The continuing collection and analysis of their sickness and mortality experience and the publication of tables and recommendations based on this by the actuaries impressed on the managers of societies generally the importance of the distinctions between insurance for life, sickness and old age. The knowledge served to spread the conviction of the need to make the orders fully regulated unions for insurance. After Neison had analysed the experience of the Foresters on the basis of whether the courts were situated in rural, town or city areas, the High Court decided to abandon tables based on the common experience of the Order and to substitute rates which reflected the influence of locality on the sickness and mortality risks.[3] The thoroughness and reliability of the actuarial work undertaken in the later years of the nineteenth century is, perhaps, illustrated by the fact that the Tunbridge Wells Equitable Society, in proposing a new deferred benefit scheme in 1971, based its calculations on the experience of the Manchester Unity of Oddfellows for the years 1893–97.[4]

Financial reform was much later in spreading to some of the smaller and less well-organized orders. Considered on the basis of their quinquennial valuations, the weakest of these were not

---

[1] P.P. 1890–1, LXXIX, Report of the Chief Registrar for 1890, p. 7.

[2] E. W. Brabrook, 'The Progress of Friendly Societies and other Institutions connected with the Friendly Societies Registry Office during the ten years 1884–94', *J. Statistical Society*, LVII, (1895), p. 291.

[3] F. G. P. Neison, *Additional Statistics deduced from the Original Records of the Sickness Experience (1871–5) of the Order*, 1886, p. 4; A.O.F., *Directory*, 1891, p. XXXII.

[4] *The Equitable*, Autumn 1971, p. 36.

likely to be able to meet much more than half of their future liabilities. The enormous variation of financial strength which existed among the affiliated orders as late as 1890 is shown in table 4.4.

Table 4.4.

A selection of affiliated orders arranged in order of solvency[1]

Society	Worth in the £	Deficiency %
Locomotive Steam Enginemen and Firemen	19s 10d	1
Manchester Unity of Oddfellows	19s 1d	4½
Philanthropic Order of True Ivorites	18s 11d	5½
Salford Unity of Rechabites	18s 3d	9
Ancient Order of Foresters	17s 1d	14½
Loyal Order of Ancient Shepherds, Ashton Unity	16s 11d	15½
Order of Druids	16s 0d	20
Nottingham Imperial Order of Oddfellows	15s 11d	21
Grand United Order of Oddfellows	14s 11d	25½
Ancient Order of Comical Fellows	14s 6d	27½
British Order of Ancient Free Gardeners	13s 6d	32½
Original Grand Order of Total Abstinence Sons of the Phoenix	12s 4d	38½
Free and Independent United Order of Mechanics	10s 3d	48½

Since the burden of sickness insurance fell on the individual lodge or court, it was essential that these units should be large enough to enable them to hope for the average experience on which their tables were based. The larger the branch, the more likely it was to contain a member who would be a competent secretary and the percentage of the members' contributions which needed to be spent on management would be smaller. The leaders of the orders sought to encourage an increase in the

[1] Based on information given by James Blossom in *Unity*, July 1891.

size of individual units but progress was steady rather than outstanding. In the 15 years following 1871 the average size of the lodges of the Manchester Unity increased from 122 to 142 members while the courts of the Foresters increased from 107 to 133. The Order of Druids sought to overcome the problems posed by small branches by operating their sick funds on the basis of forming equalized districts. Under this arrangement, every quarter, the branches in a district with a surplus paid it into a common fund while those in deficit were relieved by payments from it. The argument advanced against this arrangement which offered the undeniable advantage of equalizing risks was that individual branches lost interest in keeping a sharp watch on the claims of sick members and became more lax in their management. Apart from the feeling of local independence, the main obstacle to the formation of equalizing district funds was that while branches in poor financial shape favoured them, those which were better off and which would have to contribute their surpluses were naturally reticent.

The orders continued to grow in size during the last quarter of the century (see table 4.5) but the rate of growth of the large general orders slackened, while the teetotal Rechabites experienced a rapid period of expansion. The exceptional performance of the Salford Unity of Rechabites was probably due partly to their later foundation. This high rate of growth continued into the twentieth century. In 1910 the total adult membership in the United Kingdom reached 212,794.[1] The development of this particular order was also strongly affected by the strength of the moral and religious influences associated with the temperance movement. Neison published in 1889 a study[2] which appeared to confirm the abstainers' belief that their particular form of virtue led to a longer life. The average Rechabite aged 20 could look forward to a further 45.1 years of life, while on Neison's calculations the average Forester of the same age could only expect 40.2 years more.

[1] Richardson Campbell, *Rechabite History: A Record of the Origin, Rise and Progress of the Independent Order of Rechabites, Salford Unity*, 1911, p. 434.
[2] Francis G. P. Neison, *Rates of Mortality and Sickness according to the experience for the ten years 1878–87 of the Independent Order of Rechabites (Salford Unity) Friendly Society*, 1889.

Table 4.5.

Membership of six affiliated orders in the U.K.

	1872	1886	1899
Manchester Unity of Oddfellows	427,000	597,000	713,000
Ancient Order of Foresters	394,000	572,000	666,000
Salford Unity of Rechabites	9,000	60,000	136,000
Ashton Unity of Shepherds	46,000	72,000	103,000
Grand United Oddfellows	71,000	83,000	70,000
Order of Druids	57,000	61,000	56,000

In his final report as Chief Registrar, Ludlow summarized accurately the main developments in the orders after 1875 when he wrote that 'It is . . . among the affiliated bodies especially that the benefits of the legislation of 1875 are apparent. The conditions required by the act for the registration of branches, the contribution to a central fund, the control of a central body, have given to the organization of most of them a cohesion and vitality which they did not possess before; whilst the obligation of periodical valuation has awakened, or is awakening, one after the other to the necessity of setting their house in order by providing for a fair balancing of contributions and liabilities.'[1]

IV. Deposit, dividing and other societies

The stronger emphasis on the business aspect of friendly society affairs after 1875 was clearly reflected in the rapid growth of the largest of the unitary societies, the Hearts of Oak, and in the rise of deposit and Holloway societies. The Hearts of Oak increased from 64,421 members in 1875 to 239,075 by 1899.[2] The Royal Commission viewed the society as a well-managed insurance business and its reputation as such formed the basis of its appeal. By the end of the century, it had a system of uniform contributions to cover a great variety of benefits. The contribution was not absolutely fixed but could be varied

[1] P.P. 1890–1, LXXIX, Report of the Chief Registrar for 1890, p. 23.
[2] Hearts of Oak Benefit Society, Annual Reports.

by levy according to the claims made on the Society during the previous quarter, and averaged ten shillings. This covered sick benefits, burial money, allowance on the birth of a child, assurance of tools against fire, and other allowances. The government of the Hearts of Oak was the ultimate responsibility of the Assembly of Delegates. Since there were no local branches and members would not normally know one another, clubs sometimes came to be formed for the purpose of organizing the election of delegates.[1]

The earliest of the deposit societies was the Abbott's Ann Deposit Society founded by the Reverend Samuel Best at Abbott's Ann, Hampshire, in 1831. This Society flourished in its locality but never became more than local and was eventually dissolved in 1931. But in 1868 the Surrey Deposit Society was established on the same principles, and changed its name to the National Deposit Society in 1872. By the Second World War it had become very large indeed, with more than 1,500,000 members. Best saw deposit societies as genuine engines of individual thrift for he claimed that his society was really a savings bank, not a club. The member's money remained his own, under his own control and only under such limitations as were necessary for the protection of all. The individual member's monthly contribution was divided into two parts, one part being credited to his deposit account and the remainder to the general benefit fund. The premiums were not adjusted for age of entry or sex and persons could join at any age. But members were divided into five classes on the basis of their age and assumed state of health and when sickness benefit was paid distinctions were made. Class A members (males under 35 on enrolling) paid only $\frac{1}{4}$ of their sick allowance from their own deposit and $\frac{3}{4}$ from the general sick fund. At the other extreme members enrolled in Class E (the least insurable) had to draw $\frac{5}{8}$ths of their sick allowance from their own deposit, only $\frac{1}{8}$th coming from the general sick fund. In all cases, when the member's own deposit was used up, his claim to any sick benefit from the society came to an end. It was intended that this should be a strong incentive to members to build up their

---

[1] E. W. Brabrook, *Provident Societies and Industrial Welfare*, 1898, p. 67.

deposits and to avoid claiming sick benefit, to avoid 'pulling their own fund to pieces'.[1]

Clearly, in such societies there was no fear of insolvency since the element of insurance was so small. The great drawback was that any member suffering from prolonged sickness might find the help of the society would vanish through the exhaustion of his own deposit just when he was in greatest need. For this reason the Commissioners described them as 'essentially savings banks rather than friendly societies. That security of provision which it is of the essence of the friendly society to ensure, however it may fall short of really doing so, they do not profess to give. . . . Were they certified under the Savings Banks Act all misapprehensions of their true character would cease, and they would be recognized as an ingenious attempt, from the savings bank ground, to supply most of the objects which are aimed at by friendly societies.'[2] Before 1875 the registration of these societies was permitted by authority of the Secretary of State, but the Act of 1875 made special provision for them as a class. At the time of the Royal Commission the National Deposit Society had fewer than 1,000 members but by 1900 it had more than 45,000. From being confined largely to Surrey it had grown into a national society although most of its members were from the southern districts and London.[3] The National Deposit, it should be added, came in due course to offer what it termed 'grace pay' to many of those whose deposit, and consequently sick pay rights, were exhausted. At the same time the knowledge that a member had to draw part of his sick benefit from his own deposit led to a much lower ratio of sickness claims being experienced in the National Deposit than in other friendly societies.

The expansion of the National Deposit Society owed much to the energy of its progenitor, Canon Portal, but it is interesting to note that societies operating on these principles and without any worthwhile convivial activity did not develop a popular appeal before the latter part of the century when men were

[1] P.P. 1874, XXIII, Pt. I, RCFS, 4th Report, pp. 83–lxxxiii–xci, where the Abbott's Ann Society is described.
[2] *Ibid.*, para. 400.
[3] Brabrook, *op. cit.*, p. 67.

finding their social needs met in a variety of new ways. One of the rules of the National Deposit forbade any meetings of the society on licensed premises.

The appearance of friendly societies operating on new principles was hardly welcomed by existing societies and the journals of the affiliated orders contain a number of attacks on the 'deposit' principle. This feeling was reflected by the Reverend Frome Wilkinson in his books, *The Friendly Society Movement* and *Mutual Thrift*. In the latter he assured his readers that 'The machinery and working of the Deposit system is so complicated and intricate, that in explanation of it more space will have to be given than the importance, or small success, which has attended this ingenious attempt to combine a savings bank and a benefit society can be said to merit.'[1] Another new form of society which appeared towards the end of the century and which met with considerable success, drew equally caustic comments from Frome Wilkinson. 'There is one more benefit association on which, moved by second thoughts, we must bestow a few words, or else our publishers will most assuredly hear from the founder.'[2] This association was the Stroud Working-Men's Conservative Friendly Society, created on principles put forward by George Holloway.

Holloway set out his ideas in a paper which was awarded second prize in the Forster Prize Essay competition in 1879. Both the permanent societies such as the Oddfellows and the Foresters and the dividing societies failed to make adequate provision for their members in old age. The vast majority of members of friendly societies could never be persuaded to pay separate contributions for deferred annuities even when friendly societies offered them the opportunity. 'Pauperism is the inevitable lot of those who make no provision for old age, and a pauper's funeral . . .

> Rattle his bones over the stones,
> It's only a pauper that nobody owns.'

The answer to this problem was to blend the security of the permanent system with the popularity of the dividing societies

[1] J. Frome Wilkinson, *Mutual Thrift*, 1891, p. 54.
[2] *Ibid.*, p. 124.

107

by an equitable distribution of surplus funds, but without actual distribution. The funds thus accumulated were to become the basis of an annuity to each member in his old age, or a substantial sum of money to his legal representatives at death. In practice, the contributions were to be slightly larger than they needed to be to cover sick benefit and at the end of each year the surplus on the common fund was apportioned among the individual deferred savings accounts held for each member, the actual division being proportionate to the number of shares he held in the society. These sums once credited were to earn interest until a member retired from work or left the society.

The Working Men's Conservative Friendly Society at Stroud in Gloucestershire flourished in that town but never became a national society. The two largest societies to be built up on the principles advanced by Holloway were the Ideal Benefit Society with its headquarters in Birmingham and the Tunbridge Wells Equitable Friendly Society. By 1900 both of these societies had between three and four thousand members. They expanded very rapidly in the early years of the present century.

In discussing the emergence and growth of those types of friendly society which increased their popularity and appeal with the passage of time it is easy to forget that many local clubs continued to thrive. The very extensive Report of the Chief Registrar in 1906 gave information concerning all societies registered in 1905. The details showed that among the northern counties Yorkshire had the highest proportion of small local societies which had survived for at least 50 years. In fact, more than half of this class of society in the county had done so. The corresponding percentage in Devon was nearly 80 per cent. A considerable number of these societies had existed for more than a century.[1]

One particular form of local society flourished and grew in popularity during the later years of the last century: the dividing society. These societies were commonly called Birmingham benefit societies in East London while in Liverpool

---

[1] Lord Beveridge and A. F. Wells, *The Evidence for Voluntary Action*, 1949, pp. 197–207, set out a list of all friendly societies without branches established before 1800 and still on the register in 1905.

they were known as Tontines,[1] but they existed in all parts of the country. Members were entitled to sick pay during the year if they fell ill, their families were entitled to a payment if they died, and the fund remaining at the end of the year was divided among all the surviving contributors. Dividing societies were often called slate clubs since their arrangements were so simple that their accounts could be kept on a slate hung up in the public house where they met and were wiped out at the end of the year when the transactions were complete. Some societies kept a small sum back from the division at the end of the year with which to begin again the next year.[2]

For many years registration was refused to these societies since the law did not permit the annual division of funds as one of the objects of a society. Those that did not register omitted all mention of the practice of dividing from their rules as submitted to the Registrar. The Act of 1875, however, permitted their registration through a provision which allowed of a rule for division after all existing claims had been met.[3] The near-certain return of a lump sum to members at the end of December made these clubs very popular. The way to ensure a large sum for division was to recruit young blood annually and to prevent the older and less healthy from rejoining. The permanent societies argued that by doing this, dividing societies failed to provide for men when they really needed help and that the annual division was a gross manifestation of improvidence and lack of thrift. Since many working men who were attracted to the slate clubs could not afford both these contributions and those of a permanent society they were bound to meet with criticism. Commenting on the increase of their popularity in 1890, Ludlow confessed to some measure of apprehension at the development of this class of society 'especially when . . . it is found to compete with the affiliated orders of a permanent type'.[4]

---

[1] P.P. 1893–4, XXXIX, R.C. on Labour, Minutes of Evidence, Q. 1268. The term 'Tontine' was a misnomer; these clubs were the reverse of the scheme associated with Lorenzo Tonti since they offered no premium upon long life.

[2] Descriptions of the activities of dividing societies about 1870 in industrial regions and in agricultural counties may be found in the reports of E. L. Stanley (p. 88) and G. Young (p. 22) respectively—PP.. 1874, XXIII, Pt. II.

[3] *Ibid.*, Appendix LIV.

[4] P.P. 1890–91, LXXIX, Report of the Chief Registrar for 1890, p. 17.

The affiliated orders certainly believed that they suffered from the competition of the dividing societies. The Manchester Unity of Oddfellows sought to check them through amending the Friendly Societies' Act of 1896 in such a way as to require them to have their tables of contributions and benefits certified by an actuary approved by the government for the purpose. Those societies which failed to meet this requirement within five years were to have their registration cancelled. The Chief Registrar pointed out that the great majority of dividing clubs had no way of meeting the expenses involved in such examination and certification of tables. Moreover the enactment of this amendment would prevent the continued registration of benevolent societies, working men's clubs, cattle insurance societies and other societies whose working was such that valuation was inapplicable. While the amendment would have affected just over 1,000 dividing societies, it would also have deprived about 1,600 of the other societies of registration.[1] In spite of the disapproval of those who were sometimes referred to as the high priests of the friendly society movement, dividing clubs remained popular and showed every sign of remaining so 'as long as human nature continues to prefer a bird in the hand to two in the bush' as Brabrook put it.

The unpopularity and unsatisfactory nature of pit clubs as means of providing against the considerable hazards of sickness and death among miners has already been referred to.[2] Miners' Permanent Relief Societies were founded in most coalfields in the 1870s. One was set up in Lancashire in 1873, in the West Riding in 1877, in North Wales in 1878, in 1879 in the Midlands and in 1881 in South Wales. All of these societies took as their model the first foundation, that of Northumberland and Durham (1862). The aim of the societies was to alleviate the social and economic consequences for miners of accidents of all sorts. Disabled miners usually received sums varying from five to eight shillings weekly. If a member was fatally injured, burial money amounting to £20 or so was paid. This more than covered actual burial expenses and included some element of life assurance as well. The burial money for married members

[1] P.P. 1905, LXXV, pp. 48–9.
[2] *Supra*, p. 62.

was usually £5 with a small pension payable to the widow and orphans. The Northumberland and Durham and the West Riding Permanent Relief Societies also offered superannuation benefits.[1]

The societies were supported by joint subscriptions from employers and employees. From the point of view of the actuary, the fixing of contributions for the benefits offered was initially a question of trial and error. The results of the first useful investigation of the costs involved were not published until 1880.[2] As with other forms of society, these showed varying actuarial deficits. In practice, public gifts in response to appeals following the publicity given to mining explosions led to a certain amount of occasional income. The Northumberland and Durham Society showed a receipt of this kind amounting to £5,030 in 1881. The passing of the Employers Liability Act in 1880 led to some coalowners withdrawing their financial support on the grounds that they could not afford both the sums they might have to pay under this Act and contributions to the permanent relief societies. In other cases employers compelled their workmen to contract out of the Act.[3] In spite of these difficulties, the societies continued to expand and in 1880 a central association was set up.

The growth of the temperance movement with its strong appeal to women was reflected in the formation of small orders restricted to women who preferred temperance principles. These included the Daughters of Temperance, the Family Temperance Benefit Society, the Order of Daughters of Temperance, the Original Grand United Order of the Total Abstinent Daughters of the Phoenix, the Original Grand Order of the Total Abstinent Sisters of the Phoenix, the United Order of the Total Abstinent Sisters of the Phoenix and the South Durham and Cleveland Grand Union of the Daughters of Temperance. Most of the female tents of the Rechabites were soon amalgamated with male tents. In any case, both inside and outside of the temperance movement the number of females in

[1] Baernreither, *op. cit.*, pp. 398–420.

[2] Francis G. P. Neison, *The Rate of Fatal and non-fatal Accidents in and about Mines and on Railways, with the Cost of Insurance against such Accidents*, 1880.

[3] P.P. 1893–4, XXXIX, R.C. on Labour, Minutes of Evidence, Qs 1840–3.

friendly societies remained very small by comparison with men. Women generally seem to have shared Sir George Young's opinion that the best provision for a woman in a working man's family was the man's membership of a club and that the female friendly society appeared to be of comparatively small value. Because of the difference in the liability to sickness of men and women, the Chief Registrar believed that societies or clubs consisting of both men and women were unwise.[1]

One facility which friendly societies had come to offer and which was of increasing importance was the treatment of members by a medical practitioner when they needed his services. The arrangement commonly made was for the society to pay a small fee of about three shillings annually in respect of each member to the selected doctor who in return undertook to give the necessary service. Virtually all Oddfellows lodges and Foresters courts, along with the great majority of other societies, arranged this benefit during the second half of the nineteenth century. The arrangement for financing this benefit in the Manchester Unity was typical. Here the cost of medical attendance was charged by all lodges against their management account.[2] In many of the affiliated orders, members who resided away from their home lodge or court could arrange to receive attendance from the medical officer of a nearby lodge or court. The usual arrangement was outlined in the General Laws of the Foresters which provided that a member so situated should 'be allowed such privilege, upon being accepted by such medical officer, and by paying the same contributions into the court as may be paid by the members thereof, during which time he shall not be compelled to contribute to the medical officer of his own court.'[3]

The medical officers were invariably employed on a *per capita* contract basis or on the basis of a fixed sum. They were never offered a fee for each visit or consultation, for societies had no interest in adopting a policy which might have led to an almost open-ended commitment. As a servant of the society, the medical officer was appointed by means of an election held

---

[1] *Ibid.*, Q. 1444.
[2] *Rules of the I.O.O.F.M.U.*, 1871, Rule 61.
[3] *General Laws of the A.O.F.*, Wolverhampton 1867, no. 78 Section 2.

in the lodge or court, usually for one year at a time. A doctor who failed to give satisfaction would not be re-elected. The doctors themselves naturally disliked a system which made them so dependent on popularity among their clients. They complained that they were judged lacking and dismissed for the wrong reasons and that the system lent itself to professional undercutting of rates. If a newcomer offered to farm a club at sixpence per head less than the existing incumbent, the newcomer would be certain of election for the coming year regardless of other considerations.[1]

In some of the larger towns, the clubs often combined their medical funds to raise a large enough income to retain the services of one or more practitioners on a full-time basis and to set up dispensing centres where these might live. One organization of this type was the Leeds Amalgamated Friendly Societies' Medical Aid Association. In 1883 it consisted of 80 societies with 8,117 members. In the course of that year there were 23,180 visits and 70,713 consultations and prescriptions.[2] These medical aid associations became increasingly important and some came to be established by collecting societies and even by private organizers who made their 'turn' by charging more of the individual members than it cost them to employ the necessary number of medical men. The power of the clubs and of the medical aid associations to fix rates of remuneration for doctors led to an endless series of complaints that the profession was being exploited and to attempts at boycotting friendly society contract work in different places.[3] The further complaint was made by the medical profession that some of the people who used the services of club and medical aid association medical officers were themselves well enough off to consult doctors privately and to pay them 'proper' fees. It was alleged that in this way the willingness of the medical profession to cooperate with friendly societies and to work for low fees had been abused. Undoubtedly some of the members of these

---

[1] H. W. Rumsey, *Essays in State Medicine*, 1856, p. 158.

[2] *Friendly Societies Journal*, March, 1884.

[3] These grievances were often aired in the *Lancet* and in the *British Medical Journal*. In 1868, for instance, attempts to organise boycotts were reported at Birmingham and at Wolverhampton where a demand was made for a minimum *per capita* payment of five shillings.

societies 'being thrifty, careful men,'[1] often got on in life and naturally wished to retain their membership of the societies even when they had become more prosperous. After all, they doubtless attributed their modest prosperity in part to their membership of such mutual aid organizations as friendly societies. Belief in the virtues of self-help did not incline them to abandon its practice just when the faith appeared to have justified itself.

[1] E. W. Brabrook, *Provident Societies and Industrial Welfare*, 1898, p. 72 where some of the complaints of the medical profession are discussed.

Chapter Five
Burial and Collecting Societies

I. Local burial societies

While friendly societies as generally understood provided sick as well as funeral benefit, two groups of societies classed as such under the friendly society legislation until 1896 only offered a sum of money on death. Of these two groups, the large collecting societies were something of an anachronism among friendly societies generally. Some would have placed them in the world of industrial insurance, but the small, local burial society showed many of the characteristics of other local friendly societies. The distinction was understood well enough by contemporaries, 'The local burial societies alone really have something of the character of friendly societies. The others, though working under the Friendly Societies' Acts, are really insurance offices, started without any capital, and under the control of no shareholders, and conducted principally for the benefit of the office holders, and only incidentally for that of the assured . . .'[1] Whether small and local or large, the main aim of the members of the societies was to seek insurance against the disgrace of a pauper funeral. Burial societies were most prominent in Lancashire and the neighbouring counties. Lancashire was also the

[1] P.P. 1874, XXIII, Pt. II, Stanley, p. 27.

headquarters of most of the large collecting societies and was a county in which industrial insurance companies, such as the Prudential, transacted a great deal of business. In some parts of the county there were particularly strong concentrations of burial society insurance. Preston and its neighbourhood, for instance, had a total population of about 86,000, yet there were 108,120 members of burial societies. Thus, there must have been a good deal of double insurance.[1]

Among local burial societies the simplest form of association was to be found where the members met the agreed funeral benefit to be paid by means of a levy each time a death occurred. A slightly more sophisticated version of this arrangement flourished to some extent in the West Riding. In these societies, known locally as funeral briefs, the amount due on one or two deaths was kept in hand and at each death a levy was collected to maintain the fund. Funeral briefs with their membership limited to adults were virtually certain to break down in course of time as the original group of members grew old, for younger men preferred to form a new society of their own rather than join a brief in which levies occurred frequently. Where a brief accepted child members—as many did—it might last indefinitely, since young couples joined the brief on marriage for the sake of the children they expected to have and against whose funeral expenses they wished to guard. The levy in these circumstances was often made on each family, not on an individual basis. Young married couples who had large families stood to gain more than those who had few children. To join a funeral brief was, in a sense, a speculation on having many children; those who turned out to be childless were the losers. A large funeral brief flourished in Sir Titus Salt's model town of Saltaire.[2]

The growth of individual clubs often led them to move from the levy system to regular subscriptions and the accumulation of permanent funds. The accumulation of a fund often led to an increase in benefits offered or even the division of an apparently large sum by way of bonus among the members. The decline from this position was often rapid since the liabilities incurred

[1] P.P. 1874, XXIII, Pt. I, RCFS, para. 439.
[2] P.P. 1874, XXIII, Pt. II, Stanley, p. 2.

were virtually never ascertained actuarially and when they began to catch up on the club, the rapid diminution of the stock forced on members the conclusion that they would survive the club itself. At this stage the younger and middle-aged majority would force on the aged minority the division of what funds remained. Sir George Young claimed that 'the Burial Club which survives a generation is an exception.'[1] The local burial clubs which remained small, local and financially successful were certainly few in number. One such was the Infants' Funeral Friendly Society in Doncaster which, after many years of unregistered existence, registered in 1858. In 1871 it had 2,138 members and its capital amounted to £181. Children were enrolled between the ages of one and fourteen years. The contribution was a uniform one of a penny each month while the benefit varied with length of membership from £1 to £4. No collectors were employed, the subscription being paid at the meeting place of the society.[2]

Local burial clubs usually employed collectors to gather the subscriptions, who frequently undertook this work on a part-time basis. The Royal Commission on Friendly Societies cited a number of examples of well-run local burial societies which employed collectors but which nevertheless fulfilled their objects at very moderate cost, some of them with many numbers. The Blackburn Philanthropic Burial Society was founded in 1839 by working men at one of the local mills.[3] By 1872 it had 130,370 members and £18,725 capital. The weekly contributions were 1d or 1½d; only 1d could be paid for members under ten years of age to secure a funeral benefit of £4, and after ten years members could pay 1½d to secure a benefit of £7 10s. Most of the members were admitted at the age of 16 weeks and all but a very few lived within eight miles of Blackburn. The collectors kept as their commission 10 per cent of the sums collected in town districts and 12½ per cent in country areas. Apart from these commission payments, the expense of management amounted to no more than 2½ per cent of total expenditure. The Royal Commission cited from their

[1] *Ibid.*, Young, p. 27.
[2] P.P. 1872, XXVI, Q. 2420ff; P.P. 1874 XXIII, Pt. I, RCFS, para. 426.
[3] P.P. 1872, XXVI, Q. 2422.

Assistant Commissioner's Reports about 15 local burial societies in the north of England which had more than 1,000 members and operated economically. They listed a further 32 with more than 1,000 members—also mainly in the north—taken from the Registrar's report for 1872.

Hulme Philanthropic Burial Society was a moderately successful local society. Founded in 1842, it had 2,460 members in 1871 who lived locally. The society was managed by quarterly meetings held in a schoolroom. The two part-time collectors were appointed by the members at a quarterly meeting and were paid 12½ per cent commission on the sums they collected. The total expenses amounted to rather less than 25 per cent of income. Benefits were paid on a graduated scale reaching a maximum of £10 only after 25 years of membership. The collectors were bound to visit the corpse before any funeral money was paid to safeguard the society against fraudulent claims. The president of this society believed that local clubs were superior to large collecting societies because the members were personally known to the officers of the club, the male members had the ultimate control over it through their membership of the quarterly meeting, and such clubs were much less expensive to operate than large collecting societies.[1]

Some burial societies were established by the authorities of ragged schools with the aim of encouraging provident habits among the parents of poor children. Ancoats Burial Society was set up on the initiative of the teachers of Heyrood Street Ragged School. The society began by employing teachers to enrol members and to collect their subscriptions. It advertised to recruit part-time collectors and found that the great majority of applicants were already working as collectors for other societies, most of whose characters, it was said, 'would not bear investigation' and they could not be taken on. Collectors were paid 15 per cent of the sums they collected, the work being done in the evenings on a part-time basis. In 1871 the society had 1,300 members and its accumulated funds amounted to £158. The school made itself responsible for meeting any deficit that might arise. The management was kept entirely in the hands of a committee of teachers; the members had no part in it. The

[1] P.P. 1872, XXVI, evidence of James Anderson, Q. 17,887ff.

Manchester and Salford Ragged School Union was well satisfied with the progress made by this burial club and it informed the Royal Commission that it was going to organize a burial society at all the ragged schools in Manchester.[1]

The problem of spending part of the funds on drink and the problem of 'improper' investments which troubled the Registrar in the case of friendly societies could both be found in some of the local burial clubs. The Humane Sick and Burial Club at Ashton-under-Lyne, which had more than 7,000 members in 1870 and had its headquarters at an inn, spent 3d per member on liquor amounting to about £114 a year which it showed as 'yearly accommodation'. It also spent £7 14s for liquor on death at the rate of fourpennyworth each for the president, for the collector and for the person applying for benefit whenever a death occurred. A further sixpennyworth of drink was allowed for every committee member each time the committee met. The president explained to the Commissioners that some of the committee men 'have to come something like 3 miles but only 6d is allowed'. This society had invested £700 in 1839 by way of a mortgage on some cottages in Stalybridge. It turned out that the cottages had not been completed, one difficulty had led to another and by 1870 some £820 had been lost. The society could not foreclose and sell since the mortgagor had disappeared. No one knew whether he was dead or alive and the society did not have the necessary deed in its possession to effect a sale.[2]

II. Large Collecting Societies

The large collecting societies really had nothing in common with friendly societies proper. They were essentially commercial undertakings exploiting the contemporary abhorrence of the pauper's funeral and only incidentally encouraging anything that could be described as thrift or providence. They flourished most among the poorest class of society and very many of their insurance policies covered those with no independent income of their own—wives and children. The

[1] P.P. 1872, XXVI, evidence of John Ogden, QQ. 18,418ff.
[2] P.P. 1872, XXVI, evidence of Joseph Andrew QQ. 17,849ff.

largest of these societies had their headquarters in Liverpool. The next largest group, which was entirely composed of off-shoots at first or second hand of the Liverpool societies, was at Glasgow. The Royal Commission estimated that the total membership of large collecting societies who had passed the age of puberty as between 550,000 to 650,000 or about half of the current membership of the affiliated orders, adding that 'instead of forming the most intelligent, they would represent generally the least intelligent portion of the class insured in friendly societies'.

Table 5.1.

The ten largest collecting societies about 1872.[1]

Society	Foundation	Headquarters	Members	Funds
				£
Royal Liver	1850	Liverpool	550,000	264,795
Liverpool Victoria Legal	1843	Liverpool	200,000	49,159
Scottish Legal	1852	Glasgow	216,343	54,982
United Assurance (St. Patrick's)	1832	Liverpool	140,000	15,311
United Legal Friendly	1840	Liverpool	50,000	12,370
Loyal Philanthropic	1844	Liverpool	45,800	18,373
Liverpool Protective	1856	Liverpool	48,132	16,978
Integrity Life Assurance	1858	London	42,000	2,675
Royal London Friendly	1861	London	25,000	4,964
City of Glasgow	1862	Glasgow	24,000	7,571
St. Anne's Catholic	1847	Liverpool	20,000	1,477

These large societies were entirely under the control of their own officials and the power conflicts which persisted within them were between the central or headquarters officials and the local collectors. In the largest society, the Royal Liver, Rule 3 stated quite unambiguously that 'the committee of management shall have full power and absolute discretion to conduct the affairs of the society in such manner as they deem expedient for the interests of the society'. The committee was composed mainly of persons who had been collectors and whose period of tenure was not limited since there was no provision for their

[1] P.P. 1874, XXIII, RCFS, para. 470.

going out of office. General meetings of the members, when called, could amount to little more than gatherings of collectors. In any case the rules provided that no business could be brought to such meetings without 14 days' prior notice to the committee, and that the chairman might 'if he thinks it desirable and expedient so to do, at any time during the holding of such public meeting, dissolve or adjourn such meeting'. Thus if signs of discontent arose during a meeting, it could be dissolved immediately.[1] Similar constitutional arrangements existed in some of the other collecting societies including the United Friendly where ten of the eleven members of the central committee were collectors. The committee was permanently in office and had unlimited power of expenditure. The subtreasurer stated in 1871 that under the rules 'the committee cannot be removed without they call a meeting themselves to remove themselves, and they are not very likely to do that; it is against human nature'.[2]

Of the other two largest societies, the Liverpool Victoria Legal had a general committee consisting of eleven agents or collectors and three central officers; real authority was exercised by a subcommittee of the three officers and four agents (called managers), those for London, Leeds and Sunderland along with the principal Liverpool collector. The Scottish Legal's board of management had at one time no real control over its collectors who themselves effectively controlled the society. In the 1870s nominations to the board remained largely in the hands of the collectors who issued each year what was called a 'collector's slip'. This was a list of candidates that collectors sought to have returned to the board. The agent for the Scottish Legal in Belfast explained that collectors 'have a great power in their capacity as collectors, and they sometimes influence the members'. His own name had appeared on the collector's slip and he had been duly returned.[3]

The question of where power lay in the collecting societies was perhaps most accurately explained to the Royal Commission by the solicitor to the Royal Liver. 'In some societies the

---

[1] P.P. 1874, XXII, Pt. I, RCFS, para. 476.
[2] P.P. 1872, XXVI, evidence of Edmund Irving, Q. 22,576.
[3] P.P. 1872, XXVI, evidence of John Cherry, QQ. 14,422 ff.

collectors are practically the owners of the society, and from some evidence I have heard in this room, in certain societies the collectors do practically what they think proper. They elect their own committee, and insist on the committee being collectors. In other societies the committee of management are practically the executive of the society. In some societies I have known a single person own the society; in the St. Patrick's practically Mr. Treacy the secretary, who got the thing up from nothing to what it was, was owner of the society.'[1] The Commissioners remarked that a somewhat similar position was held at one time in the Royal Liver by its first secretary, John Lawrence, in the United Legal Friendly by its sub-treasurer, in the Scottish Legal by its secretary and manager and in the City of Glasgow Society by John Stewart.

The case of John Stewart in some ways typified the collector-entrepreneur to whose acumen and industry the large collecting societies owed their existence and growth. Stewart was a collector working for the Royal Liver in Glasgow. He saw his opportunity to use his existing contacts to form an independent society and in 1862 along with a number of collaborators set up the City of Glasgow Friendly Society 'as it was well-known that the rights and privileges of the Scottish members (of the Royal Liver) have been consistently ignored'. Stewart became the secretary of the new society and supplied the initial capital which the venture required. An office was opened at 16 Hope Street near the Royal Liver's office at number 30. Most of the collectors of the new society were Royal Liver men who, of course, transferred their clients with them. In the words of the centenary publication of the City of Glasgow Society 'people who called at 16 Hope Street were amazed at the huge piles of Royal Liver Contribution Cards lying on the counter of the City of Glasgow office.' By December 1862 the Society had formally minuted that Stewart was to be established as permanent secretary. His salary was to be the very considerable one of five per cent on total contributions above £10 weekly. The personal and proprietorial nature of the government of this society was demonstrated in 1864 when another society offered Stewart £400 a year to bring his new society to them. He turned the

[1] P.P. 1872, XXVI, evidence of Charles Bretherton, Q. 23,394.

offer down and the City of Glasgow board increased his rate of commission by a further 1¼ per cent on the total contributions 'in gratitude'.[1] It was perhaps also typical of the 19th century collecting society that within six years of its foundation the City of Glasgow experienced a split. Stewart's rule as manager and treasurer, which had become his office by this time, was challenged by the secretary. After some weeks of dispute during which the society's offices were captured by first one side then the other, Stewart regained possession and the dissentients set up a new collecting society, the Glasgow Reformed Friendly Society. This recruited its initial membership from those City of Glasgow members whose collectors had joined the dissentient party. The society tried to hold them by sending a letter to 'parties and families who had been improperly decoyed to other societies'.[2]

The very heavy running costs of collecting societies troubled many concerned with social questions. Consequently the profits of those who operated them attracted a good deal of attention. The term profits was used in this context by the solicitor to the Royal Liver who maintained that surpluses arising from members' payments should go to the managers since they were really profits arising from wise management. He described the collecting societies as 'trading' societies and 'the profits of what I call a trading friendly society are taken by way of salary instead of dividends; that is the practical result of the system'.[3] According to its accounts for 1871 the Royal Liver Society collected premiums of £176,053, of which 40 per cent was set aside for management. In the past this had been as high as 55 per cent. Of the 40 per cent, the collector received 27½ per cent, most of this being the standard commission of 25 per cent to each collector on his total collections, while the rest was entrance fees for new members gained and perquisites. The treasurer and eight members of the board of management received £4,920—two of them £800 each and the rest £520. But apart from these salaries many of the board still held collectors' books which brought them in another £150 or so

---

[1] J. House, *Friendly Adventure*, Glasgow, 1962, pp. 12–17.
[2] *Ibid.*, p. 20.
[3] P.P. 1872, XXVI, evidence of Charles Bretherton, QQ. 23,397ff.

each. The actual collecting was usually done by a deputy with whom the profit was shared. Members of the board also had valuable patronage in that they could and did give very profitable collectors' books to relations. The only danger to the governing group of the society was from possible rival groups of ambitious collectors seeking to share more fully in the sweets of office. The managers could in fact raise their salaries as often as they pleased out of the contributions. They had only to keep the collectors happy and this they achieved by periodical increases in their salaries or perquisites.[1]

The Royal Liver was possibly the best run of the large Liverpool collecting societies. At the other extreme during much of the last century was the United Assurance Society (or St Patrick's Society), a society that was strong among Irish immigrants and was under the patronage of the Roman Catholic Clergy. When run by the entrepreneur who built it up, Treacy, there was never a committee meeting nor an audit. Claims were unpaid or disputed on frivolous pretexts and Treacy apparently made off with £7,000 or so belonging to the society. As the scandal grew more notorious an attempt was made by some priests to bring about reform. A series of encounters in public meetings and in the law courts over the years failed to check Treacy, who used the Society's funds to engage congenial lawyers and thus held on to his salary until the end of his life. After his death his adherents still held office and appointed a new secretary on condition that he should pay an annuity to Treacy's widow who occupied a house built for her with the society's funds. The defeat of the would-be reformers was marked by a banquet for all the collectors and a gold watch costing £40 as a present for a defending attorney, all paid for out of the funds. The Assistant Commissioner in 1871 wrote that 'though the society is guilty even yet of such minor offences as cooked balance sheets, fictitious entries of capital and the embezzlement by committeemen of sums exceeding £70, which defalcations have extended unchecked over years, yet there is nothing now worth noticing compared with the grandiose villany of former years.'[2] Little wonder that this Assistant

[1] P.P. 1874, XXIII, Pt. II, Stanley, pp. 27–9.
[2] P.P. 1874, XXIII, Pt. II, Stanley, p. 30.

Commissioner, E. L. Stanley, was later to suggest to the Social Science Association that it would be possible to get rid of the lavish and fraudulent collecting societies if only the Manchester Unity of Oddfellows would establish a family funeral fund to be worked through the organization of its lodges and which could thus cover the whole country.[1]

The essential element in the entire system was the collector or agent. It was very successful collectors who became the entrepreneurs who established and ran the societies; it was the moderately successful who sold the burial insurance and gathered the contributions, ever anxious to extend a business to which their incomes were so directly geared by the commission system. The collectors themselves were drawn from among the working class and little in the way of education was sought in recruits. The ability to sell and to bring in the premiums was the quality that mattered. A member of the committee of the Royal Liver explained that 'The fact of intelligence and education has no bearing whatever as to the character or ability of a collector in making a book; it has nothing to say to it; in fact, we find that the more refined and educated a man is, the less hope we have that he will succeed among the working classes. We find that a man who is educated only to a certain point, just to the standard of the poor people, and who is able to meet them from time to time, is just that character of man who will get the business in a society like ours.'[2]

To the working man of little education but possessing the qualities associated with the good salesman, the prospects offered by the position of collector in a large collecting society were very attractive. They included the entrance fees of members, which were usually 2d a head, 25 per cent on all contributions collected, the entire contributions for the first six weeks from each new member, transfer fees of 3d per member half-yearly for the trouble of copying members' names from the old book to a new book, a profit on the sale of sets of rules (3d out of 6d in the case of the Royal Liver) and sometimes a payment for the sale of contribution cards. By far the largest single

---

[1] *Trans. of the National Association for the Promotion of Social Science,* 1874, p. 806.
[2] P.P. 1872, XXVI, evidence of James Atherton, Q. 22,385.

element among these sources of income was the 25 per cent on contributions. The best collectors' books brought in up to £400 a year for their owners, some of the work of collecting being farmed out by the official collector to one or more deputies or to members of his family. This was a very fortunate position for a labouring man earning little more than £1 per seek to aspire to. Many collectors made much less than £400 a year, but the actual rate of remuneration for the collections made was clearly generous.[1]

The hardest part of a collector's work lay in making the book in the first place, that is to say in persuading people to enrol and to pay their contributions. The value of the book, that is, of the collector's business, was reflected in the sums which others were willing to pay for it and these seem to have gone as high as £600 to £700 on occasion. In the course of normal business competition between the societies, rival canvassing campaigns were undertaken and 'during the heat of contest, a cloud of skirmishers is, as it were, thrown out in the shape of canvassers, to prepare the advance of the regular collectors'. The canvassers in these campaigns usually received the entrance fees. Apart from these major competitive selling efforts, canvassing was an individual matter for collectors.[2] Gladstone described collectors as 'preachers and denominational missionaries, who, animated by the golden vision of 25 per cent on the premiums paid, find their way into every cottage in the country and become eloquent in the praise of the institutions to which they belong'.[3] So far as the members were concerned, the collector was the sole embodiment of the society. He not only collected the contributions, but was the distributor of any rules or, indeed, of any benefit which might be obtained. The influence of the weekly collector over the members was considerable.

One reason why this influence was so considerable was the ignorance and poverty of the class among whom the collecting societies recruited their members. The Vice-Chairman of the Royal Liver Society really summarized the condition of the membership when he explained that the position was the same

[1] P.P. 1874, XXIII Pt. I, RCFS, para. 490 ff.
[2] *Ibid.*
[3] *Parliamentary Debates*, Third Series, CLXXIII, 1565, 7 March 1864.

in all parts of the country, 'they are all much of the same class, principally the very poorest'.[1] A large proportion were Irish immigrants, many did not know their age accurately, and the inability to read or write made them ready victims of fraud. In any case, the rules were hardly pressed upon the members. In the United Assurance they were only given to the member after he had become one, in other words, he discovered the terms of his contract after he had entered into it. The Royal Liver made the rules available at a charge of 6d or the equivalent of six weeks' subscriptions. There is much evidence of collectors packing general meetings of societies in both Liverpool and Glasgow in their own interests with members whose expenses and 'free' beer were paid for out of the funds by collectors who guided them in their voting.[2] All members who lived at a distance from the headquarters of such societies that still kept up a pretence of self-government by public meeting would not even be troubled by these formalities.

In any case, a considerable proportion of the adult members of collecting societies were women. Widows, for instance, who could not enter a sick club, would welcome the opportunity of avoiding the prospect of their funeral being on the parish. It was said that those living in out of the way hamlets were particularly gullible. One collector in Norwich, when one of his subscribers, an old lady, died in benefit, hit on the idea of going to the village where she was born and telling the story of her funeral. He was rewarded for his acumen by a number of new members. 'They all said it was time something should be done for them, and I could not get out my cards fast enough. Now at —————————, the week before, I could not get a life; they all said the parish would bury them.'[3] The payments which agents received for new members in any case exposed them to the temptation of seeking new recruits rather than to maintaining

---

[1] P.P. 1872, XXVI, evidence of Henry Liversage, Q. 1,359.

[2] P.P. 1872, XXVI, evidence of Robert McKinnon, Q. 11,545 for a description of a meeting of the Scottish Legal in Glasgow where each collector 'took his seat beside his own party, and he would hold up a white handkerchief, and if they did not vote the way he indicated, they had to find their way back to the locality they came from themselves, and even to look out to pay their own lodgings for the night' but if they voted right, they got their travelling expenses and lodgings.

[3] P.P. 1874, XXIII Pt. II, Young, p. 25.

the existing subscribers in membership, and complaints against this particular malpractice were widespread. Defaulting collectors and tricky rules were the grievances apparently most felt by the members, the majority of whom seem to have had little knowledge of the form of government or the overall expense of operating the societies.

The effect of a collector failing to turn up regularly to gather the contributions was, of course, to throw his members out of benefit. Some societies at certain times themselves took steps which had the effect of doing this. During litigation in the United Assurance it closed its Dundee office for a year, thereby throwing many members out of benefit. The Royal London Friendly apparently withdrew its agent from Belfast and the members there lost any claim to benefit. Whatever the cause, lapsing of membership could be a source of profit to collectors and societies alike. Because of the frequency of lapses, it was argued by some officials that it was possible for a society undertaking only burial insurance to manage without any accumulated fund. In the Royal Liver it was reckoned that lapses amounted to about 13 per cent of the members each year, thus giving an average period of membership of eight years. The Royal Commission concluded that 'a general burial society thus lives by its lapses, in other words, by confiscation of the premiums of its members'.[1]

There can be little doubt that the large collecting societies were the weakest of the engines of thrift supposedly devoted to encouraging self-help in Victorian Britain. The poor among whom they flourished could only be induced to save at all by collectors calling regularly. Defenders of the societies pictured the collectors as friends of poor families, visiting them regularly in their homes, discussing their troubles with them and acting generally as father-figures whose advice was sought on a variety of topics. Very many collectors certainly lived up to this image and felt quite consciously that they were serving society well by inducing the habits of self-help and providence among the least provident classes in the country. Yet the very system operated by the collecting societies militated against the interests of those they claimed they were seeking to serve. The

[1] P.P. 1874, XXIII Pt. I, RCFS, para. 505.

main reason for the abuses found in the societies was their lack of responsibility and answerability to either members or shareholders. The local burial societies were under the control of their members, consequently their management expenses were modest and their largely part-time officials were immediately answerable to their clients.

Perhaps the most obvious yardstick for comparison with the large collecting societies was the Prudential Company which began industrial insurance business in 1854 and was the first company to take infant lives on to the books. The growth of business in the Company's industrial department was remarkably rapid, as may be seen in Table 5.2 and by the end of 1872 it had over a million life policy-holders. It was much better run

Table 5.2.

Policies issued by the Prudential Insurance Company in its industrial department.[1]

Date	No. of policies	Date	No. of policies
1857	6,839	1864	109,907
1858	12,442	1865	148,108
1859	17,778	1866	163,423
1860	33,133	1867	140,740
1861	48,274	1868	264,027
1862	42,808	1869	287,026
1863	68,363	1870	296,935

than the large collecting societies in that its book-keeping system was much more efficient, it supervised its collectors much more closely and it tried to prevent any lapse in contributions from insurers which were not due solely to their own default. The book-keeping was such that the exact number of members was known weekly: by comparison the collecting societies could never give more than an approximation. From

[1] R. W. Barnard (ed.), *A Century of Service: The Story of the Prudential 1848–1948.* 1948, p. 38.

1870 the Company only paid commission to collectors for new business on the net increase they were able to achieve, in other words, all lapses were deducted. The consequence of this was that while in 1869 the equivalent of 41 per cent of new business lapsed, in 1870 only 29 per cent did so. The collectors were closely supervised and the Company had an efficient audit department. This greater efficiency sprang really from one cause, the exclusion of collectors and officials from control of the concern. The company was controlled by its shareholders and no officer was permitted to hold a share.

One abuse to which the growth of burial insurance of infants was said to have given rise was the murder of very young children by their parents so that the latter could collect the burial benefit. In an effort to stamp this out, legislation was enacted in 1850 forbidding the insurance of a child under ten beyond the sum likely actually to be incurred for funeral expenses with a maximum limit of £3.[1] The Select Committee on the Friendly Societies Bill of 1854 examined the position and concluded that the number of instances where child murder had been committed in order to obtain funeral benefit were so few that there was no need to legislate to deal with this specific topic.[2] The Act of the following year raised the permitted limits for funeral benefit to £6 for a child under five and £10 for a child between five and ten years of age. Burial payments on the death of a child were required to be made only on production of a certificate signed by a qualified medical practitioner.[3] The Select Committee and the legislation which followed by no means put an end to the general fears that were felt. Edwin Chadwick expressed his misgivings in an address to the Social Science Association at Sheffield in 1865. He stated that he had come across child murder for the sake of burial money when investigating provision for the destitute. He warned his audience that 'close and sustained investigations into the sources of crime established the general conclusion that, given the profit, given the opportunities or temptations, by exposures or want of pre-

---

[1] 13 & 14 Vict. c.115.
[2] P.P. 1854, VII, Report from the Select Committee on the Friendly Societies Bill, pp. iv–v.
[3] 18 & 19 Vict. c.65, s.10.

cautions, for obtaining it by crime—you may confidently assume the existence of the practice of the crimes, and that it is in default of investigation if they are not detected.'[1]

The Royal Commission investigated this question and reported its findings fully.[2] Evidence was sought from coroners. 75 of them were unable or unwilling to give an opinion while the answers from 45 were strongly affirmative. The coroner for Liverpool, Aspinall, said that he had not the slightest doubt that an immense amount of parental neglect of a most scandalous character went on daily in Liverpool 'and I am really disposed to think that the neglect is greater than it would be, on account of the prospect, at the end of the child's term of lingering, of the club money.' He described in detail the techniques adopted to obtain death certificates from medical practitioners and the weaknesses of the criminal law in dealing with such cases. The Commission also obtained mortality statistics for Liverpool, Manchester and certain other large centres and found a very marked jump in the rate of mortality in Liverpool among children after they had passed the age of one year. This it connected with the fact that by the rules of most societies infants only came into full benefit after 52 weeks of membership.[3] Proof was also given of insuring the same child in several societies, thus multiplying the benefits accruing in case of death.

The Commission noticed in passing that the very large number of policies on the lives of infants issued by the Prudential Company were legally worthless. The Life Insurance Act of 1774 enacted that no insurance should be made on the life of another unless the policy holder had an insurable interest.[4] The Friendly Society Acts expressly permitted the insurance of infants on certain terms as a concession from this general provision, but while collecting societies could take advantage of this, the Prudential certainly could not for as a joint stock company it was clearly not able to act under friendly society legislation. The Commissioners reiterated their assistants' judgement that life assurance companies' contracts on infant lives were

[1] C. Walford, *The Insurance Cyclopaedia*, 1870, Vol. I, pp. 407–8.
[2] P.P. 1874, XXIII Pt. I, RCFS, paras. 567–84.
[3] P.P. 1874, XXIII Pt. I, RCFS, paras. 576–8.
[4] 14 Geo. 3. c.48, s.1.

illegal 'and rest like stockjobbing transactions merely on the basis of good faith and of credit.'[1]

III. The attitude of the State

The practices associated with the collecting societies and industrial assurance generally worried governments on different occasions in the second half of the nineteenth century. Gladstone's anxieties in the 1860s led him to try to establish a sound and reliable alternative for working men, an annuity and insurance scheme operated through the Post Office. An earlier attempt on these lines in 1853 having failed to attract the necessary support, his Government passed a rather wider measure in 1864.[2] In the course of an eloquent illumination of the collecting society and insurance company scene, Gladstone drew the attention of the Commons to such abuses as the very high proportion of lapses. 'If the poor man fails . . . to pay one premium the policy drops and he loses everything he has paid. . . . Has the House the smallest idea of the number of these lapsed policies? Had I not had it in positive figures I could not have believed it. It will appear a strange relation to those who hear me when I state, that the number of these lapsed policies in the Friend in Need Society during five years was 18,000 out of 86,000 policies made. . . . The Royal Liver Society issued 135,000 policies last year, and had in the same time 70,000 lapsed policies.'[3] He went on to demonstrate to the House the excessive sums spent on management and the consequently slender reserves which collecting societies accumulated. The Liverpool United Loyal Society had been enrolled for 21 years, 'ample time to consider its ways', yet with an annual income of over £10,000 its accumulated capital only amounted to £3,900. 'The next case is that of the Royal Liver which is fourteen years old; the society, I think, which issued 135,000 policies last year. Its income for premiums is £77,000, and what does the House suppose to be the expense of managing, raising, and dealing

[1] P.P. 1874, XXIII Pt. II, Stanley, p. 211.
[2] 27 & 28 Vict. c.43.
[3] *Parliamentary Debates*, Third Series, CLXXIII, 1577, 7 March 1864.

with that amount—£36,000. With an income of £77,000 the accumulated capital after fourteen years' business, according to their own balance sheet, is £39,000.'[1]

The Act empowered the Postmaster General to conduct life assurance business with the sums insurable subject to an upper limit of £100 and a lower of £20. Customers were to pay their premiums at a selected post office at intervals of not less than a week. No collectors were to be employed. Policies acquired a surrender or paid-up value after five years.[2] The scheme did not prove popular and the number of contracts did not average more than 400 or so a year. Burial insurance had to be sold to working men and women; it was not the sort of thing they were prepared to go to the post office to buy. Moreover it was argued that the financial terms offered were poor value. E. L. Stanley pointed out that a mechanic could do far better with his money than buy a post office annuity. The same money put in a building society or cooperative society would accumulate interest at five per cent whereas the annuity was based on tables allowing interest at only three per cent.[3] Moreover, the actual contributions required to purchase an annuity were so large as to be beyond the reach or the will of labouring men. In order to try to compete with the undoubted convenience of home collection of the societies, it was suggested that postmen should collect contributions for government annuities and burial insurance. This suggestion was never found acceptable since it was held that the first duty of a postman was 'to use all despatch in the delivery of his letters'.[4]

In 1868 Lord Lichfield introduced a bill in the Lords 'to amend the laws relating to friendly societies, and to small government annuities, and the assuring of payment of money on death'. The proposals would have given policyholders security against lapse without notice and would have prevented their transfer from one society or company to another without their consent; the insurance of infant lives would also have been

---

[1] *Ibid.*, 1578.
[2] 27 & 28 Vict. c.43.
[3] E. L. Stanley, 'What legislation should follow the Report of the Commission on Friendly Societies?' *Trans of the National Association for the Promotion of Social Science*, 1873, p. 808.
[4] P.P. 1874, XXIII Pt. I, RCFS, Appendix XV, p. 46.

restricted. The insurance companies and collecting societies which would have been affected opposed the bill vigorously and denounced it as an attempt to destroy 'the working men's spontaneous thrift movement'.[1] Much money was spent by such societies as the Royal Liver, the Liverpool Victoria Legal, St Patrick's and the Royal Oak in fighting Lord Lichfield's bill. The money thus spent came from members' funds. The sub-treasurer of the Royal Oak justified this political expenditure on the grounds that the bill would have ended their burial insurance for infants and 'if that part of our business had been knocked off, we might as well have shut up at once'. Through getting children as soon as possible after birth an entry was secured to the family 'and we get whole families through it'. He claimed that it was this that kept the establishment going.[2]

The Royal Liver took the leading part in opposing the bill and a little later tried to sponsor a bill on this topic itself which had a very different intent. According to Tidd Pratt's report, this was hawked about among Members of Parliament for introduction to the House of Commons without finding anyone to adopt it. The Registrar commented on the illegality of spending the funds of societies in promoting legislation. The Royal Liver then adopted a rule allowing the committee of management to 'apply for or oppose any bill or proceeding in or emanating from Parliament which they consider desirable for the interest of the society'.[3] According to the Friendly Societies' Acts, promoting or opposing legislation was not one of the purposes for which such societies might be established. The rule could hardly have been held legal since the Royal Liver was a registered friendly society. The Earl of Lichfield eventually withdrew his bill in the face of the opposition.

In its Fourth Report of 1874 the Royal Commission followed up its illuminating revelations with six recommendations aimed particularly at burial insurance.[4] These were:

that the amalgamation of societies not being branches of the same body, be subjected to special provisions;

---

[1] Dermot Morrah, *A History of Industrial Life Assurance*, 1955, p. 39.
[2] P.P. 1872, XXVI, evidence of Edmund Irving, QQ. 22,558–60.
[3] *Rules of the Royal Liver Friendly Society*, 1870, Rule 8.
[4] P.P. 1874, XXIII Pt. I, para. 925.

that the mode of transforming societies into joint stock companies be regulated;

that special provisions be enacted for societies receiving contributions in more than one district, otherwise than through other societies or branches of societies as their agents;

that the insurance of the lives of infants under a given age (say three years) be prohibited, and that additional precautions be taken with reference to the certificates of their deaths;

that the existing system of government insurance through the post office for death and deferred annuities be extended, so as to cover the whole ground now occupied by what is termed industrial assurance;

that the law be amended so as to enable companies to carry on legally the business of industrial assurance within the same limits and subject to the same restrictions as friendly societies.

Section 30 of the Friendly Societies Act of 1875[1] was designed to meet the case of the large collecting societies, applying as it did to societies receiving contributions by means of collectors at a greater distance than ten miles from the registered office. It provided that such a society must furnish every member with a copy of its rules together with a printed policy when he first insured. No forfeiture of a policy could be enforced for default in paying contributions before a written notice had been delivered to the member allowing him at least fourteen days to pay his arrears. No collector was to be a member of a committee of management or to take part in the proceedings of any meeting. At least one general meeting was to be held every year and the balance sheet was to be available to members at least a week before the meeting. The annual returns were to be certified by an accountant who was not to be a member of the society. All societies, including unregistered ones, were made subject to restrictions on the burial insurance they could grant for infants. Minors under 16 could not become members of future adult societies, and minors under three could not become members of any future society—those between three and sixteen could join societies for juveniles only. But this last restriction did not apply to existing societies which could continue taking infant lives. Children under five were not to be insured

[1] 38 & 39 Vict., c.60.

for more than £6 and those between five and ten could not be insured for more than £10.

The provisions of the Act hardly brought about the reform which the Royal Commission had hoped to see. Some large societies continued to break up and leave their members without the benefit for which they had paid. The United Assurance was the worst case of collapse. In 1880 it had 181,000 members, in 1883 154,000 and when it broke up in 1885 it had 148,627. But by that time, its total capital resources amounted to no more than £5,203. A number of new societies continued to be formed every year, usually by discharged collectors. They might get several hundred or even a thousand members before collapsing and vanishing from sight.[1] On the other hand the largest and better run increased considerably in membership. By 1888 their actual membership amounted to one half of that of all registered friendly societies in England although they numbered only 47 in a group of 25,000 registered societies. The fact that those founded before 1875 could still admit infants who comprised so large a proportion of their members gave them a built-in advantage over any newcomer which could not enjoy this privilege. In 1888 the four largest collecting societies in England and Wales had between them 88 per cent of the funds and 90 per cent of the members.[2] These were the Royal Liver, the Liverpool Victoria Legal, the Royal London and the Blackburn Philanthropic Burial. In Scotland, the Scottish Legal had grown in like manner and had about 400,000 members by this date. By the 1880s it became clear that the largest amongst these societies were beating the medium sized. Between 1880 and 1887 the membership of the four largest increased by 52.75 per cent and their funds by nearly 66 per cent while the moderate sized were showing a decline.

Under the Act of 1875 it was possible for the Chief Registrar to hold an inquiry into the affairs of a society if requested by a proportion of the members. A reforming group within the Royal Liver gained a public inquiry into its affairs, aided by the editor of *Truth* who both exposed the existing state of affairs

---

[1] P.P. 1888, XII, evidence of J. M. Ludlow to Select Committee on Friendly Societies, p. 48.
[2] *Ibid.*, p. 7.

and supplied the necessary £50 which the Treasury required before permitting it. Of the total income of the Royal Liver for 1884 of £360,000 only £1,533 could be placed to reserves owing to the very high expense of management. E. L. Stanley who was appointed as inspector showed that the existing managers treated the society's funds as their own property. There were two secretaries who divided nearly £12,000 a year between them. A further £5,304—or £884 each—was paid to the other six members of the committee of management. The old story of packed meetings, bribery, corruption and even the purchase of favourable editorial comment in newspapers was revealed by the inquiry.[1] The inquiry itself ended abruptly when the solicitor to the society absconded and various account books that were wanted disappeared with him. The outcome was a compromise between the reformers and the committee by which the two secretaries and three of the committee retired and the leader of the reform group, E. F. Taunton, became the new secretary at a reduced salary of £1,000 a year. The reformers enforced various economies including the dismissal of more than a hundred clerks.

The complaints against collecting societies and analyses of their troubles in the 1880s really centred on the same problems as those which the Royal Commission had investigated earlier. The requirement for an annual general meeting of members to provide some check on the management could be of little value when there were 100,000 or more members. Even where such meetings were conducted with the utmost propriety they could only be a farce so far as any real representation of the members was concerned. In fact the only real influences in the large collecting societies remained the collectors on the one hand and the central management on the other, with a perpetual struggle for mastery between the two. The management charges remained very high and the process of collection from door to door would naturally tend to be expensive—even without the excessive inflation of charges which it was in the interests of the collectors and managers to seek. In 1886 the Chief Registrar,

---

[1] P.P. 1886, LXI, Report to the Chief Registrar on the Royal Liver Friendly Society by E. L. Stanley.

writing in his report of Section 30 of the Act of 1875, commented that he had 'no doubt that it is unsatisfactory, but he dares not hope that any amendment will make it otherwise'.[1] In any case it could not be too frequently repeated that insurance in a collecting society or industrial assurance company was the most costly form that such provision could take and that persons who effected such insurance placed themselves at the mercy of others who were interested in getting as much out of them as they could.[2]

The continuing dissatisfaction with collecting societies and industrial insurance led to the appointment of a Select Committee by the Commons in 1888. The evidence which the Committee took repeated many of the points made by witnesses to the Royal Commission in 1871. The officials of such societies were everything, the members were nothing. Ludlow suggested to the Committee that since a general meeting was a farce for societies with more than 10,000 members, the principle of government by delegates should be made compulsory in its place. He also suggested that the Chief Registrar should have wider powers to order an inspection as well as powers to require the dissolution or winding-up of a society after inspection.[3] Among other abuses which remained common was that members were still being transferred from one society to another without their knowledge, since when collectors moved from one society to another they often took their members with them. This remained possible as the members usually knew the club by the name of the collector, for example, 'Mr. Jones' club'. Ludlow had no doubt but that the practice of the societies tended to increase infant mortality.[4]

The reformed Royal Liver Society was said by the Chief Registrar to be infinitely better conducted 'with all its faults' than most of the other smaller collecting societies.[5] It had now begun to provide paid-up policies after premiums had been

[1] P.P. 1886, LXI, p. 8.
[2] *Ibid.*, p. 10.
[3] P.P. 1888, XII, Report of the Select Committee on Friendly Societies, evidence of J. M. Ludlow.
[4] *Ibid.*, QQ. 14, 37–9.
[5] *Ibid.*, QQ. 232.

paid for at least 21 years.[1] E. L. Stanley suggested to the Committee that there was really little the state could do to secure better administration of these societies by direct interference. The best course was to maintain the freedom for combination and to impose very stringent punishments for fraud and malversation of money. Subject to that, the public should be left to buy their own experience and to 'burn their fingers if they must'.[2]

The Select Committee concluded that collecting societies when well managed were of value since there was no other means of inducing large numbers of the working class to make some provision for their burial even though the cost of management was very high, amounting to nearly half of the premium income. The principal recommendation of the Committee was for a new bill which would cover all collecting societies and industrial assurance companies. Many of the existing provisions of Section 30 of the Act of 1875 should continue but the existing ten mile limit would be abolished and all societies employing collectors would come under the new Act. No collector was to serve on a management committee or as a trustee or manager. The Chief Registrar should have power to order inspections whenever he felt this advisable and the inspectors should have power to administer oaths and to require the attendance of witnesses. The Registry ought also to make an order directing the manner of disposing of the funds. Surrender values should be obligatory after subscriptions had been paid on policies for five years. In the case of collecting societies, as distinct from insurance companies, registration should be made compulsory and they should only be permitted to use the term 'friendly society' in their title if it were preceded by the word 'collecting'. No new collecting society should be registered until the applicants had deposited with the Registry the sum of £500. This sum was to be retained until the annual income from members' subscriptions amounted to £1,000 and the first valuation had been made. If the valuation showed a deficiency, then the society was to be dissolved and the promoters were to be repaid

---

[1] P.P. 1888, XII, Report of the Select Committee on Friendly Societies, evidence of E. L. Stanley, Q. 541.
[2] *Ibid.*, Q. 311.

their £500 less the cost of meeting any claims from members.[1] The Chief Registrar's office needed to be strengthened. The Committee proposed that the sole official authority in which all powers and duties concerning the administration of the new act should be concentrated should be known as the 'Central Office'. In other words, the control of industrial assurance companies should be removed from the Board of Trade and transferred to this new office. The future adequate staffing of this office ought to be the subject of separate inquiry.[2] There was some criticism of the Chief Registrar for not intervening more actively in the affairs of societies when members made complaints as, for instance, in the case of the United Assurance Society in 1883.

The report from the Select Committee was not followed immediately by legislation. In 1890 the House of Lords set up a Select Committee to investigate the question of infant mortality. Its main recommendation was that a proposal to pay burial insurance money directly to undertakers instead of parents should not be adopted. In 1896 new legislation, largely of a codifying nature, was enacted. The special provisions applying to collecting societies and industrial assurance companies were taken out of the Friendly Societies Act[3] and placed in a separate measure, the Collecting Societies and Industrial Assurance Companies Act.[4] Although the separation of the legislative provisions into two measures served as a tidying-up operation, many of the more far-reaching suggestions of the Select Committee of 1889 were not adopted. The definition of a collecting society laid down in the act of 1875 as one that received contributions by means of collectors at a distance of more than ten miles from the registered office was left unchanged. The transfer of control of the companies from the Board of Trade to the Chief Registrar was another important recommendation that was not acted upon. Others which were not taken up included the imposition of an obligation to grant a surrender value after payment of premiums for five years and

---

[1] P.P. 1889, X, Report from the Select Committee on Friendly Societies, pp. ixv–xvii.
[2] *Ibid.*, p. xx.
[3] 59 & 60 Vict. c.25. *supra*, p. 89.
[4] 59 & 60 Vict. c.26.

the requirement for a deposit of £500 by persons seeking to register new societies.

The main effect of the new legislation was to make existing legal requirements much clearer and to bring industrial insurance companies under the same regulations as collecting societies in such matters as burial insurance on the lives of children. The recommendations that when new societies had a deficiency they should be wound up by the Chief Registrar and that he should be able to intervene to order inquiries or institute other proceedings on his own initiative were not enacted. The position remained that the Chief Registrar could only act if asked to do so by a certain number of members—in societies of more than 10,000, at least 500 members were needed before such a request could be effective. In practice it was usually only through collectors themselves that 500 signatures could be obtained. Therefore, such applications were usually initiated by dissatisfied collectors, and were incidents in the continuing struggle in collecting societies between the incumbent managers whose aim was to hold on to office, and those collectors who were seeking it.[1]

Against this background, very rapid growth continued and by the early years of the 20th century the three largest collecting societies had about 2,000,000 members each. The actual figures

Table 5.3.

Collecting Societies, 1891–1903.[2]

	1891	1899	1903
No. of societies	43	46	43
No. of members	3,875,215	5,922,615	6,973,136
Funds	2,713,214	5,207,686	7,220,932
Funds per member	14s 0d	17s 7d	20s 8d

[1] E. W. Brabrook, *Provident Societies and Industrial Welfare*, 1898, p. 83.
[2] E. W. Brabrook, 'On the Progress of Friendly Societies and Other Institutions connected with the Friendly Societies Registry Office', *J. Statistical Society*, LXVIII, 1905, p. 325.

returned for 1905 were Royal Liver 1,957,139 members, Liverpool Victoria Legal 2,102,018 and the Royal London 2,073,651.[1] The rate of growth during the last years of the 19th century is illustrated by the figures in table 5.3. A large proportion of the members were, of course, children and the period of membership usually terminated long before death. The Royal Liver Society, for instance, experienced in 1905 47,000 deaths and 682,000 lapses from other causes; new entries for the same year amounted to 851,000. The collecting societies could hardly be considered as foremost among the agencies for mutual thrift or self-help, but their continued success showed that they met a need among the poorer section of the community.

[1] P.P. 1906, CXII, Pt I, Report of the Chief Registrar, p. 90.

Chapter Six
Building Societies

I. The emergence of building societies

As organizations for promoting thrift and housing, the building societies emerged alongside friendly societies but their appeal was always much more limited in the 19th century. While virtually all classes of society could find some sort of friendly society with subscription rates low enough to enable them to join, this was never true of early building societies. Their rates of subscription for members were not suited to the poorer working men, but, as with many friendly societies, building societies attracted strong support among tradesmen and other members of the lower middle classes.

The activities undertaken by building societies were described with typically incisive phraseology by the Friendly Societies' Commission 'Building societies do not build; they simply make advances on building. They are, in fact, investment associations, mainly confining themselves to real securities.'[1] While this described the position by the 1870s, the Commissioners themselves explained that some of the earliest societies did actually build. The articles of a society established in

[1] P.P. 1872, XXVI, RCFS, 2nd Report, para. 13.

Birmingham in 1781 'for building on lands belonging to William Jennings Esq.' included these provisions:

> that each subscriber for 3 shares should have one or more houses built of the value of 200 guineas, each subscriber for 2 shares have one or more houses, value £140, and each subscriber for 1 share should have a single house, value £70;
> that the committee should have power to contract for the leasing of the land to be built upon;
> that the land intended for building upon should be laid out in lots and balloted for by subscribers; separate leases were to be executed but these were to remain in the hands of the committee until the proposed buildings were completed.

Building clubs were said to have developed New John Street and Pritchett Street, Birmingham. In his *Century of Birmingham Life*, J. A. Langford stated that building clubs were responsible for houses in Cheapside, Woodcock Street and Islington Row.[1] Birmingham and its surroundings may well have seen some of the earliest building societies, but similar societies undertaking the actual construction of houses in these early years might also be found in Lancashire and Yorkshire. It has been suggested that what were possibly the first back-to-back houses in Leeds were erected by a terminating building society. The articles of agreement of Crackenthorpe Garden Building Club were drawn up on 3 November 1787 and provided for the division of Crackenthorpe Gardens into 52 building plots. A number of the original conveyances from the building club to the first owners have survived and have come to light as a result of the recent compulsory purchase of these properties by the municipal authorities, for clearance.[2]

One of the most fully documented of these early societies is Longridge Building Society, the records of which are in Lancashire County Record Office. The Society's articles are of interest because they show clearly both the form of organiza-

---

[1] *Ibid.*, p. 7. footnote; S. D. Chapman and J. N. Bartlett 'The Contribution of Building Clubs and Freehold Land Societies to Working-class Housing in Birmingham' in S. D. Chapman (ed.), *The History of Working-Class Housing*, 1971, p. 237; J. A. Langford, *A Century of Birmingham Life, 1741–1841*.

[2] M. W. Beresford, 'The Back to Back House in Leeds, 1787–1937' in S. D. Chapman (ed.) *op. cit.*, p. 102.

tion of an 18th-century society and its activities. The first article required the appointment of a committee of three members to be chosen by the subscribers for the purpose of 'contracting for land sufficient for such houses, and convenient gardens thereto, providing materials, setting the work, letting the houses as they become habitable, and transacting all other business relative thereto, to the best advantage of the society'. Each committee-man was to be allowed sixpence for each monthly meeting he attended. Other articles provided that subscribers should attend monthly at the house of John Swarbrick (the White Bull) to pay their subscription of 10s 6d along with 3d for the expenses of the meeting. As with contemporary friendly societies, the club money was to be 'deposited in a box provided for that purpose, with four locks, and lodged with the said John Swarbrick. Each officer to have a key and to attend each monthly meeting'. The Society had 20 members among whom the houses were allocated by ballot, the deeds of each proprietor being lodged in the Society's box until the whole venture was completed. In order to speed up the rate of building, loans were raised to augment the cash available from subscriptions and the 20 houses were completed within about five years.[1] The Society did not oblige members to occupy their houses; they might let them if they wished since article V stated that 'Each member shall have liberty to enter upon his own house, or put a tenant therein, on a rent to be fixed by the committee.' This Society seems to have been typical of its contemporaries in not requiring owner-occupation.

As a result of his investigations, S. J. Price concluded that by 1825 well over 250 building societies had been founded[2] but it is impossible to be at all certain about total members of societies at this time. By 1825 some societies must have fulfilled their function, provided their subscribers with houses and duly terminated; others would have collapsed for some reason without completing their intended course. There was a considerable increase in the number of foundations in the years following the Napoleonic Wars. The successful establishment of one society

---

[1] S. J. Price, *Building Societies: their origin and history*, 1958, pp. 32–44.

[2] *Ibid.*, p. 58. Price lists 63 societies known to have functioned between 1775 and 1825, pp. 59–67.

in a town led to the formation of other societies as at Bradford where seven societies were founded between 1823 and 1835.[1]

All of these societies were similar to the Longridge Society in that they followed the terminating pattern. The object was to enable their members to subscribe and act jointly until each had acquired his property, when the society would terminate. Perhaps the most difficult problem in operating these societies was to decide the order in which members were to take possession of the houses built by their society—or to receive advances from the common fund with which to purchase a house, as came to be the case with increasing frequency. Clearly those who gained possession at an early date were better placed than those who had to wait until later. A ballot was quite often used; sometimes a child would be employed actually to draw the numbers in an attempt to avoid arousing any suspicion of rigging. Some societies decided the matter by taking the order in which members had originally joined the society, but the effect of this was to discourage anyone from joining once the society had begun to transact business. By 1830 the most usual method of determining which member should receive the next advance was by some form of auction. Members were invited to make bids and the highest bidder was given the advance. In effect the advance went to the member prepared to allow the highest rate of discount. This system of allocating advances came to be accepted as normal by the middle of the century.[2]

The Longridge Building Society was typical of the early societies in its form of organization. Early societies had a very limited membership, a committee to organize their business and trustees in whom the assets were vested. As with friendly societies, the members met monthly at a public house to pay their subscriptions and to pass a convivial evening in each other's company. There were the usual rules against 'quarrelsomeness' and other unacceptable behaviour with comparatively large fines for offenders. Unlike contemporary friendly societies where drink was paid for from the club subscriptions themselves, a separate subscription to meet the cost of drink

---

[1] *Ibid.*, pp. 66–7.

[2] H. F. A. Davis, *Law and Practice of Building and Freehold Land Societies in England Scotland and Ireland*, 1870.

appears in the rules of some early building societies frequently enough for it to have been the usual arrangement.[1] This more systematic additional provision of a special subscription to pay for liquid refreshment confirms the impression that the early building societies were designed to meet the needs of the better-off among working men and tradesmen.

Some terminating societies framed their principles of operation on extremely shaky foundations and found themselves unable to fulfil their objectives, since these were too ambitious. The reason for these difficulties was sometimes strong local competition, and sometimes a lack of understanding. Scratchley found a number of societies as late as the 1840s which proposed to last for only ten years, the shares of which were £120 and the payments of investors ten shillings per month. In order to achieve their aims with these figures, it would have been necessary to keep subscriptions fully invested at an interest rate of 14½ per cent. Yet the borrowers' payments in the same societies did not bring in more than seven or eight per cent or even less since the prospectuses showed that borrowers in the first year would receive advances of £60 per share and would pay in return 14 shillings a month. Thus the promised results could not be attained and the societies had to extend their lives, or failed at an earlier stage.[2]

II. *The Benefit Building Societies Act of 1836*

The legal standing of early building societies was confused and when societies got into difficulties this became a matter of considerable importance. As in the contemporary unregistered friendly societies, it was difficult or even impossible to get redress against the malversation of funds by officers of the societies. In an effort to clarify their position some of the building societies registered under the Friendly Societies Act of 1793 and its successors. Such registration also carried with it valuable exemption from the currently heavy stamp duties.

[1] Examples of this may be found in the Articles of Agreement of the Amicable Building Society, Birmingham, 1781, Article I and in the Articles of Longridge Building Society, 1793, Article II. These sets of rules are printed in Price, *op. cit.*, pp. 33–5, and 575–8.
[2] A. Scratchley, *Treatise on Benefit Building Societies*, 1857 edition, pp. 33–4.

Building societies

Before 1836 the registration of building societies as such was not recognized as appropriate under the Friendly Societies Acts and there is some evidence that building societies which registered sought to represent themselves as fulfilling the legally defined objects of friendly societies in their rules or articles. The Bradford Union Building Society, for example, had a rule which stated that its members 'do form ourselves into a society and by contribution of our own savings to a common fund and on the principle of mutual insurance for the maintenance of ourselves, wives and children in sickness, infancy, advanced age or any other natural state or contingency, we do hereby undertake to build 33 cottages or dwelling houses'.[1] This society was registered as a friendly society in 1824.

The great majority of building societies remained outside the friendly society legislation and found themselves in a vulnerable position in 1836 when the government sought to consolidate the law concerning stamp duties. The sequence of events leading to the Building Societies Act of 1836 remains obscure. According to the evidence given by Josiah Hosking—who was connected with 20 societies in Liverpool—to the Royal Commission in 1871, the Chancellor of the Exchequer proposed in 1835 to charge duty on all companies transferring shares. Building societies in Manchester and Liverpool feared that this duty would be levied on societies and sent a delegation to see Spring-Rice, the Chancellor, to press their views. Spring-Rice accepted their case and felt the societies needed legislation of their own which was introduced in the next session, 1836.[2] Some of the details of Hosking's account may not be accurate; the date of 1835 is particularly doubtful since the government attempted the reform of stamp duties in the following year, but there seems to be little doubt that it was fear of stamp duties which stimulated the representations leading to the Act of 1836.[3]

During the first half of May, 1836, petitions were received by the Commons from a number of societies in South Lancashire

[1] E. J. Cleary, *The Building Society Movement*, 1965, p. 15; E. Naylor, *Bradford Building Societies*, 1908, p. 22.
[2] P.P. 1871, XXV, RCFS, Q. 6456.
[3] Cleary, *op. cit.*, pp. 26–7, discusses Hosking's evidence as well as the different reasons for representations given by Naylor, *op. cit.*, p. 20.

for the insertion of a clause in the Stamp Duties Bill exempting benefit building societies from the duty on the transfer of shares. These included the Mason's Arms Society, the Bay Horse Society, and the Black Bull Society, all of Bury; the Duke of Clarence Society, and the Provident Society of Salford; the Pendleton Association, and the Manchester and Salford District Association.[1] Clearly these and other representations met with a favourable hearing, for in June and July the Benefit Building Societies Bill made its way through Parliament, apparently attracting little attention, and received the Royal Assent on 14th July.[2]

The Benefit Building Societies Act of 1836[3] assimilated building societies more closely to friendly society legislation than was the case with any of the other members of the group of organizations with which the Registrar had to deal. It enacted that all the provisions of the existing friendly societies acts[4] 'so far as the same or any part thereof may be applicable to the purpose of any benefit building society, and to the framing, certifying, enrolling and altering the rules thereof' were to 'extend and apply to such benefit building society, and the rules thereof in such and the same manner as if the provisions of the said acts had been herein expressly re-enacted'.[5]

The only exception to this assimilation was that building societies were not given the right to invest funds in savings banks or with the Commissioners for the National Debt at the concessionary interest rates of which friendly societies were able to take advantage. The reason for this exception was the loss which the Treasury encountered through subsidizing concessionary interest rates to savings banks.[6] According to Hosking, Spring-Rice saw in government encouragement and support for building societies a way of limiting the Treasury's losses on its support of savings banks. He was reported to have told building society representatives that 'as a matter of finance we lose every year by the savings banks, and if we encourage

---

[1] *House of Commons Journal*, vol. 91, pp. 326, 347, 357, 366.
[2] *Ibid.*, p. 664.
[3] 6 & 7 Wm. IV, c.32.
[4] 10 Geo. IV, c.56, and 5 & 6 Wm. IV, c.40.
[5] 6 & 7 Wm. IV, c.32. s.4.
[6] *Infra*, pp. 219–22.

these societies we shall benefit the government funds, by getting people to save in these societies instead of in savings banks.'[1] Thus there may have been some hope on the part of the government that the cost to the Treasury of extending to building societies that exemption from stamp duties which friendly societies enjoyed would be more than balanced by providing savers with an attractive alternative to the subsidized savings banks.

The Act recited that building societies had been established 'principally among the industrious classes for the purpose of raising by small periodical subscriptions a fund to assist the members thereof in obtaining a small freehold or leasehold property'. It went on to offer the right of registration to societies which limited the value of each share to £150 and the monthly subscription to 20 shillings for each share. It did not seek to limit the number of shares which any individual might hold. The Act drew generously the limits within which building societies might make their own rules and govern their own affairs. Moreover those societies which had been established prior to 1st June 1836 were entitled to the protection and benefits of the Act on having their rules certified and deposited without being 'required to alter in any manner the rules under which they are now respectively governed'.[2] These generous terms offered to existing societies were indicative of the generally helpful attitude intended by the government in this piece of legislation. The Act remained in force for nearly 40 years. The changes made in the law after 1836 in so far as it concerned friendly societies found no reflection in that governing building societies so that by 1870 the provisions of the two Friendly Societies Acts[3] which had been drawn upon by the Act of 1836 continued to apply only to building societies. Moreover the Act of 1836 was described by the Royal Commission as 'probably one of the worst drawn which yet remain on the statute book'. The language of its first and leading section was said to be incapable of grammatical construction and the Act 'so bristles throughout with doubts' that almost every line of it had

[1] P.P. 1871, XXV, RCFS, Q. 6456.
[2] 6 & 7 Wm. IV, c.32, s.7.
[3] 10 Geo. IV, c.56, and 5 & 6 Wm. IV, c.40.

had to be brought to the courts for interpretation at some time.[1] The Act was not founded on the report of a select committee and appeared 'to have slipped unheeded through Parliament'.[2] One matter that was not dealt with at all in the Act was the question of the borrowing powers which societies should be able to exercise. From their very beginnings building societies had in practice borrowed as a way of speeding the provision of houses for members in the early years of a terminating society's existence. Towards the end of their span of life terminating societies often found they had a surplus of funds which they sometimes loaned to other societies. In 1838 the Registrar, Tidd Pratt, issued an official handbook entitled *Instructions for the Establishment of Benefit Building Societies* which contained a model rule which authorized trustees to borrow money 'when there shall not be any moneys lying in the hands of the bankers to the credit of the society'.[3] Evidence given to the Royal Commission in 1871 showed that the Registrar changed his mind more than once on the question of borrowing. A witness from the Sun Permanent Building Society explained that the rules of his society were submitted to Tidd Pratt in 1853 and that he insisted on the power to borrow being excluded from them. Amendments to the rules which included the power to borrow were submitted in 1856 and Tidd Pratt then approved the rule granting this power.[4] The vagueness of the Act of 1836 and the total omission from it of important issues in building society administration undoubtedly threw a considerable burden of decision-making on the Registrar and the courts.

III. Mid-century growth and development

But the inadequacy of the legislation of 1836 really sprang from the tremendous amount of growth and development shown by building societies in the three decades following its enactment. No regular returns were required even from registered societies in this period and although returns were twice called for by the House of Commons, they were obviously incomplete and

[1] P.P. 1872, XXVI, RCFS, 2nd Report, para. 20.
[2] *Ibid.*, para. 22.
[3] *Ibid.*, para. 96.
[4] P.P. 1871, XXV, RCFS, W. R. Warner, QQ. 2956–7.

unreliable. The second of these was required by the House in 1889. Since a building society, once it had registered, had no further contact with the registration authorities, there was no record of any dissolutions. Hence the only way of trying to assemble the material for the return was by posting inquiry forms to the addresses given at the time of initial registration, although many of the inquiry forms were bound to be returned by the Post Office as many of the societies would have long since disappeared, while others had changed their addresses. In these circumstances the Royal Commission reported in 1872 that it was unable to offer any complete statistics. The Building Societies Protection Association sent its own list of societies to the Commission, but several large societies were omitted from this. The Commissioners attempted to estimate numbers of members and the size of the financial transactions of building societies, largely on the basis of intelligent guesswork. In this way they came to the conclusion that by 1869 there were about 2,000 building societies with a total of 800,000 members.[1] E. J. Cleary has recently suggested that the total number of societies in 1869 was nearer to 1,500 with a membership not greatly in excess of 300,000.[2]

The Commissioners also found no sound basis on which to assess accurately the extent of the financial transactions of the societies. In the event it based its estimate on the material provided by the Building Societies Protection Association and 'as a mere estimate' put forward these figures for building societies as a whole:

total subscribed capital	£9,000,000
total loan and deposit capital	£6,000,000
total assets	£17,000,000
advanced on mortgage	£16,000,000

The very rapid growth of the building society movement in the 1840s has been illustrated by Cleary. On the basis of the details given in the *Building Society Directory* he was able to show that 767 terminating and 81 permanent societies were

[1] P.P. 1872, XXVI, RCFS, 2nd Report, para. 24.
[2] Cleary, *op. cit.*, pp. 286–9 where a careful attempt is made to build up an estimate of total numbers by using the various pieces of evidence available.

established in the decade preceding 1853.[1] The most significant element in this rapid growth was undoubtedly the emergence of the permanent building society, which may have owed its origin to the practice of forming terminating building societies in series in order to accommodate fresh groups of applicants in succession. In place of forming a new society for each successive group, it appeared simpler to keep the original society in existence and to continue admitting members at any time. The individual could join or leave when it suited him to do so. The member lost nothing from the newer form of organization since it remained true that 'A permanent society is a terminating society to every individual from the date at which he enters.'[2]

Some of the advantages offered by a permanent as compared with a terminating society were set out in the first report of the Leeds Permanent. The directors dwelt on the difficulty which terminating societies encountered in attracting new members a few years after their foundation because of the size of the premium they were required to pay on entry. By contrast, mortgage loans or withdrawal of accumulated savings were freely available in a permanent society. While the main object of the founders of the Leeds Permanent was said to be to enable the industrious classes and 'more especially the working man' to purchase or erect his own dwelling, the directors 'felt it to be their duty on the present occasion to state that no society in the Kingdom offers better facilities to all parties for obtaining county votes in a more easy manner than this, not being connected with any political party or sect.' During the year it was claimed that 60 people had been put in the position of being able to claim the franchise.[3]

The £2 freeholder—even if his land was mortgaged—could claim the right to vote and after the Reform Act of 1832 this right was extended to copy and lease holders of houses worth

---

[1] *Ibid.*, pp. 44–5. A number of commentators noticed the rapid growth of the societies in the middle years of the century. According to the *Edinburgh Review*, for instance 'Another mode of investment which has lately become a great favourite both with the middle and working classes, is afforded by what are termed Benefit Building Societies'—CXCIV, April 1852, p. 421.

[2] P.P. 1871, XXV, RCFS, H. I. Brown, Q. 4085.

[3] *First Report of the Leeds Benefit Building and Investment Society*, 16 January 1850.

£10 per annum in the boroughs or of land with an annual value of £10 in the counties. A series of lawsuits in the early 1840s cleared away certain doubts concerning the legal validity of spreading the franchise by buying land mainly with the aim of breaking it up into small parcels in order to create the right to vote. A marked growth in the number of freehold land societies followed, many of them established by one or other of the political parties with the aim of facilitating the enfranchisement of their own supporters through land purchase. Even so, there can be little doubt but that the building societies did more to add to the number of electors than the freehold land societies in the 20 years preceding the changes made by the Reform Act of 1867. As the committee of the Leeds Permanent recognized, the drive to acquire the franchise played a significant part in stimulating building society development in the middle years of the last century. The freehold land societies themselves were constituted on the permanent principle and this stimulated the spread of the permanent idea among building societies. Indeed, a number of land societies registered as benefit building societies[1]. The interest of politicians in the spreading of the franchise also led a number of them to take an active part in the management of ordinary permanent societies.

The main reason for the growth of the permanent society to its predominant position in the later 19th century lay in the way in which it separated the investor from the borrower and met the needs of both in a more adaptable manner than a terminating society could do. The contrast between the two forms of society was brought out clearly by James Higham, Secretary of the Fourth City Mutual Building Society which was organized on permanent principles. He explained that from the standpoint of an investor, his society was willing to take a monthly subscription or to accept the full amount of a share (£60) as a single payment. Whichever the investor chose, the paid-up share remained as an investment and the member received interest on it indefinitely, whereas in a terminating society the members had to withdraw their money and find another investment on the stipulated date for the close of a society. The greater flexibility permitted to the borrower by a permanent

[1] P.P. 1872, XXVI, RCFS, 2nd Report, para. 52.

society could be equally attractive, for when taking a loan he could choose the length of time over which he repaid it up to a maximum of twenty years. The closing date of a terminating society meant that after such a society had been established for a few years, the length of time over which it could arrange for the repayment of an advance was very limited and it was particularly difficult for working men to pay off advances over comparatively short periods.[1]

The complaint was made that permanent societies tended to become investment associations which charged borrowers more than strictly mutual societies would have done in order to pay bonuses or higher rates of interest to investing members. Some societies certainly operated in this way, but others sought to minimize their profits only ensuring that the income from borrowers exceeded the payments to savers by a sufficient margin to pay for the management expenses. Some of these societies were able to charge borrowers the same rate of interest as subscribing investors were paid by the process of accepting deposits at a lower rate of interest. Thus in its first year the Leeds Permanent charged borrowers and paid share subscribers five per cent but it only paid four per cent on the loans it accepted on deposit. In the case of this society, it is of some interest to find that a considerable source of loan finance were friendly societies, thirteen of which deposited funds with the Leeds Permanent in the first year of its operation.[2] The practice of this particular society was singled out for commendation by the Royal Commission twenty years later when it remarked that the equalization of interest rates between borrowers and investors—as distinct from depositors—was achieved by 'the excellent Leeds Permanent Society'.[3]

At the other extreme from the Leeds Society was the position taken by Frederick Ingoldby, chairman of the Planet Society. He believed that borrowing members ought to be excluded from all privileges of membership such as voting at the annual meeting. He claimed that they might on some occasion outvote

[1] P.P. 1871, XXV, RCFS, Q. 2877.

[2] *First Report of the Leeds Benefit Building and Investment Society*, 16 January, 1850.

[3] P.P. 1872, XXVI, RCFS, 2nd Report, para. 44.

investors on some question such as the appropriation of the reserve fund or might decide to divide the profits among themselves. 'We think that their interest, supposing that they are not investors as well as borrowers, should cease when they have had their advance. We attach great importance to that point.'[1] The number of societies appearing to adopt this attitude in practice if not in theory was sufficiently great for the Commission to remark that permanent societies became often mainly agencies for the investment of capital, rather than for enabling the industrious to provide dwellings for themselves.

The growth of permanent societies was often alleged to have had the effect of converting the building societies into middle-class organizations. William Harle who had organized a number of terminating societies in the North-East, asserted that the great bulk of investors were not working men but 'females' and 'industrious tradesmen'.[2] The loans made by the large permanent societies were sometimes very large. The South Yorkshire Society, for instance, advanced as much as £10,000, £12,000, £15,000, £20,000 and £30,000 in single advances to the owners of factories and works.[3] On the other hand the London Building Societies Protection Association gathered statistics of the size of mortgage advances made by its members and these showed that 69,879 were below £300 while 9,393 exceeded that figure. Thus the Commissioners concluded that the societies did still mainly carry on their business with the working class 'or with a class but slightly superior in station'.[4] These conclusions were supported by the position of the Leeds Society in the 1860s. Five-sixths of its mortgage advances were for sums below £400. Very few investors had more than three shares—or 7s 6d weekly subscription—and the majority had only one. The President of the Society had no doubt but that the great majority of investing members were working men, earning weekly wages. 'On Friday, there are a large number of police in the office, that being the day on which the police wages are paid. A great number of them deposit 2s 6d a week

[1] P.P. 1871, XXV, RCFS, Q. 7163.
[2] *Ibid.*, Q. 8198.
[3] *Ibid.*, Q. 7719.
[4] P.P. 1872, XXVI, RCFS 2nd Report, para. 47.

with us.' By 1870 this society had a number of branch offices away from Leeds and that in Hartlepool was said to be very successful since many of the men working at the iron works there were small savers usually contributing 2s 6d weekly.[1] The extent to which working men invested in and borrowed from the permanent societies appeared to vary a good deal from one society to another and between different areas. But the position of the management was much clearer for permanent societies were almost invariably under the direction of the middle class. Among those occupations most heavily represented among the directors and sponsors of building societies could be found solicitors, auctioneers and land agents, and builders. The Royal Commission concluded it was at least safe to say that members of the middle class by then entered the building society movement in much larger numbers, took a much larger share in its direction and derived much greater benefit from it than they had done thirty years earlier.[2]

The elaboration of the ways in which building societies came to be used to meet the needs of the middle class may be seen from the links developed by insurance companies. One of the earliest accounts of the possible valuable connections that could be created between life insurance institutions and the societies was published in 1846.[3] Three years later Arthur Scratchley included in his book on building societies a chapter on 'Life or Fidelity Insurance applied to Building Societies'.[4] In 1853 the British Life Office introduced a building assurance policy by which:

(1) the subscriptions which purchased the property also assured the life of the purchaser for the same sum as the outstanding debt so that in case of death, at any time prior to the completion of the subscription term, his family was entitled to the property without further payment;
(2) the purchase money was advanced by the Office immediately the first subscription was paid.

---

[1] P.P. 1871, XXV, RCFS, T. Dawson and T. Fatkin, QQ. 5125 and 5065.
[2] P.P. 1872, XXVI, RCFS, 2nd Report, para. 48.
[3] J. H. James, *A Treatise on Benefit Building Societies*, 1846.
[4] A. Scratchley, *A Treatise on Benefit Building Societies*, 1849.

Thus under this scheme, the insurance company actually undertook the business of the building society itself by making the advances.[1]

Scratchley took matters a stage further and put forward a scheme for applying life assurance to investors as well as to borrowers. His scheme applied to investors in permanent building societies who had undertaken to pay a monthly subscription for a given number of years and at the end of the period were to receive the full value of the shares for which they had been subscribing. Without some form of insurance, when an investor died, his family were merely entitled to claim the amount of his past subscriptions. By paying a very small insurance premium, a man in good health might under this scheme enable his dependants to receive his shares paid in full if he died before completing his term of subscription.[2]

From another point of view, the permanent society was for many simply a savings bank. This was one aspect of the building society movement which attracted the attention of the leaders of teetotalism. Their reforming interests have been broadly described as humanitarian, educational and counter-attractive. Temperance reformers were eager to inculcate thrift not only through savings banks 'but also through building societies and the freehold land movement'.[3] In that the Chancellor of the Exchequer, Spring-Rice, had sought to encourage building societies to develop into attractive rivals to the Treasury-subsidized savings banks, he appears to have achieved his object. Many of the permanent societies built up a considerable savings business in the middle years of the century. The Queen's Society at Birmingham, for instance, accepted subscriptions as small as 6d, and members were urged to bring what they could as often as they could. There was no entrance fee and no charge of any sort. Savers were given a passbook predated for eight or ten years showing every pay day. If members came in between the set dates, the society entered their savings in a day book and on the fortnightly pay-day entered the sum which had been paid between one pay-day and

[1] C. Walford, *Insurance Cyclopaedia*, vol. I, 1870, p. 404.
[2] Scratchley, *op. cit.*, pp. 135-6.
[3] Brian Harrison, *Drink and the Victorians*, 1971, p. 175.

another.[1] The Industrial Permanent Building Society at Greenwich established a 'savings bank department' for the receipt of small deposits on which it paid 4 per cent interest.[2]

While permanent societies developed and even came to predominate in some parts of the country such as London and the South-East during the 1850s and 1860s, terminating societies continued to serve a useful purpose. Even in 1870 it was said that in some Lancashire towns, Sunderland, and South Wales, terminating societies were being founded in great numbers and were preferred by the working classes in those places to the permanent ones. According to a solicitor to a number of terminating societies in Oldham, the people there did not like permanent societies because they liked 'to see an end of a society, and to manage it'. They believed that they could not tell so readily how matters stood in a permanent society.[3]

If the growth of permanent building societies was the principal development which had occurred since the Building Societies Act was passed in 1836, the other main development which had not been foreseen by the legislators of that year was the growth of the loan or deposit system. The considerable demand for money in the early years of the existence of a terminating society was often met by borrowing from bankers. As the society moved into an easier cash position in its later years, the debts were repaid. While permanent societies also borrowed from bankers, their need for borrowed funds was of a longer term nature and they met this need by accepting funds from members of the public on deposit. Societies generally paid for deposits at a rate of interest somewhat lower than that paid to shareholders. In the 1860s and 1870s four per cent seems to have been fairly usual with rates tending to fall in the 1870s and subsequent years. The Temperance Land and Building Society, for instance, paid five per cent for this money originally, then found four per cent sufficient and in 1870 reduced this to three per cent, finding it then had more money in hand

---

[1] P.P. 1871, XXV, RCFS, James Taylor, Q. 3657.
[2] *Ibid.*, Peter Blake, Q. 3613.
[3] *Ibid.*, William Ashcroft, QQ. 6282–4.

than it could employ profitably.[1] The popularity of this form of investment with members of the public was very marked. The Royal Commission recognized this, and pointed out the attraction of a building society—with its money secured on property and a constant flow of cash from monthly repayments—as compared with a bank whose securities might be of a much more fluctuating and uncertain character.

There was, of course, no specific provision for this particular development in the Act of 1836 and the Registrar's office was still striking the actual word 'deposit' from any building society rules which came before it—even though enormous sums were in fact being accepted as deposits. The explanation of the office's policy given by the Assistant Registrar served to confirm the impression that new legislation was needed. Present practice was to permit 'merely the naked power to borrow money. Now under that power to borrow I suppose there is nothing to prevent their receiving money in any sum, and in any shape, and upon any conditions as to payment, either by way of cheque or otherwise, as these societies do . . .'[2]

In suggesting that the activities of building societies deserved that legal countenance which only new legislation could give, the Royal Commission argued that the societies had promoted the investment in property of many millions of pounds yearly, that they had had great influence in training members of the working class 'to business habits', and that they had enormously encouraged the building of houses for the working and lower middle classes. The claim was not made that the activities of the societies had led to any improvement in the standard of working-class accommodation and this was, perhaps, wise, for when societies were hard-pressed to find enough borrowers—as some undoubtedly were from time to time—they were not always as particular as they might have been in insisting on a high standard in the properties they accepted as security for mortgages. Yet it is worth noticing that some of the surveyors employed by societies were aware not only of the social but also of the financial advantages of trying to ensure that advances should only be made on houses offering a reasonable standard

---

[1] *Ibid.*, Henry Phillips, QQ. 6112–3.
[2] *Ibid.*, E. W. Brabrook, Q. 3306.

of amenity and comfort. Messrs Perkin and Backhouse, surveyors, reported to the committee of the Leeds Society in 1850 that they had had to survey small cottage dwellings without cellars, pantries, closets, cupboards or even their own privies. They added, 'Now such miserable accommodation is inadequate and unfit to the requirements and comfort of a man with a wife and family, and our object in calling your attention to this class of buildings is for the purpose of inducing you to consider well the advances of money which you are asked to make upon such property, for we are persuaded that as the sanitary movement progresses, the improvement in the erection of cottage dwellings will be such, that occupiers ere long will have the opportunity of inhabiting more commodious and better homes at a rental some little above what they are now paying, and thus cottages deficient in accommodation will become indifferently tenanted, whilst those of a superior class will no doubt be eagerly sought after.'[1]

There could be no doubt but that the importance of the building society movement claimed for it a more appropriate legislative framework. The Royal Commission considered whether special legislation was needed or whether the societies might not more properly be assimilated to the existing Companies Act. This was a view which had support in some quarters, not least from the Chancellor of the Exchequer, Robert Lowe. Companies could fulfil all the functions of a building society such as advancing money on property, issuing shares, contracting loans and so forth. On the other hand, the number of shares in a company could not be varied without considerable difficulty and the shares always formed a definite number. The fluctuating membership and the changing number of shares which were of the essence of a building society could hardly be conveniently accommodated within the existing company pattern. The Commissioners concluded that the legal form of the building society needed to be maintained and that the law respecting it needed amendment and consolidation.[2]

All the main recommendations of the Royal Commission were broadly favourable to the societies. Registration should

[1] *Report of the Leeds Benefit Building and Investment Society*, 1860.
[2] P.P. 1872, XXVI, RCFS, 2nd Report, paras. 79 and 80.

continue to be with the Registrar of Friendly Societies. The analogy of type between building societies and other bodies in relation with the Registrar was such that it would only be harmful to detach a single member of the group and place it under a new officer. The effect of registration should be to incorporate a society, giving it full corporate powers, thus enabling it to dispense with the existing system of trusteeship and to deal with property directly.[1] Exemption from stamp duty on mortgages should continue but ought to be limited to mortgages not exceeding £200. This limit was suggested since it was roughly in line with the maximum sums on which fiscal concessions could apply in the case of friendly societies, industrial and provident societies and savings banks.[2] The rules of societies should contain provisions covering such matters as withdrawals, redemptions, the power to borrow and the power to issue preferential shares. It was also suggested that the power to borrow should normally be limited to two-thirds of the total value of the amounts secured on mortgage.[3] Finally it was recommended that the Registrar be given power to settle disputes when requested by both parties and to wind up societies on the vote of a meeting of members.[4]

Before the Royal Commission had been set up, local building societies in the North-East had persuaded the Member of Parliament for Sunderland, Gourley, to introduce a bill which would put beyond any doubt the borrowing power of societies. The London Association of societies prevailed upon Gourley to make certain changes in his bill which received their support at a meeting in October 1869. The Building Societies Protection Association—as this group centred on London was called—had ahead of it a period of campaigning lasting until 1874 before any new legislation actually reached the statute book.[5] Gourley's bill was referred to the Royal Commission on Friendly Societies

---

[1] *Ibid.*, paras. 81 and 94.
[2] *Ibid.*, para. 77.
[3] *Ibid.*, paras. 121 and 120.
[4] *Ibid.*, para. 127.
[5] The Building Societies Protection Association was established to enable the member societies to act together in making representations to the government. This society was the direct lineal ancestor of the present Building Societies Association.

which was set up in 1870 and the question of further parliamentary action went into abeyance until the Second Report of the Commission was issued in 1872. From that date until the Gladstone ministry went out of office two years later, little progress was made. H. A. Bruce, the Home Secretary, made it clear that the sort of measure the government wanted to see was one which would have made building societies subject to the provisions of the Companies Act and they would have come under the Board of Trade rather than the Registrar of Friendly Societies. At least two Government bills were introduced in 1873 which would have had the effect of assimilating building societies to the company structure. Both of them were strongly opposed by building society interests and their supporters, who were still pressing the government to accept Gourley's bill in a modified form.[1]

The deadlock was eventually broken by the return of the Disraeli ministry in 1874 with Assheton Cross as the new Home Secretary. Cross had been one of the spokesmen for the building societies in the previous Parliament and the way was now clear for progress to be made with new legislation. A bill based on Gourley's original proposals as advocated by the Building Societies Protection Association was introduced into the Commons by McCullogh Torrens who was currently president of the Association. The bill was referred to a Select Committee which included a number of its sponsors. The committee made very few alterations. There followed a meeting between the sponsors and the Chancellor of the Exchequer at which they agreed to give up exemption from stamp duties on mortgage deeds in exchange for concessions on borrowing powers— although exemption from stamp duties on other deeds and documents was maintained. The bill was finally enacted at the end of July 1874.

The Building Societies Act of 1874[2] provided the legal framework within which building societies have since developed. S. J. Price wrote in 1958 that while there had been various amending acts, 'nevertheless the 1874 Act remains the linchpin

---

[1] Cleary, *op. cit.*, pp. 93–6; Price, *op. cit.*, pp. 226–9.
[2] 37 & 38 Vict., c.42.

on which building society practice is based'.[1] Most of the provisions were also in accord with the recommendations of the Royal Commission. Building societies were placed under the Chief Registrar of Friendly Societies. Existing societies could continue under the Act of 1836. Every newly-registered society became a corporate body and there was no longer any need to appoint trustees to hold mortgaged property on behalf of a society.[2] The legal right of societies to receive money on deposit or by loans up to an amount not exceeding two-thirds of the current value of mortgages was enacted as recommended by the Royal Commission. In the case of terminating societies an alternative limit of twelve months' subscription on the shares issued was permitted.[3] Annual accounts were to be prepared and a copy was to be sent to the Chief Registrar.[4]

The Act of 1874 did not go as far as the Royal Commission had recommended in certain respects. It did not give the recommended powers to the Chief Registrar in the matter of certifying or rejecting proposed rules and it did not give him the legal authority he needed to police building societies. While the new law provided well-run societies with the facilities they needed, it failed to provide the means of preventing less well-run societies from pursuing courses likely to lead to disaster thereby endangering public confidence in all building societies. The act of 1894 became necessary precisely because that of 1874 failed to enact these 'policing' measures proposed by the Royal Commission.

IV. *Economic difficulties, 'mushroom' societies and the legislation of 1894*

The economic circumstances with which building societies were confronted from 1875 for most of the remainder of the century were much more difficult than those of the previous quarter century. The immediate consequence was a slowing down of the rate of growth of the large and well established

---

[1] Price, *op. cit.*, p. 230.
[2] 37 & 38 Vict., c.42, s.9.
[3] S.15.
[4] S. 40.

permanent societies. The more difficult economic and financial background also helped to bring out more rapidly and more starkly the shortcomings of the Act of 1874 than might otherwise have been the case. The third quarter of the century had been a period of rising commodity prices and property values. From 1875, falling prices, falling interest rates and declining property values were characteristics of the British economy which made sound building society operation more difficult.

The impact of these circumstances may perhaps be seen most clearly through the figures reported by one or two of the larger societies. During the first few years after 1875 the new trend in commodity prices appeared to have little impact on the Halifax Building Society; its total assets doubled between 1875 and 1880. By 31st January 1889 they stood at £1,146,393 yet ten years later they had only reached £1,209,312. The figure for 1900 was £1,461,257.[1] Comparable figures for the Leeds Permanent Society showed a similar picture. Between 1868 and 1878 total assets nearly trebled to £1,128,162 but ten years later the total had only struggled as far as £1,382,163.[2] In the case of the Halifax Society profits just exceeded £10,000 in 1879–80. By 1885–6 they had almost halved to £5,199 and only reached £10,000 again in 1903–4.[3]

The general fall in interest rates made the shares of building societies comparatively more attractive as investments just when the demand for mortgages was falling. The purchase of one's own house by means of a repayable loan appeared to be a much less attractive prospect while the house was steadily losing value on a declining property market. In order to attempt to 'induce borrowers in much larger numbers and to obtain outlets for the very large funds which have been lying in the hands of the bankers for several years', the Halifax Permanent adopted a new table for borrowers in 1883 in which the mortgage loan would be repayable over a longer period—nearly twenty years. In their Report for 1885 the directors of the society stated that they had had to reduce the rate of interest payable to investing

[1] These figures represent the combined totals of the Halifax Permanent and Halifax Equitable which joined to form the Halifax Building Society and are from Annual Reports.

[2] *Leeds Permanent Building Society Annual Report*, 1898.

[3] Oscar R. Hobson, *A Hundred Years of the Halifax*, 1953, p. 45.

members to four per cent. During the 1880s the directors had been driven to making advances to public bodies including school boards at a lower rate of interest than that provided by the tables in use by the Society. Between 1880 and 1882 a total of £20,000 was loaned to Halifax School Board for the construction of schools.[1]

In order both to limit the inflow of cash and to increase the attractiveness of borrowing, the Leeds Permanent Society reduced the rate of interest it offered on its deposit accounts from 4 to 3½ per cent in 1881 while the interest offered on new share accounts was reduced from 4½ to 4 per cent. The interest charged to borrowers was also cut to 4 from 4½ per cent. In 1884 a new table was introduced to enable borrowers to repay their mortgage loans over the greatly extended period of 42 years if they so wished. Interest rate reductions continued to be made during the rest of the century until the rate charged to borrowers fell to 3½ per cent in 1895 when that offered to new investors fell to 3 per cent.[2]

The need to find some more profitable use of building societies' funds than depositing them in banks led many societies into advancing cash for less reliable securities than they would have wished and to advancing a larger proportion of the total valuations of mortgaged properties. The latter was a particularly dangerous practice at a time of falling property values. According to the return ordered by the House of Commons in 1893, the Halifax, for instance, had in possession on 9 November properties on which the total debt due amounted to £126,493. This was a considerable sum when set against the figure of just under £1,000,000 for total mortgage assets.[3] Societies were more strongly than ever tempted to lend on industrial property which seemed able to absorb considerable sums in large mortgage loans. To make such a loan put the lending society in the position of being dependent on the future prosperity of the borrower's business and a number of societies learned to their cost just how dangerous a situation this could

---

[1] *Ibid.*, p. 46.

[2] Leeds Permanent Building Society, relevant *Annual Reports*.

[3] P.P. 1894, LXXVIII, Return relating to properties in possession of each building society on the date of the last annual account.

be. The Sheffield and South Yorkshire Building Society went into liquidation in 1886 with liabilities to investors amounting to £193,000 against which the principal assets were loans amounting to £117,885 on the security of Dunraven Colliery. This colliery had not flourished and the society having accepted it as security had had to take it over itself—only to make further losses. It was eventually sold for £26,000 in 1890.[1]

The difficulties which building societies encountered in the 1880s and early 1890s are indicated in table 6.1. For most of the 1880s total assets and liabilities remained reasonably steady, the

Table 6.1.

Building societies 1883–93, comparison of liabilities and assets.[2]

		Increase or Decrease £
Liabilities to shareholders	—	4,299,229
Liabilities to creditors	—	4,847,126
Profit and loss balance	—	18,371
Total liabilities	—	9,164,726
Mortgage assets	—	9,741,821
Other assets	+	577,095
Total assets	—	9,164,726

actual diminution began to show in the overall figures from 1890 when public confidence in building societies came to be undermined by the collapse of such societies as the Portsea Island and the Liberator.

One group of building societies which was not, at least in theory, troubled by interest rates were those established on principles first set forth by Thomas Bowkett, a medical practi-

[1] Cleary, *op. cit.*, p. 127.
[2] *J. Statistical Society*, LVIII, 1895, p. 295.

tioner, in the 1840s. His ideas were set out most clearly in his book, *The Bane and the Antidote*, which was published in 1850. His aim was to reduce the cost of building society finance so that poorer working men would be able to buy houses through them. The principle was that a subscriber lent the society a small sum annually for a long time and in return the society lent him a large sum for a short time—free of interest. In a typical society 100 persons would subscribe 9½d a week each or £2 1s 2d a year. 'Leaving the 1s 2d out of the question to pay the current expenses, they have at the end of the year £200; they draw lots for it, and the one to whom it falls has the £200 lent to him without interest, provided that he expends it on freehold property.' He was then to repay one-tenth of the sum each year for the next ten years. After that he was to continue his normal subscription until 100 houses had been purchased when the total subscriptions would be returned to each member and the society would terminate. The actual life of a society would be from 25 to 27 years, a house being purchased every time the sum of £200 had accumulated in the society.[1] Societies operating on these principles met with only limited popularity in the 1840s and 1850s. The main drawback was the length of time which unlucky members would have to wait for their loan, the actual priority being decided by lot. A weakness was that members who became disappointed at not getting a loan in the early years might withdraw their subscriptions. The absence of interest was intended to counteract this tendency at least in part since the only 'payment' for a member's money was an interest-free loan and if he withdrew in the early years he forfeited all hope of any return on his subscription. The possibility of an early loan and the gambling attraction inherent in this helped to attract members initially.

The person who popularized Bowkett's ideas was R. B. Starr who became a professional building society promoter. Largely through the efforts of this ingenious salesman, more than 1,000 Starr-Bowkett societies had been founded by 1892.[2] After early collaboration with Bowkett in the 1860s, Starr went his own way. He took out the copyright of his own published versions of

[1] P.P. 1871, XXV, RCFS, Thomas Bowkett, QQ. 4120–7.
[2] P.P. 1893–4, XXXIX, R.C. on Labour, Appendix LVI, para. 69.

Bowkett's principles. His reward came in the fees he charged from the secretary, solicitor and surveyor on their appointment to one of his societies. To ensure they in turn were able to reap their necessary rewards, the rules were drawn in such a way as to make the dismissal of these office-holders by the members virtually impossible. Starr's societies had to buy their rule books and printed stationery from his printing company and, from 1882, they had to insure their properties with the Starr-Bowkett and General Insurance Company. The hostility of the rest of the building society movement and a series of lawsuits brought by Starr to enforce the payment of copyright fees resulted in unfavourable publicity but did not check the foundation of new Starr-Bowkett societies. Indeed, Starr fought back by founding the *Starr-Bowkett and Building Society News* in 1882. Starr's commercial success led to the appearance of rival groups of societies such as the 'Self-Help' (numbering 53), the 'Model' (260), the 'Perfect Thrift' (137), the 'Popular' (about 50) and others all floated by rival promoters.[1]

In his evidence to the Royal Commission on Labour, the Chief Registrar, E. W. Brabrook, showed a moderately critical attitude. He believed the main attraction of these societies to working men lay in their small contribution linked with the chance of an early appropriation through the lottery system which they used for deciding who should have the next loan. The buying and selling of these rights to interest free loans for considerable sums and the increased tendency to speculation were described by Brabrook as one of the chief evils of this class of society. He also objected to their rules making the officers virtually irremovable and restraining the members from altering the rules. In 1893 he commented that the promoter's remuneration had reached £70 or £75 whereas a few years earlier it had stood at £30 or £35, but 'Even Starr-Bowkett societies have induced many men to put away small savings that would otherwise have been wasted, and have conferred upon many men the advantage of a freehold house at a very low cost.'[2]

His predecessor, Ludlow, was much more critical. There was nothing objectionable so far as the ballot for an advance (or

[1] Cleary, *op. cit.*, pp. 107–11.
[2] P.P. 1893–4, XXXIX, R.C. on Labour, Appendix LVI, paras. 72–82.

'appropriation')⎤merely served to determine the order in which borrowers who sought to buy houses actually received funds. But there was nothing to ensure that the money was spent in this way so that balloting for appropriations often became 'sheer gambling'. 'Men join a building society without the slightest intention to buy or build, simply as a lottery from which they may draw an appropriation and re-sell it and, if they draw it, perhaps begin by getting drunk on their luck.' Moreover some societies—'the most rickety'—bought up their own appropriations as a means of attracting new members since the society itself could always afford to pay ballot-winners a better price for its own appropriations than could any individual. 'And thus it has happened repeatedly, that so-called building societies have lived through several years and died without ever making a single genuine advance, having done nothing but declare sham advances by ballot and buy them back. In other words, the ballot, or ballot and sale system, is spreading over the whole country a vast network of lotteries to tempt the working and lower middle classes.'[1] The formation of Starr-Bowkett societies in significant numbers was effectively ended by the Act of 1894 which made balloting illegal in newly-established societies.

The formation of large numbers of Starr-Bowkett and similar societies goes far to account for the considerable number of building societies registered under the Act of 1874 in the following years.

The Chief Registrar reported that by the end of 1890 the total number of societies which had been incorporated under the 1874 legislation and which had ceased to exist was as high as 1,237 or 34 per cent of the total number incorporated. Of these 466 ceased to exist without any formal or legal dissolution— letters to them had simply been returned by the post office marked as 'not known'. The 2,333 incorporated societies still in existence had over 600,000 members with funds of £50,582,365. Since nearly £15,000,000 of this represented borrowed capital, the sum held by investing members as shares was about £35,000,000, representing an average holding of about £60, 'sufficient to show that although building societies are a

---

[1] J. M. Ludlow, 'Building Societies', *Economic Review*, III 1, 1893, p. 71.

favourite investment of the working classes, they are not confined to them'.[1] Statistics relating to unregistered societies, their foundation, size or dissolution, do not exist. Yet these particulars relating to registered societies were sufficient to show that these widely-used savings agencies were not merely suffering from adverse economic circumstances, but that their members were in some respects needlessly exposed to financial risk through the inadequacy of the legislation of 1874. The shortcomings of the law were being commented on well before the failure of the Portsea Island Society in December 1891 or the much more spectacular failure of the Liberator Society in 1892.

Table 6.2.

New building societies registered and incorporated, 1874–1894.[2]

Permanent societies	583
'Starr-Bowkett' societies	799
'Model' societies	267
'Mutual' societies	154
'Perfect Thrift' societies	137
'Economic'	89
'Richmond'	87
'Popular'	50
Other terminating societies	1,185
Total	3,351

The Portsea Island Society was one of the larger societies at the time of its demise with liabilities of £624,000. On liquidation its assets amounted only to £435,000. The cause of the society's difficulties was falsification of the accounts by its secretary who himself borrowed £90,000. Supervision of his activities by the directors was inadequate. They were said to

[1] P.P. 1893–4, XXIX, R.C. on Labour, Brabrook, Q. 1463.
[2] *J. Statistical Society*, LVIII, 1895, p. 295.

have signed blank cheques at each meeting and left it to the secretary to fill them in. The secretary responsible for the loss was prosecuted and convicted. The accounts of the Society were so confused that it could not be ascertained whether any particular depositor had a legal claim on the Society or not. Hence a private act of Parliament was obtained which put shareholders and depositors on the same footing and what remained of the assets was distributed equally among all classes of claimants alike.[1] Dishonesty in the officers and lack of adequate supervision caused the downfall of a number of societies.

The Liberator Society was founded in 1868 and later incorporated under the Act of 1874. Its founder was Jabez Balfour, a prominent Nonconformist whose father was a director of the Temperance Permanent Building Society. Balfour made the most of these connections and brought well-known Nonconformist and temperance figures—including four MPs—on his board of directors. From the start investors felt confidence in such a society so that in its tenth year its assets passed £1,000,000. The main object of the society was said to be 'to assist in the building of Nonconformist chapels and to afford facilities to persons desirous of purchasing house property on equitable terms.' Until about 1880 the Society operated on normal principles. Balfour controlled various companies, including two concerned with property development and house building and these borrowed from the Liberator. Balfour's other companies included the London and General Bank and J. W. Hobbs, a building firm. At the time of the crash the total mortgage assets of the Liberator amounted to £3,423,000 and over £3,000,000 of this had been loaned to Balfour's companies. All had been well while the Liberator had continued to attract investments since current subscriptions were used to pay the interest due to investing members. Anxieties concerning the Liberator seem to have spread among some members in the earlier part of 1892, but it was Balfour's London and General Bank Company which was the first to go under. Investors then began to seek the withdrawal of their funds from the Liberator on a large scale. The Society could not meet the demands and a

[1] E. W. Brabrook, *Building Societies*, 1906, pp. 47 and 123.

winding-up order was issued in October.[1] Something of a general run on other building societies followed, perhaps the worst pressure being that which fell upon the Birkbeck Building Society which was saved by a loan of £500,000 from the Bank of England. The need for new legislation to protect members of building societies could no longer be neglected. A total of four bills were introduced with this aim in view and all were referred to a Select Committee in the spring of 1893.

The shortcomings of the Act of 1874 were said by the Chief Registrar to have been the consequence of failing to carry out the recommendations made in the Second Report of the Royal Commission on Friendly Societies in 1872. The recommendations on building societies were not as fully enacted as those concerning other organizations under the care of the Registry.[2] The 1874 legislation was framed largely in the interest of the Committees of the larger societies. It failed to safeguard adequately the rights of members and it failed to provide an efficient system of penalties to ensure that such requirements as it laid down were actually complied with. In the case of friendly and cooperative societies, legislation had given members four checks upon the management. The first of these was the right to inspect the books at reasonable hours. The second the right of a proportion of members to apply to the Registrar for the appointment of inspectors to inquire into the affairs of a society, the inspectors having power to require the production of all books and documents and to examine the officers of a society on oath. The third was the right of a proportion of the membership to apply to the Registrar for the calling of a special meeting of the society. The fourth was the right in friendly societies for a similar proportion of members to apply to the Registrar to investigate the affairs of a society with a view to dissolution or winding up if they felt its funds to be insufficient to meet existing claims. None of these rights could be claimed by members of building societies who were inadequately protected against their organizations' officers.[3]

Moreover, the law's requirements of building societies were

---

[1] *Ibid.*, p. 129; Price, *op. cit.*, p. 285ff.
[2] P.P. 1893–4, XXXIX, R.C. on Labour. Brabrook QQ. 1481–7, 1606.
[3] *Ibid.*, J. M. Ludlow, QQ. 1934–5.

difficult to enforce because no 'efficient system of penalties'—such as was recommended by the Friendly Societies Commission—had ever been enacted. While there was no legal limit to the operations of a building society, the maximum penalty that could be imposed on summary conviction for obtaining by false representation possession of a society's moneys or wilfully misapplying them was a fine of £20. In the case of friendly and cooperative societies, actions for the enforcement of penalties could be commenced not only on the initiative of the authorities of a society, but also on the complaint of any member authorized by the Registrar or on the initiative of the Registrar himself. No such possibility existed under the Building Society Acts, 'and a weak or dishonest committee or board of directors may easily screen a dishonest official'.[1] Between 1874 and 1891 the *Building Society Gazette* reported 31 cases of defalcations by officials of the societies. The actual extent of the problem was a good deal greater than these figures might suggest for wherever possible many societies would have preferred not to move openly against officials lest the resulting publicity should lead investing members to seek to withdraw their holdings and thereby imperil the financial stability of their society.[2] Even the requirement for an annual return from registered building societies was much less useful than in the case of the other forms of organization under the Registry for each society was permitted to make an annual return in its own form and up to its own date. This made it impossible to collate really accurate collective results for any given period and facilitated fraud by enabling officials to draw up their returns in the form least likely to reveal any malpractices. The Chief Registrar had no authority to determine any of the particulars to be included in an annual return.

The extent of the Liberator's loans to Jabez Balfour's companies raised in vivid form the risks to societies which made large advances to individual borrowers. In 1872 the Commissioners recorded that it had been suggested to them that the amount of individual advances should be limited.[3] If this had

[1] J. M. Ludlow, 'Building Societies', *Economic Review*, III 1, 1893, pp. 72–3.
[2] Cleary., *op. cit.*, p. 121.
[3] P.P. 1872, XXVI, RCFS, 2nd Report, para. 115.

been done it would not only have led to greater safety but would also have brought building societies more closely into line with other voluntary associations for mutual aid which were all subject to kindred limits on their transactions. It would also have served to make them 'more genuine representatives of the thrift and aspirations of the working class'. It was suggested that any society which did not limit the total sum to be advanced to any one person to £500 should be deprived of exemption from stamp duties and should be required to pay at least the minimum fee for the registration of companies, £2.[1]

From the four bills with which it was faced the Select Committee took that proposed by the Government for detailed examination and introduced changes in it which would have the effect of increasing further the power of the Chief Registrar to regulate building societies. The Building Societies Association and those MPs sympathetic to it opposed strongly a number of the new provisions now proposed and the end of the parliamentary session led to a postponement of the matter until 1894. The Association maintained its opposition to many features in the official bill, but by this time the Government was determined to bring about reform, and the bill was enacted.

The Building Societies Act of 1894[2] filled most of the gaps which critics had pointed to in the Act of 1874. It required the rules of a society to set out information as to funds, the terms on which shares were issued, borrowing powers, and the way in which loans were to be met.[3] The Chief Registrar was to determine what the annual statement of accounts should contain. The number and aggregate amount of mortgages was to be stated in four groups up to £5,000; particulars of each mortgage exceeding that figure were to be given in a schedule to the accounts.[4] Sections 4 to 9 gave much wider powers to the Chief Registrar. On application by a certain number of members the Chief Registrar could appoint an inspector to examine a society's affairs or call a special meeting of a society. He was also given power to cancel or suspend the registration of societies

[1] Ludlow, *op. cit.*, p. 82.
[2] 57 & 58 Vict., c.47.
[3] S.1.
[4] S.2.

or to order their dissolution in certain circumstances. The practice of balloting for advances was prohibited in all new societies and power was given to existing societies to discontinue the practice if they so wished.[1] Advances on second mortgages were prohibited and the powers of investment of societies were widened to include any 'trustee' security.[2] Unincorporated societies certified under the Act of 1836 were obliged to register under the later legislation and become incorporated unless they were originally certified before 1st January 1857.[3] Approximately 60 societies which had been formed within 20 years of the passing of the Act of 1836 were therefore exempted from this requirement. The reason for this exemption was the existence of the Birkbeck Building Society which was established in 1851 and which had become much more a bank of deposit than a building society. Its deposits were nearly twelve times greater than its mortgage assets and it could never have hoped to adapt its affairs in such a way as to meet the requirement of the Act of 1874 that deposits should not amount to more than two-thirds of total mortgage assets.

The passing of the Act of 1894 helped to restore public confidence in building societies generally. The impact of the legislation in strengthening the societies may be seen in the returns which the Chief Registrar published during the years which followed. Possibly the most influential single section of the Act in this regard was section 2 which provided that the Chief Registrar should prescribe the form in which the accounts of a society were to be presented. The form was in fact voluntarily filled up every year by 42 of the 62 unincorporated societies still under the Act of 1836 which were permitted by law to furnish a statement of account in any form of their own. The special scheduling of certain assets which this section also required had a considerable and beneficial effect on the societies. The first schedule was of mortgages exceeding £5,000, the second of properties in possession and the third of debts where repayments were at least twelve months in arrears. The societies which failed most disastrously had often been those

[1] S.12.
[2] S.13 and S.15.
[3] S.25.

which had the largest amount of properties in possession and of mortgages on which the repayments were in arrears. Hence the need to reveal the exact position each year had a salutary effect on societies as may be seen in table 6.3. The advantages of

Table 6.3.

Specially scheduled assets of building societies, 1897–1903.[1]

	1897	1903
1. Large mortgages	£1,992,000	£2,067,000
Percentage to total assets	5%	4%
2. Properties in possession	£4,770,000	£2,397,000
3. Mortgages in arrear	£332,000	£195,000
Percentage of 2 and 3 to total assets	13%	5%

lending small amounts to many householders were certainly enhanced in the minds of building society managers and it is hardly a coincidence that the directors of the Halifax added to their usual call in the annual report for a much larger number of borrowers the words 'if possible borrowers for smaller amounts'.[2]

By 1905 the power of inspection conferred on the Chief Registrar by Section 5 had been used in thirteen cases and was proving very effective since it enabled investigations to be made into several cases of fraud. The power to dissolve a society on the application of a number of members was used six times in the first decade under the new Act. The prohibition of the practice of balloting for advances in new societies put a stop to the creation of societies for granting advances on the Starr-Bowkett principle. The provision made for existing societies to discontinue advances by ballot was only taken advantage of by three societies. The measure effectively terminated the business of many building society promoters. Between 1883 and 1891 an average of 194 new societies were incorporated annually; this

[1] *J. Statistical Society*, LXVIII, 1905, p. 331.
[2] Hobson, *op. cit.*, p. 52.

average dropped to only 22 for the period from 1898 to 1914.[1] The abolition of balloting largely accounted for the reduction in the number of societies and of members between 1895 and 1903 which is shown in table 6.4. For the rest, the table serves to illustrate the growth in assets and liabilities and the general improvement in the building societies themselves and in the degree of public confidence which they came to enjoy again by the end of the century.

The figures given in table 6.4 give some idea of the extent of building society activity by the end of the century, but it is impossible to form an adequate impression of the extent of

Table 6.4.

Building societies, 1895–1903.[2]

	1895	1903	Dif-ference
Number of society returns	2,625	2,124	−19%
Number of members	637,635	601,204	−6%
Amount received	£29,853,449	£40,734,866	+36%
Due to shareholders	£35,165,641	£38,312,729	+9%
Due to depositors and other creditors	£17,718,606	£24,161,484	+36%
Undivided profit	£3,074,881	£3,836,273	+25%
Large mortgages	£1,302,791	£2,067,260	+59%
Properties in possession	£2,752,542	£2,488,352	−10%
Mortgages in arrear	£353,463	£196,564	−44%

their operations without trying to make an estimate of the impact of their activities on house ownership during the century. There are no statistics on which to base any overall estimate of the number of persons the societies might have enabled to become owners of their own houses in the first 30

[1] Cleary, *op. cit.*, p. 152.
[2] *J. Statistical Society*, LXVIII, 1905, p. 336, (based upon Annual Reports of the Chief Registrar).

years or so of the century. But in 1896 the Chief Registrar estimated that at least 250,000 persons had been enabled by the building societies to become 'proprietors of their own houses' since 1836. After making allowance for large mortgages and taking the average mortgage at £300 he showed that the number of mortgages existing in 1896 would have amounted to 115,000.[1]

[1] E. W. Brabrook, *Provident Societies and Industrial Welfare*, 1898, p. 164.

Chapter Seven
Cooperative Societies

I. Early Cooperatives

According to the historian of the cooperative movement in the 19th century, 'the instinct of cooperation is self-help'.[1] This was certainly true of the retail cooperative society movement during the second half of the century. Like most of the friendly and building societies, the consumer cooperatives were governed by their members and operated within a legal framework administered by the Registrar of Friendly Societies. Essentially the cooperative store was a combination of small retail buyers which went into the market to get what its members wanted at wholesale prices and returned the surplus or profit to them by way of dividend.

A few early cooperative societies may have been established on the initiative of philanthropists in the last years of the 18th century. In 1794 Dr Shute Barrington, Bishop of Durham, established a cooperative store at Mongewell in Oxfordshire for the benefit of the poor in that and three nearby villages.

---

[1] G. J. Holyoake, *The History of Cooperation*, 1908, p. 587. According to Smiles Cooperative societies' 'have promoted habits of saving, of thrift, and of temperance'. *Thrift*, 1875, p. 105.

According to Barrington 'a quantity of such articles of consumption as they used was procured from the wholesale dealers as bacon, cheese, candles, soap, and salt, to be sold at prime cost, and for ready money. The bacon and cheese, being purchased in Gloucestershire, had the charge of carriage.'[1] The shop was tended by an infirm old man who needed only to be paid one shilling weekly since he had his house rent discharged and parish pay. Barrington calculated that on total transactions of £223 14s 2d in 1796 the saving to the poor amounted to £48 1s 0d, and commented that 'many, in every parish, would lend their assistance to carry this plan into execution, if it were known that the *rates* would be lowered at the same time as the poor were benefited.' The poor received full weight and good quality articles and they avoided getting themselves into debt with the local shopkeeper. Comparable philanthropic cooperatives were established by the local clergy at Greenford and at Hanwell in Middlesex in 1800.

But apart from such isolated endeavours, the history of the cooperative movement before the foundation of the Rochdale Equitable Pioneers Society in 1844 was hardly concerned with self-help in the commonly understood sense. During the first part of the century the cooperative movement was dominated by the influence of Robert Owen and the social philosophy accepted and propagated by cooperators or socialists. Various attempts were made to establish communities of cooperators who accepted the validity of the moral and ethical ideals of Owen. Holyoake considered that 'world-makers' was a more relevant term with which to describe these people than 'utopianists'. They were social projectors and world-making was therefore a fair description of the ambitious schemes they put forward.[2] The obstacle which world-makers encountered was the absence of the necessary capital with which to purchase land and establish the new communities. As a possible solution to this difficulty the idea was advanced of opening cooperative stores the profits of which would be accumulated so as to raise the funds required. This scheme for fund-raising was advocated

[1] Holyoake, *op. cit.*, pp. 313–14.
[2] *Ibid.*, p. 15.

strongly in the late 1820s and it has been remarked that 'thus did storekeeping enter the cooperative movement'.[1] In the early 1830s more than 400 cooperative societies were in existence. Whether they were in trading or manufacturing—as some were—their rules proclaimed that their ultimate objective was to settle communities on the land with the profits they hoped to make.[2] It was unlikely that these societies even if they had met with trading success would ever have accumulated sums of the order needed to attain their objects for the actual presence and availability of a large sum of money might well have led a good many members to find more immediately desirable ways of spending it. In fact the societies were to become caught up in Owen's Grand National Consolidated Trades' Union. When this organization collapsed, many of the idealistic cooperatives went under.

The final endeavour to establish a cooperative community on idealistic lines was that at Queenwood in Hampshire. Two agricultural properties amounting to more than 500 acres were obtained and a community was established, named by Owen 'Harmony'. By 1845 the Queenwood enterprise proved to be a failure, after £37,000 had been spent on it. The property and remaining assets were disposed of in accordance with the directions of the Court of Chancery in 1846. The failure of this settlement marked the end of the cooperative movement as understood in the first half of the 19th century. In Holyoake's words, 'Cooperation, after 30 years of valorous vicissitude, died, or seemed to die, in 1844–5.'[3]

II. From Rochdale to the Royal Commission

The transition from the earlier cooperative movement to the later may be traced in the development of the Rochdale Equitable Pioneers Society itself. The origins of this society were as idealistic and Owenite as those of other early societies as

---

[1] Sidney Pollard, 'Nineteenth Century Cooperation: from Community Building to Shopkeeping'. *Essays in Labour History*, (ed. Asa Briggs and John Saville), 1960, p. 83.

[2] C. R. Fay, *Cooperation at Home and Abroad*, 1908, p. 277.

[3] Holyoake, *op. cit.*, p. 259.

may be seen from the definition of the objects of the Society in the original rules, namely:

'To form arrangements for the pecuniary benefit and improvement of the social and domestic condition of its members by raising a sufficient amount of capital in shares of one pound each to bring into operation the following plans and arrangements:
The establishment of a store for the sale of provisions, clothing, etc.

The building, purchasing or erecting of a number of houses, in which those members desiring to assist each other in improving their domestic and social condition may reside.

To commence the manufacture of such articles as the society may determine upon for the employment of such members as may be without employment or who may be suffering in consequence of repeated reductions in their wages.

As a further benefit and security to the members of this society, the society shall purchase or rent an estate or estates of land, which shall be cultivated by members who may be out of employment or whose labour may be badly remunerated.

That as soon as practicable, this society shall proceed to arrange the powers of production, distribution, education and government; or in other words to establish a self-supporting colony of united interests or assist other societies in establishing such colonies.

That for the promotion of sobriety a temperance hotel be opened in one of the society's houses as soon as convenient.'

The founders were also much concerned with political issues such as the best means of obtaining the People's Charter.[1] A cooperative society had foundered in Rochdale as recently as 1841 and one of the founders of the Pioneers, Charles Howarth, suggested an innovation in the method of working which was designed to secure the permanent interest of the members in the welfare of the society. This was that the profits made from sales should be divided among all the members who made purchases

[1] Holyoake, *The History of the Rochdale Equitable Pioneers*, 1900, pp. 12 and 68.

in proportion to the amount they spent. Initially the share of profits due to them would remain in the hands of the directors until it amounted to £5, they being registered as shareholders of that amount. Thus members would not have to try to find the capital for their society out of their pockets and they would become shareholders at no apparent cost. If the enterprise failed they would seem to have lost nothing; if it flourished they might expect to accumulate for themselves further shares of the profit.

The revolutionary impact of this innovation in the method of working and its future significance for the cooperative movement proved to be of immense importance. The story of the opening of the Rochdale Pioneers' store in Toad Lane in 1844 is legendary. At the end of the first quarter the society paid a dividend of 3d in the £. The second dividend was 4d, the fourth 7d, the fifth 9d, the sixth 11d, the seventh 1s 2d, the eighth 1s 4d. For some years the dividend came into the range of 2s to 2s 6d.[1] The strong appeal of the trade dividend kept members loyal to their store and gave them an immediate interest in its success. It was argued that it was the most equitable way of remunerating the organized consumers since those members who contributed most to the store by buying most from it had the right to reap the largest share of its profits.

Under the rules adopted at Rochdale the division of profits was made quarterly from the net proceeds of all retail sales after meeting expenses of management, interest on loans, reduction in value of fixed stock, dividends on subscribed capital, increase of capital for the extension of the business and 2½ per cent of the remainder (after the above were provided for) applied to educational purposes. Of the objectives outlined in the original set of rules, the more idealistic came to attract less and less attention or support. In 1861 a special resolution passed at the October quarterly meeting was entered in the Minute Book and assented among other things that 'the present cooperative movement (intends) . . . by a common bond, namely that of self-interest, to join together the means, the energies, and talents of all for the common benefit of each.'[2]

---

[1] *Ibid.*, p. 73, quoting from an account sent by John Kershaw, one of the last surviving Pioneers, for the use of Holyoake in 1891.
[2] *Ibid.*, p. 161.

The Rochdale Pioneers certainly had not sought to repudiate in any way the earlier ideals of cooperators, and societies stressing the old ideals continued to be established in the late 1840s, one of the best-known being the Leeds Redemption Society. This society was strongly influenced by James Hole and along with kindred organizations, it did not seek merely to bring about a series of reforms in the life of the country. This approach appeared to be totally inadequate. What was required was not improved conditions in the existing political and social structure but a total reconstruction of society. The appeal of Redemption Societies with their communitarianism was that they appeared to offer a practical path of advance to secure drastic reform without revolution. The Redemptionists regarded themselves not as an isolated experimental group, but as part of a widespread international communitarian movement.[1]

The financial and worldly success that so obviously attended the Rochdale Pioneers' Society led to widespread imitation and by 1850 more than 200 societies were established, mainly in the North of England.[2] There is some evidence that a number of the older cooperative societies changed to the new system. This was what happened in the Stockport Great Moor Society—which had been established in 1832—after a conflict between those members wishing to maintain the original no-dividend system and others who sought to follow the Rochdale model, the latter group triumphing in 1847.[3] The great majority of the many new cooperative societies founded in the years following 1850 were of the dividend paying store variety. By this time cooperators saw in the stores themselves a way of improving their lot in the existing form of society whose continuance was implicity taken for granted. Cooperative stores were no longer seen as a means towards abolishing the existing social and political system and replacing it by an idealistic society.[4]

In the two decades preceding the appointment of the Royal Commission on Friendly Societies in 1870, the greatest growth

---

[1] J. F. C. Harrison, *Social Reform in Victorian Leeds: The Work of James Hole, 1820–95*, Thoresby Society Monograph No. 3, 1954, pp. 12–13.

[2] P.P. 1893–4, XXXIX, R.C. on Labour, Minutes of Evidence, Q. 33, J. T. W. Mitchell.

[3] Fay, *op. cit.*, p. 280.

[4] Pollard, *op. cit.*, p. 102.

in the Rochdale-type of store-keeping and dividend paying societies occurred in the industrialized counties of Lancashire and Yorkshire. The predominance of these two counties in the cooperative movement at that time may be seen from the details shown in table 7.1. As with friendly societies the slowest development in the early years was to be found in the predominantly agricultural counties, more particularly in the southern half of the country. The argument has been advanced that an important cause of the survival and growth of the dividend paying society was the rise in the purchasing power of the working man and his widening margin of expenditure during much of the second half of the 19th century. It has been pointed out that in the five years to the end of 1848, the membership of the Rochdale Pioneers' Society grew to 140 and the society's capital to £397, but that in the next five years the membership grew to 720 and the capital to £5,848—or £8 per member, thus possibly reflecting the early impact of this development.[1]

The overall growth of the movement by 1872 was shown by the figures given in a House of Commons return of 1873: some details from this are shown in table 7.2. As with official figures of this period which purported to show the extent of other self-

Table 7.1.

Distribution by counties in 1870 of cooperative distributive societies which were still in existence at the end of the century.[2]

County	No. of Societies
I Northern:	
Durham	28
Northumberland	18
Cumberland	13
Westmorland	5
Yorkshire	121
Lancashire	112
Cheshire	17

[1] Pollard, *op. cit.*, p. 107.
[2] Cd. 698, Board of Trade, *Report on Workmen's Cooperative Societies in the United Kingdom*, 1901, table details extracted from statistics, pp. 70–159.

County	No. of Societies
II North and West Midlands:	
Leicestershire	13
Rutland	—
Lincolnshire	2
Nottinghamshire	9
Derbyshire	17
Gloucestershire	3
Herefordshire	—
Shropshire	2
Staffordshire	5
Worcestershire	1
Warwickshire	7
III South Midland and Eastern:	
Middlesex	—
Hertfordshire	2
Buckinghamshire	3
Oxfordshire	3
Northamptonshire	21
Huntingdonshire	—
Bedfordshire	—
Cambridgeshire	2
Essex	5
Suffolk	5
Norfolk	1
London (12 mile radius)	6
IV South-Eastern:	
Surrey	1
Kent	4
Sussex	2
Hampshire	—
Berkshire	3
V Southern and Western:	
Wiltshire	5
Dorset	1
Devonshire	4
Cornwall	4
Somerset	4
VI Wales	9

help organizations, the qualification must be made that not all societies made the returns requested. The Secretary to the

Table 7.2.

Industrial and Provident Societies at the close of 1872.[1]

	No. of members	Share capital	Dividend paid to members	Amount allowed for educational purposes
		£	£	£
England and Wales	301,157	2,786,965	715,577	6,461
Scotland	38,829	181,793	108,790	235
Ireland	564	1,814	1,038	nil
Totals	340,550	2,970,572	825,405	6,696

Royal Commission attempted to make allowance for this incompleteness and estimated total membership at 347,000 persons. He believed that these were almost invariably heads of families and that they must, therefore, have represented at least four times that number or 1,388,000. So far as England and Wales were concerned, he suggested that industrial and provident societies might have had a total membership of 320,000 persons with over £3,000,000 capital and doing £11,500,000 a year of business at an average profit of over 7 per cent, 88 per cent of this being divided amongst the members.[2] The four largest societies in 1872 were shown by the House of Commons Return as the Halifax Industrial with 7,400 members and sales during the year of £235,730, the Leeds Industrial with 6,756 members and sales of £180,750, the Bury District with 6,460 members and sales of £193,952, and the Rochdale Equitable Pioneers with 6,444 members and sales of £267,572. Of all the societies included in the return, the growth shown by these had been exceptional.

The extent of the development of profitable cooperative operations in the northern counties by the 1870s was no doubt partly due to the answer which the stores seemed to provide to needs of working people in these industrial settlements. A feature of the manufacturing districts of Lancashire and Yorkshire in much of the 19th century was the great number of small

[1] P.P. 1873, LXI, 349.
[2] P.P. 1874, XXIII, Pt. I, 4th Report, Appendix I, p. 241.

provision shops, many of them dealing in drapery goods as well as food, and with customers drawn almost entirely from among the operative class. With these shops the credit system often predominated. Many customers had what was called a 'Strap Book' which was always taken when anything was fetched and balanced when the operatives received their wages—usually weekly but sometimes fortnightly. A balance was usually left due to the shopkeeper, thus many operatives were always more or less in debt. When trade slackened and employment became less plentiful, the debts increased and some customers became irretrievably involved in debt. The policy of not granting any credit which the cooperatives usually adopted meant that their members were at least removed from the temptations of indebtedness. The dividend came as an additional and tangible reward for prudence.

The attraction which the cooperative store held for the individual operative and his wife may be illustrated by these examples from Rochdale in 1853. The cases were published in the *Leader* newspaper and to conceal the identities of individuals were designated by numbers. Number 12 joined the Rochdale Pioneers in 1844 having never been out of a shopkeeper's book for 40 years. He spent over £1 weekly at the shop and his debts had amounted to as much as £30 at times. Since joining the Pioneers he had paid in contributions £2 18s, had drawn from the Society as profits £17 10s 7d and still had £5 left in the fund. Thus he had had better food, gained £20 and had such a society been open to him in the early part of his life, he would have become worth a considerable sum. Number 22 joined the Society at its beginning, having never been out of a shopkeeper's debt for 25 years. His average expenditure at the shop had been about 10 shillings weekly and he was usually indebted to the extent of 40 or 50 shillings. He paid contributions of £2 10s to the Society, drew from it in profits £6 17s 5d and still had left in the funds £8 0s 3d. He believed that the credit system had made him careless about saving and prevented his family from being as economical as they would have been had they been compelled to pay ready money for their necessities. Number 131 joined the Society in 1844 having never been out of debt to a shopkeeper for 14 years. He spent on an average nine shillings per week and generally owed 20 to 30 shillings. He paid into the Pioneers contributions amounting to £1 18s 4d, had drawn £1 12s 1d in profits and still had £3 1s 10d in the funds. He believed that the credit system was one reason why he was always poor and that since joining the society his domestic comforts had greatly increased and had he not belonged to the society in 1847, he would then have been obliged to apply to the parish officers for relief. 'Thus the members derive all the advantage of a sick as well as a benefit society. It is thus that the society gives to its members the money which they save.'[1]

It is no exaggeration to see the increasing success of the cooperative stores as arising partly out of the growing appeal of self-help generally. Holyoake, as much the prophet as the historian of the cooperative movement, contrasted cooperation which was 'the discovery of the means by which an industrious man can provide his own dinner without depriving anyone else of his', with state socialism which was 'one of the diseases of despotism, whose policy it is to encourage dependence'.[2] The comparative failure of contemporary cooperative societies for purposes of manufacture was partly due to the difficulty of building in to their working arrangements anything so powerfully motivating yet simple as the dividend on purchases. Apart from this, the successful manufacture of flax or shoes required a greater technical knowledge of markets and of changes in demand, price, season or fashion than cooperators possessed. Capital and judgement were both lacking.[3] Cooperative manufacture only really began to flourish later on when the Co-operative Wholesale Society itself became large enough to find it worthwhile to run factories and workshops to provide goods needed in the cooperative stores.

III. Legislative framework

Cooperative societies were obviously the creations of their members and did not owe their existence to governmental

[1] These examples were reprinted from the *Leader* by Holyoake, *The History of the Rochdale Equitable Pioneers*, pp. 42–3.

[2] Holyoake, *The History of Cooperation*, pp. 606–7.

[3] John Holmes, 'Cooperation, its Progress and Present Position', *Trans. of the National Association for the Promotion of Social Science*, 1871, p. 585.

initiative in any sense, yet the legislature was in a position to hinder or to facilitate their progress to the extent that it provided or denied a suitable legal framework against which to operate. As with friendly and building societies, one of the most pressing needs to become apparent was the ability to protect their property against fraud or theft by legal process. The first enactment by which cooperative societies were apparently able to obtain legal recognition was the Friendly Societies Act of 1834 which authorized societies to be established under it for 'any other purpose' (than those specified) 'which is not illegal'.[1] But cooperative societies only seem to have taken a definite place in the system with the enactment of the so-called 'frugal investment clause' in the Friendly Societies Act of 1846. This authorized the establishment of societies among other purposes 'for the frugal investment of the savings of the members, for better enabling them to purchase food, firing, clothes, or other necessaries, or the tools or implements of their trade or calling, or to provide for the education of their children or kindred, with or without the assistance of charitable donations: provided always that the investments in any such investment society shall not be transferable, and that the investment of each member shall accumulate, or be employed for the sole benefit of the member investing, or the husband, wife, children, or kindred of such member, and that no part thereof shall be appropriated to the relief, maintenance or endowment of any other member or person whomsoever, and that the full amount of the balance due according to the rules of such society to such member, shall be paid to him or her on withdrawing from the society, and that no such last-mentioned society shall be entitled or allowed to invest its funds, or any part thereof, with the Commissioners for the Reduction of the National Debt.'[2]

While the Act permitted cooperative societies to register with the Registrar of Friendly Societies and so gain the right to protect their property by suing if need be, it hampered their operations in other directions. While a registered society could sell goods to its own members, it might not sell to any other person. Thus a society at Leeds had a corn mill and produced flour

[1] 4 & 5 Wm. IV, c.40, s.2.
[2] 9 & 10 Vict., c.27, s.1.

which it sold to its members, but the bye-product—bran—it found itself accumulating since the members had no use for it while the public at large which would have purchased it could not do so since the law prohibited its sale to any save members. 'And the result was an accumulation of over 600 bags of bran, bending down the floor of the warehouse, and heating, to the danger of combustion; useless to them and a loss, directly negativing the advantages of their otherwise economic working.'[1] The inadequacy of existing legislation to meet the growing requirements of the multiplying cooperative societies was fully established in evidence given by J. M. Ludlow and other Christian Socialists before the Commons' committee on investments for the savings of the middle and working classes in 1850. The committee found that the law still did not afford adequate protection or any 'summary mode of enforcing the rules agreed to for mutual government', it went on to urge the 'pressing need for new legislation to remove the existing difficulties'.[2]

The need for reforming the legislative structure had been pressed by a number of leading Christian Socialists including J. M. Ludlow and the bill which was introduced by H. A. Slaney owed a good deal to them.[3] The bill became law as the Industrial and Provident Societies Act of 1852[4] and was the first to be expressly designed to meet the requirements of the cooperative societies. The Act authorized the foundation and registration of societies 'for any purpose or object for the time being authorised by the laws in force with respect to friendly societies or by this Act, by carrying on or exercising in common any labour, trade, or handicraft, or several labours, trades, or handicrafts' with the exception of mining, quarrying and banking.[5] A series of limitations were required to be written into the rules of any society registering under this Act. These included the conditions on which non-members could be employed, how loans and interest thereon were to be secured, and a limit of six

---

[1] Holmes, *op. cit.*, p. 582.

[2] P.P. 1850, XIX, 172, Select Committee on the Savings of the Middle and Working Classes, Report and Evidence.

[3] The bill is described as 'Ludlow's bill' by N. C. Masterman, *John Malcolm Ludlow*, p. 109.

[4] 15 & 15 Vict., c.31.

[5] S.1.

per cent on any interest payment that might be made. The total amount owing on loan was limited to four times the total of paid up subscriptions, dividends were not to be paid out of capital, and the rules had also to state the terms on which members might withdraw including the extent to which they could be compelled to fulfil any standing obligations. The interests of members in societies were not to be transferable. Disputes were to be referred to arbitration and enforced through the courts. All provisions of the laws relating to friendly societies were to apply unless the Registrar certified that any provision was not applicable, and the exemption from stamp duties enjoyed by friendly societies was not to be extended to industrial and provident societies. No individual member could hold a share capital in a society of more than £100. Societies were not to be deemed to fall within the Joint Stock Companies Act of 1844 and the liability of individual members for the lawful debts was not to be regarded as restricted save that no former member was to be held liable after the expiration of 2 years from leaving a society.[1] Finally, an annual statement of assets and liabilities was to be prepared and submitted to the Registrar by each society.[2]

The total effect of this Act was therefore to recognize co-operative societies as virtually trading friendly societies but without fiscal privileges. As with the latter, property was to be vested in trustees who had power to sue and to be sued. The legal framework thus created stood with only minor amendments until 1862 and the growth of the cooperative movement under these arrangements was considerable. One of the shortcomings was the absence of limited liability and this was finally introduced by the Industrial and Provident Societies Act of 1862.[3] In some respects this Act was a companion statute to the Companies Act of 1862[4] and served to extend to cooperative societies concessions appropriate to them. The granting of incorporation with limited liability was undoubtedly a momentous change and of greatest immediate value to the larger and

---

[1] S.11.
[2] S.10.
[3] 25 & 26 Vict., c.87.
[4] 25 & 26 Vict., c.89.

faster growing societies. The certificate of registration now made the society a body corporate, having a perpetual succession and a common seal with power to hold property and with limited liability. The limits of liability for members of industrial and provident societies were the same as those applying to members of limited companies. No contribution was to be required from any member exceeding the amount (if any) remaining unpaid on the shares which he held and no past member was to be liable even to this extent once he had ceased to be a member for a period of at least a year.

The other important innovation introduced by this Act was the conferment on societies of power to invest capital in another society provided that no such investment be made in any society not registered under the Act. It was this provision which made it possible to establish the English and Scottish Cooperative Wholesale Societies on a cooperative as distinct from a joint-stock basis. The new Act increased the maximum shareholding of an individual member from £100 to £200. In general terms the Act of 1862, as further amended by those of 1867 and 1871[1] assimilated industrial and provident societies rather to companies under the Companies Acts than to societies under the Friendly Societies Acts. Instead of the general incorporation of the provisions of the Friendly Societies Acts, after 1862 only those provisions of the Acts remained applicable which related to the jurisdiction of the Registrar: the cheap and simple system of registration, methods of dealing with disputes, and with cases of fraud. The societies were further assimilated to the company pattern in such matters as freedom of dealing in land, liability on bills of exchange, the legal obligation of their rules upon members and the obligation to keep before the public their trading names indicating the fact of limited liability. The most important differences between the societies and companies were the absence of any fixed amount of capital—the societies were likened to the French concept of *sociétés à capital variable*[2] —and the limitation of individual interests to £200.

The importance of providing a suitable legal framework within which the cooperative societies could operate had thus

[1] 30 & 31 Vict., c.117 and 34 & 35 Vict., c.80.
[2] E. W. Brabrook, *Provident Societies and Industrial Welfare*, p. 140.

been fully appreciated by the time the Royal Commission made its inquiries in the early 1870s. While the Industrial and Provident Societies Acts of 1852 and 1862 may be regarded as important measures removing blockages which were stemming the flow of the cooperative movement, the impact of the Acts of 1876 and 1893 was much less vital. The Industrial and Provident Societies Act of 1876[1] which followed the Report of the Royal Commission was almost a transcript of the Friendly Societies Act of the previous year[2] with the exception of incorporation, limited liability and its consequences. Thus the tendency to assimilate the law to that for companies was now reversed.

In 1893 the Cooperative Union obtained a consolidating and amending Act.[3] The amendments this measure introduced were few in number but some were significant. It increased from five to ten shillings the minimum deposits which societies could receive at one time and it reduced the number of members who might apply to the Registrar to appoint inspectors, or to call a special meeting, to one-tenth of the total membership, or to 100 where the total membership exceeded 1,000. The provisions for free inspection of the books by every person having an interest in the funds were considerably restricted except where the right was granted by a subsequent amendment of the rules.

IV. Development in the last quarter of the century

The period of most rapid expansion of the cooperative societies was the last quarter of the century, rather later than that of friendly societies. Between 1874 and the end of the century the recorded membership of all cooperative societies increased from 403,010 to 1,681,342 or from 1.2 to 4.1 per cent of the population of the United Kingdom. The increase in the value of the total amount of business turnover of the societies was more rapid than that of their membership, rising from about £15,000,000 in 1874 to about £68,000,000—excluding the

[1] 39 & 40 Vict., c.45.
[2] 38 & 39 Vict., c.60.
[3] 56 & 57 Vict., c.39.

banking activities of the C.W.S. A more detailed picture of the growth of cooperative societies towards the end of the 19th century is given in table 7.3.

Table 7.3.

Membership and Capital of Retail Cooperative Societies in the United Kingdom.[1]

Year	No. of Societies	No. of Members	Capital Share	Loan
			£	£
1881	971	547,212	5,380,246	671,771
1884	1,128	696,282	6,653,390	840,571
1887	1,153	828,073	8,561,098	908,998
1890	1,240	961,616	10,310,743	1,132,585
1893	1,421	1,169,094	12,529,359	1,388,876
1896	1,462	1,359,865	15,388,499	1,517,298
1899	1,531	1,623,111	18,937,595	2,530,934

By this time the constitutional and working arrangements of most of the societies had come to be standardized, many societies having adopted the model rules prepared by E. V. Neale, general secretary to the Cooperative Union. These provided that membership should be open to all over the age of 16, that each member was entitled to one vote irrespective of the number of shares he might happen to hold and that the management should be in the hands of a committee of management. These committees usually consisted of from ten to fifteen members elected by the shareholders at the general meeting, only a fraction of the committee retiring each year so as to provide continuity of policy. The members of the committee were usually unpaid, but in some of the larger societies a small fee was allowed to meet out-of-pocket expenses. In most societies the office of secretary was part-time, secretaries undertaking the considerable burden of work involved in their spare time but a few of the largest societies made full-time appointments. Secretaries and treasurers were subject to periodical retirement and re-election by general meetings. With the growth of the C.W.S.

[1] Statistics from annual returns to the Chief Registrar of Friendly Societies.

Bank an increasing number of societies abolished the separate office of treasurer and appointed the Bank as treasurer.

The capital structure of societies consisted mainly of share and partly of loan capital. Shares had a nominal value of £1 and were either paid for in full on allotment or by instalments, usually at the rate of 3d per week per share. In many of the larger societies an initial subscription of one shilling was the only cash payment demanded, the balance of the cost of a member's share being met by crediting his share account with the sums to which he became entitled as his share of the profits. While legislation limited the number of shares which a member could hold to £200, loan capital could be invested up to any limit fixed by a society's rules. In some of the older-established societies, the capital available tended to increase beyond an amount which could be profitably employed and in these cases the rules limited the amount of share capital that a member could hold to £100 or even to £10. The first share taken up by a member was usually a transferable share or one which he could only dispose of by finding someone else to take his place on the share register. Subsequent shares were often withdrawable and these the member could have repaid to him at short notice. Members tended to look upon withdrawable shares in much the same light as a savings bank account and to draw upon them when needing cash.

The rate of interest payable on share capital was always fixed and the most usual figure was five per cent. Towards the end of the century there was a tendency to reduce this figure to four per cent or even lower as societies found themselves possessed of more capital than they could usefully employ. This was partly a reflection within the cooperative movement of the general decline in interest rates at this time which also became apparent in the rates offered by building societies and savings banks. Because the view was so strongly held that the societies existed to serve the consumer and not the investor some societies required members who did not purchase goods up to a certain figure to forgo interest on their shares or even to withdraw from membership.

The appeal of the cooperative societies as self-help institutions lay partly in the way in which they acted as automatic savings banks. Members whose shares were fully paid up continued to allow the interest on their shares along with the dividends on their purchases to accumulate as additional shares, thus earning compound interest. When the maximum share limit was reached the money was credited as loan capital advanced by members to their societies. In this way a member's capital was constantly increasing without any savings actually being made by him from his ordinary income. 'The account books of almost every old-established society would show numerous instances of members who, having invested in cash only one or two shillings, and having in the course of a number of years withdrawn many pounds sterling, still have a substantial balance standing to their credit.'[1] This process of capital accumulation led the movement as a whole to have more capital than it needed for its own purposes and conferences were held from time to time to decide how best to employ the surplus. At the end of 1899 nearly £10,000,000 was invested by retail cooperative societies outside their own businesses. £4,465,041 of this was invested in domestic property, some of the houses being let to members and others being held on mortgage as security for advances to members who had used their cooperative society as an alternative to a building society. £3,816,067 was invested in other cooperative organizations including the cooperative wholesale societies and the balance was invested in a variety of railway and canal undertakings, cotton mills and other businesses.[2]

The management committee of each society had the duty of ascertaining the disposable profit available after meeting all prior charges including the interest payable on shares and grants to charitable or educational funds. The profit was converted into a dividend expressed as so much in the £ on all purchases members had made during the relevant period. The actual mechanism involved giving each customer a metal token indicating the value of his purchase each time he bought at the store. At the end of the half-year the tokens were produced by the member and used to calculate his share of the profits. The

[1] Cd. 698., Board of Trade, Report on Workmen's Cooperative Societies in the U.K., 1901, p. xvi.
[2] *Ibid.*

success of the cooperatives hinged on their selling goods at full retail market prices and thus being able to accumulate attractive profits and dividends. There were grounds for believing that in areas where competition was lacking and the cooperatives had almost monopolized retail trading as they did in some mining districts, the societies kept their prices high in order to increase the dividends.[1] Some reformers were anxious to see a lowering of prices in an effort to bring in to the cooperative stores the poorest classes. These latter were usually obliged by their very poverty to purchase at the lowest prices they could find in the ordinary shops since they were in no position to wait for a prospective dividend. As with other agencies of self-help, those who were very poor could hardly make use of the facilities available since they lacked the means to do so. Within family groups it was said to be the women for whom the dividend had the strongest draw and who as wage-spenders objected to purchases which contributed nothing to the half-yearly or yearly bonus.[2] The average rate of bonus paid to members of all societies during the last five years of the century amounted to 2s 8d in the £. Details of dividend payments for the year 1900 are given in table 7.4.

One of the forms which the opposition of private traders took to the cooperative stores was to put pressure on wholesalers to stop them supplying the cooperatives. In order to overcome this difficulty, and in order to avoid competing against one another in the open market, some of the retail societies had sought to establish cooperative wholesalers. The Christian Socialists attempted something on these lines in London in 1850 and the Rochdale Pioneers set up a wholesale department to serve itself and other societies in 1855, but both of these failed for a variety of causes, one of which was the state of the law. The societies managed to reform this in 1862 when the new Industrial and Provident Societies Act gave them power to establish and control federations for their common benefit. The immediate sequel was the establishment of the Cooperative

---

[1] Private traders with whom the cooperatives competed tended to accuse them of charging high prices and paying their dividends from these excessively high prices. P.P. 1893–4, XXXIX, Minutes, Q. 5197, R. Walker (Trades' Defence Association of Scotland).

[2] Fay, *op. cit.*, p. 319.

Table 7.4.

Rates of dividend on purchases made by members of retail cooperative societies in 1900.[1]

Rate of dividend per £	No. of members in societies paying rate stated	Percentage of members
6d and under	4,589	0·3
Over 6d and up to 1s	20,457	1·3
Over 1s and up to 1s 6d	76,471	4·7
Over 1s 6d and up to 2s	264,335	16·3
Over 2s and up to 2s 6d	293,635	18·1
Over 2s 6d and up to 3s	596,019	36·8
Over 3s and up to 3s 6d	205,784	12·7
Over 3s 6d and up to 4s	130,481	8·1
Over 4s	20,400	1·3

Wholesale Society[2] based on Manchester the next year, the Scottish Wholesale Society being founded five years later in 1868. The chairman of the C.W.S. told the Royal Commission on Labour in reply to a question, that the relation between the English and Scottish Wholesale Societies was that 'they work together in harmony'.[3]

Membership of the C.W.S. was confined to registered societies which were required to hold 3 shares for every 20 or fraction of 20 members and were entitled to one vote for every 500 members. Membership conditions for the Scottish society were slightly different, but in both cases the wholesale societies were managed by committees elected by the members, a small proportion retiring each quarter but being eligible for re-election. A peculiar feature of the English society was that its quarterly meetings were divided into meetings held in different parts of the country; member societies could send their delegates to whichever they found convenient. The agenda at

[1] Cd. 698, Board of Trade, Report 1901, pp. 16–17.
[2] Founded as the 'North of England Cooperative Wholesale Industrial and Provident Society Limited', it took its present name in 1873.
[3] P.P. 1893–4, XXXIX, R.C. on Labour, Minutes, Q. 162, J. T. Mitchell.

each was identical and the votes given at each meeting were added together, the result depending on the total numbers. The C.W.S. commenced business in 1864 with 50 member societies and its rate of growth may be seen from table 7.5. The Scottish

Table 7.5.

Membership, capital and sales of the C.W.S. 1864–1900.[1]

Year	No. of members in shareholding societies	Total capital £	Sales £	Dividend per £ of sales d
1864	18,337	2,455	51,857	$1\frac{1}{2}$
1867	59,349	26,313	331,744	3
1870	89,880	44,164	677,734	$2\frac{1}{4}$
1873	168,985	200,044	1,636,950	2
1876	276,522	417,985	2,697,366	$3\frac{3}{8}$
1879	331,625	494,330	2,645,331	$2\frac{3}{4}$
1882	404,006	632,203	4,038,238	$2\frac{5}{8}$
1885	507,772	841,175	4,793,151	$3\frac{3}{8}$
1888	634,196	1,116,035	6,200,074	$2\frac{7}{8}$
1891	751,269	1,636,397	8,766,430	$3\frac{1}{2}$
1894	910,104	1,891,102	9,443,938	$2\frac{3}{4}$
1897	1,053,564	2,472,321	11,920,143	$2\frac{3}{4}$
1900	1,249,091	3,187,945	16,043,889	4

Wholesale Society had 288 federated societies by 1900. Its capital was £1,676,765 and sales for the year amounted to £5,463,631. In both societies the surplus remaining after paying all charges and interest on shares at the fixed rate of five per cent was divided among the customer societies as a dividend on purchases, thus accruing ultimately to the benefit of the individual members of the retail societies.

The need for banking facilities for the cooperative movement soon became apparent and from 1868 the C.W.S. was actively exploring possible ways of meeting these needs. One of the main obstacles was the Act of 1862 which had specifically excluded banking from the business which a cooperative society

[1] Percy Redfern, *The Story of the C.W.S., 1863–1913*, 1914, pp. 418–19.

or federation of societies might conduct. This exclusion was not withdrawn until 1876 when banking was permitted if certain conditions were met—the most important of these being that societies engaged in banking should possess no withdrawable share capital. In a paper he read to a cooperative conference in 1870, J. M. Ludlow recommended the establishment of a bank under company legislation 'in the closest possible connection with the Wholesale Society'. Eventually the C.W.S. quarterly meeting resolved that 'as a means to commence and gradually develop a banking business, authority be given to the Committee to receive loans from the members withdrawable at call, and subject to 1 per cent below the minimum Bank of England rate of interest, the same to be used in our own business or lent out on approved security.'[1] This was apparently in contravention of the law but out of deference to it the new department was not to be called a bank but the 'Loan and Deposit Department'. With the change in the legal position in 1876 this clumsy title was dropped. Turnover in that year reached £10,000,000 with a profit of £3,500 divided among the society-customers. In the early days a smaller dividend was paid upon debit than upon credit balances even though it is the interest paid on the former which generates profits for a banker. The comment of the historian of the C.W.S. may well be justified namely that 'thrift being so essentially a cooperative virtue, evidently it was not considered right to encourage debtors'.[2] In 1900, 621 cooperative societies transacted their banking business through the C.W.S. bank and the profits amounting to £11,445 were distributed as dividend at the rate of one per cent on average debit and credit balances. Some statistics illustrating the growth of the banking department are given in table 7.6.

In the last few years of the century the C.W.S. prepared a scheme through its banking department by which it advanced capital to federated societies at $3\frac{1}{2}$ per cent on the security of title deeds of houses for selling or letting to their members. A number of local societies had already entered the housing field; some had begun to provide houses for letting while others

[1] *Ibid.*, p. 66.
[2] *Ibid.*, p. 70.

advanced mortgage funds in the same way as building societies.

Table 7.6.

The C.W.S. Banking Department, 1873–1900[1]

Year	No. of current accounts	Receipts	Overdrafts and advances	Profit
		£	£	£
1881	136	11,920,414	116,684	1,336
1884	174	14,948,675	438,145	1,572
1888	226	18,738,754	387,013	4,984
1892	314	28,986,245	605,623	7,309
1896	421	37,804,732	1,185,517	8,321
1900	621	62,860,606	1,394,359	11,445

There was a sharp conflict of opinion among cooperators as to which of these ways of providing better housing for their members was preferable. The C.W.S. loan scheme was therefore drawn up in such a way as to be suitable for both. By the end of the century, over 4,000 houses had been built and let to members while mortgages had been granted on more than 16,000. Ten local societies were prepared to advance as much as 95 per cent of the value of the houses mortgaged. It was claimed that 'practically any responsible cooperator' was able to obtain a 20 years' loan at a gross charge of about four per cent.[2]

Although life and burial insurance organizations carved for themselves a profitable field of activity, often at the expense of those they purported to help,[3] the cooperative movement did little to introduce its principles into that area. The Cooperative Insurance Society was founded in 1867 and had to register under the Companies Acts since a society for carrying on the business of insurance could not register under the Industrial and Provident Societies Acts at that time. Much of the society's

[1] Cd. 698, Board of Trade, Report, 1901, p. 20.
[2] Redfern, *op. cit.*, p. 327; D. McInnes, *How Cooperative Societies can supply their members with dwelling houses*, Cooperative Union Pamphlet, 1899.
[3] Chapter Five *passim.*

business consisted of insuring cooperative stores against fire and fidelity risks. Life insurance premiums are shown in the accounts of the society from 1886 when they amounted to only £118. The life business grew only slowly and by 1900 the life premiums represented 5,623 out of a total income of £31,435.[1] To some extent the registration of the Cooperative Insurance Society under the Companies Acts led to it developing many of the characteristics of other insurance companies and it was independent of the main cooperative movement until a closer association with the C.W.S. was brought about in the early years of the present century.

Alongside its value as a wholesaler and as a central organization sponsoring specialized services for the cooperative form of self-help, the C.W.S., and its Scottish opposite number, came to exert a considerable social influence. Through delegate meetings to transact regular business, a constant healthy circulation of ideas was established and maintained, and the experience of the central institution was placed at the service of the most remote local societies. The steady improvement in standards in the cooperative movement seems to have owed much to this. It was claimed that this was shown by conditions in districts which had refused to join the federal bodies. Societies in the county of Forfar had held aloof from the Scottish Wholesale Society and in the 1890s it was said that 'cooperation had stood still in consequence during the past 30 years, each society in its own rut'.[2]

As with friendly societies, cooperatives were in their very nature schools of self-government for their members and from the beginning emphasis had been placed on the importance of applying some of the profits to educational purposes. The Rochdale Pioneers, for instance, set aside 2½ per cent of their profits for an educational fund and from this created a library and news room in the 1850s. From 1850 to 1855 the society ran a school for young persons at a charge of 2d monthly and from 1855 provided a room for adult classes.[3] The importance of accepting the prior claim of educational expenditure on profits

[1] Cd. 698, Board of Trade, Report, 1901, p. 58.
[2] R. H. I. Palgrave (ed), *Dictionary of Political Economy*, vol. I, 1894, p. 419.
[3] Holyoake, *The History of the Rochdale Pioneers*, pp. 50–1.

was frequently emphasized by leading figures in the cooperative movement. Societies were urged to set aside at least 2½ per cent of their net profits for education by the C.W.S. *Almanac* for 1883 which added that 'though societies may and do succeed without this, yet it is because the older generation still lives and guides them, but when the day arrives that they no longer take part in their management, the societies will run a great risk of suffering thereby.'

In 1887 the cooperative movement granted a total of £23,256 for educational purposes, the main items of expenditure being:[1]

reading rooms   £9,891 (297 reading rooms)
libraries   £3,873 (202,013 volumes)
lectures   £ 957 (269 lectures)
classes   £1,410 (3,717 students in 184
                              classes)
distribution of literature £ 539

A report presented to the Cooperative Congress in 1898 by its committee on education divided the educational work of the movement into three branches: education in the principles and methods of cooperation, provision for the acquisition of knowledge on general subjects, and arrangements for recreation and pleasure. A total of £57,622 was spent on education by the cooperative societies in 1899.

Along with this lively interest in education the societies proclaimed neutrality in religious and political matters. During the first half of the century many of the Owenite societies had apparently torn themselves to pieces through political dissension so it must have seemed a necessary precaution for the Rochdale Pioneers and other cooperative societies to state formally in their rules that the political and religious opinions of individuals were of no concern to other members. By definition, cooperation was simply a method of trading, open to all regardless of their political or social views.[2] Although the co-operative movement maintained its neutrality until after the end

---

[1] P.P. 1893-4, XXXIX, R.C. on Labour, Minutes of Evidence, Q. 45, J. T. W. Mitchell.

[2] Catherine Webb (ed.) *Industrial Cooperation: the Story of a Peaceful Revolution*, 1904, p. 69; A. M. Carr–Saunders, P. Sargant Florence, R. Peers, *Consumers Cooperation in Great Britain*, 1938, p. 40.

of the 19th century, it was not surprising to find some of its leading figures supporting the causes of Liberalism and Nonconformity. But the avoidance of political and religious controversy did not exclude formal or actual adherence to the principles of temperance. Most cooperative societies avoided all connection with the drink trade and sold no alcoholic beverages. When Gladstone visited an Oldham cooperative in 1867, he was told that 'temperance men were generally cooperators and that many of the board of directors were such.'[1] When the President of the C.W.S. gave evidence before the Royal Commission on Labour in 1892, he was asked to explain how the movement promoted temperance as well as thrift. He replied, 'I will give you an instance of a man who used to spend his money regularly at the beerhouse. His wife became a member of the store, and he was also induced eventually to become one, and he became more sober from seeing his money was being saved, and then he began to tell other people. It was the old story of "Buy your own cherries". . . . I only state that to show that the tendency is, when a man's wife begins to save, that the man himself begins to save. I am sorry it is not always the case, but in many cases it has the effect of making him more sober and steady and thrifty.'[2]

[1] Brian Harrison, *Drink and the Victorians*, 1971, p. 336.
[2] P.P. 1893–4, XXXIX, R.C. on Labour, Minutes, Q. 158.

Chapter Eight
Savings Banks

I. Early savings banks

Savings banks were distinguished from all the other agencies of thrift and self-help which have been discussed in this volume by their distinctive form of management. The user members of the banks, the depositors, had no legal right whatever to any say in the management of the institutions to which they might entrust their savings. Outside the Post Office Savings Bank—where the management was, of course, vested directly in the state—the management function was discharged by trustees and managers. The Chief Registrar of Friendly Societies contrasted building societies and savings banks in these terms: 'As compared with a well-constituted building society, a trustee or Post Office savings bank is as the infant to the grown man; in the one the depositor hands over the money to the trustees or to the postal authorities to take care of it for him, in the other he becomes a member with the same right as any other member to watch over the safety of his investment and to take part in the management of it. The judicious investor in a building society has therefore made great advances in self-education over the mere depositor in the savings bank.'[1] In essence, the savings banks were

[1] E. W. Brabrook, *Building Societies*, 1906, p. 157.

established by members of the influential classes in an effort to provide the means by which the lower orders might come to make provision for themselves, thus achieving the dual aim of lessening the burden of the poor rate and becoming more prudent and sober working men.

A concern over the harmful effects of the poor law on those who might come to need relief from the rates is present in many of the pamphlets and articles of the early years of the nineteenth century advocating savings banks. Henry Duncan, Minister of Ruthwell in Dumfriesshire and founder of one of the earliest savings banks, explained that the only way by which 'the higher ranks can give aid to the lower in their temporal concerns, without running the risk of aiding them to their ruin, is to afford every possible encouragement to industry and virtue,—to induce them to provide for their own support and comfort,—to cherish in them the spirit of independence, which is the parent of so many virtues,—and judiciously to reward extraordinary efforts of economy, and extraordinary instances of good conduct'.[1] The *Edinburgh Review* believed that the establishment of savings banks was particularly desirable in England since it was in that country that the poor law, 'by the certainty of its bounties' was increasing the natural improvidence and thriftlessness of the labouring classes and thus creating much of the misery which it was devised to remove.[2] Other advocates of savings banks saw in them a device for increasing the number of people who would feel they had a stake in the security of the country and would therefore be deterred from 'compassing the disturbance of their native land'. The importance of public peace would be felt with that strong conviction which individual interest always inspired.[3]

Schemes for local, county and national savings banks were put forward. Whitbread introduced into the Commons a bill in 1807 in which he proposed to set up a national bank for the use of the labouring classes alone in which working people might

---

[1] Henry Duncan, *An Essay on the Nature and Advantages of Parish Banks*, 1816, p. 1.

[2] *Edinburgh Review*, 'Publications on Parish or Savings Banks', XXV, 1815, p. 142.

[3] *Quarterly Review*, 'On improving the Condition of the Poor', XII, 1814, pp. 158–9.

deposit up to £20 a year and not more than £200 in all. The money was to be invested in government stock and the whole scheme to be operated by the Post Office.[1] Much of the later interest in Whitbread's proposal was due to the way in which it anticipated Gladstone's Post Office Savings Bank Act of 1861. Malthus advocated a scheme of county banks and this was felt by the *Quarterly Review* to be simpler. In every county town there should be a savings bank established, offering public security for the deposits it received. It should have agents throughout the county who could receive money for deposit. No addition needed to be made to the number of public servants for this purpose since even every village was covered by a tax collector who might also collect savings bank deposits. The clergy could do much by way of explaining the aims of the county savings banks while, the *Quarterly Review* suggested, the Tract Societies might also lend their aid.[2]

On one point all the advocates of savings banks seem to have been in agreement: the classes whose savings the banks were to hold could afford to save in normal times against periods of hardship or difficulty later on. George Rose analysed the different groups who ought to save under these headings:

Apprentices—on completing their apprenticeship should save five to ten shillings weekly instead of spending all their earnings;

Journeymen—in many trades their earnings were considerable and the failure to save was often the consequence of ignorance rather than of improvidence or thoughtlessness;

Domestic servants—whose wages were frequently more than sufficient for their necessary expenses;

Carmen, porters, servants in lower conditions—might very generally be able to make small deposits. Even day labourers might be expected to deposit a small sum weekly while they remained unmarried. In support of his claim that even many day labourers could save if they were so minded, Rose gave a number of examples of labourers he had come across when seeking depositors at Christchurch. One remarkable day-labourer named Saunders who was aged 33 had already accumulated £100. Even by the age of 27 he had saved £50 although

[1] *Parliamentary Debates*, VIII, 887, 19 Feb 1807.
[2] *Quarterly Review*, XII, pp. 155–7.

never earning more than ten shillings a week.[1] Day labourers were paid so little that they could save nothing unless they made almost superhuman efforts.

Some of what are usually described as the earliest savings banks in this country were really charitable institutions. As part of her social work Mrs Priscilla Wakefield founded a benefit society for women and children at Tottenham in 1798. Honorary members paid subscriptions which helped to meet the cost of benefits. In 1801 a loans fund was added and so was a savings bank which offered five per cent interest on deposits. Special arrangements were also made to encourage children to deposit their pennies and this was, perhaps, the first Penny Bank. The work of Mrs Wakefield received some publicity from the Society for Bettering the Condition and Increasing the Comforts of the Poor which explained that great attention was paid to the moral character of those admitted as members and that a notorious irregularity of conduct incurred expulsion.[2] This account of the work at Tottenham had some influence on George Rose in founding Southampton Savings Bank and on the foundation of the Edinburgh Savings Bank.

The Reverend Joseph Smith established a charitable bank in 1798 in his parish at Wendover. Along with two of his wealthier parishioners he undertook to receive such deposits as any working people felt they could make and to repay the money in the winter months with the addition of one third which would be allowed as interest on their deposits. Deposits were only received on Sunday evenings and there were about 60 subscribers. The Wendover bank inspired a number of other Sunday banks including one at Hertford founded by the local minister in 1808. This institution collected about £300 annually in small deposits and paid it back on the first day of each year with interest of twelve per cent from charitable sources.[3]

Perhaps the earliest savings bank to be founded on the later trustee pattern in England was the Provident Institution of Bath. The Marquis of Lansdowne was its President and it was established in 1815. The sums deposited were invested in

[1] George Rose, *Observations on Banks for Savings*, 1816, pp. 19–22.
[2] A. Scratchley, *A Practical Treatise on Savings Banks*, 1860, p. 5.
[3] *Ibid.*, pp. 5–6; H. Oliver Home, *A History of Savings Banks*, 1947, p. 27.

public funds and initially each depositor's rate of interest varied according to the price of government stock on the day on which the investment of his savings was made. The Provident Institution at Bath was in one sense born out of an earlier unsuccessful attempt to widen a bank for taking the wages of industrious domestic servants only which had been founded in 1808.[1] Both the new bank at Bath and the Edinburgh Savings Bank—which was founded in 1814—were far removed in practice from the earlier semi-charitable institutions and from Duncan's Parish Bank at Ruthwell whose closely paternalistic rules were criticized by some early supporters of the savings bank movement as being a deterrent to possible depositors. Duncan claimed that his was the first genuine savings bank in that it was the first to be self-supporting. The existence of what was called the auxiliary fund to which honorary and extra-ordinary directors were required to contribute and which was used to pay premiums to those who were most regular with their deposits or who had exhibited superior industry or virtue casts some doubt on Duncan's claim. The savings bank placed its funds with the British Linen Bank at five per cent; it allowed four per cent to depositors, this being increased to five per cent if they had at least £5 deposited, were of at least three years' standing and met one of five conditions, namely, that they wanted to get married, were at least 56 years of age, died, or in case possession of the money 'should appear to the Court of Directors, after due inquiry, to be advantageous to the depositor or his family.' In order to stimulate further the spirit of thrift, the rules provided for a small fine to be inflicted on any depositor who failed to deposit a certain sum each year. Duncan also commended the paying of a small premium to those depositors who saved regularly and in the 1816 edition of his *Essay on Parish Banks* drew attention to the system followed by the Dumfries Bank which paid a premium to those who saved on a regular three-weekly basis.[2]

Among those who feared that this particular approach would be more likely to alienate than to attract most working men was

[1] William Lewins, *A History of Banks for Savings*, 1866, p. 25.
[2] Henry Duncan, *An Essay on the Nature and Advantages of Parish Banks*, 1815, p. 19; Lewins, *op. cit.*, pp. 29–40.

the Committee of the Highland Society which thought that one of the greatest recommendations of the Edinburgh Savings Bank which had induced many to become depositors was that those joining it were not bound to continue unless they wished to do so. The very fact that they could take their savings when they wished had led to very few of its depositors wishing to discontinue. The *Edinburgh Review* criticized 'the benevolent projector of the Parish Bank at Ruthwell' for fining those who failed to deposit a minimum sum each year; the very idea of 'such an inquisitional power' would deter many from entering.[1] The Edinburgh Savings Bank paid a uniform rate of interest on all deposits.

The Provident Institution for the town of Southampton and its vicinity was established in November 1815 and began to transact business on 1 January 1816. It was modelled on the banks at Bath and Edinburgh and the person mainly responsible for its establishment was George Rose who was named as President. One of the trustees was Palmerston. Deposits of not less than a shilling could be accepted and interest was to be paid at the rate of four per cent once an account reached 12s 6d. Deposits could be withdrawn on one week's notice. The rules provided for any 'officiating minister, or other responsible person' in the county of Hampshire to receive deposits intended for the bank.[2] The possible impact of this arrangement was reduced by a further provision that the bank could accept no responsibility for any sums so deposited until they had actually been paid over in Southampton. Another bank founded in 1816 which developed the Southampton plan of rural banking facilities much more successfully was the Exeter Savings Bank. Within a year the village clergy in 60 places were acting as agents and remitting deposits to the parent bank in Exeter.

The principal difference between the savings banks at Bath and Southampton was that the latter agreed to pay a fixed rate of interest and to repay the deposit in full regardless of the price of government stock.[3] The bank thus stood the risk that might

---

[1] *Edinburgh Review*, XXV, p. 143.

[2] The rules of the Southampton Savings Bank are printed in G. Rose, *Observations on Banks for Savings*, 1816, pp. 6–14.

[3] Scratchley, *op. cit.*, p. 9.

arise from any movement in the prices of the funds. The main reason for moving to this system from that at Bath where each depositor was paid whatever his deposit produced was the extreme inconvenience arising from market fluctuations. This problem of the investment of funds arising from deposits could only be satisfactorily solved through legislation since at this time the only possible home for these funds was government stock with its ever changing price levels.

II. Legislation and the progress of the savings banks, 1817–50

George Rose's interest in savings banks and particularly his experience of the problems arising out of the establishment of the Southampton bank convinced him of the need for some measure of protection and aid from the state. In April 1816 he sought leave in the House of Commons to bring in a bill 'to afford protection to banks for savings'. This bill was very modest in that it sought only to cause trustees to enrol their savings banks with Quarter Sessions and to deposit their rules with the Clerk of the Peace. Officers entrusted with money were to give security and depositors were not to be prevented from applying for parish relief. Rose was regarded as something of an authority on the problems of the poor and of the industrious classes, since he had carried the Act of 1793 through Parliament which offered certain legal benefits to friendly societies.[1] His bill was generally welcomed in the House and given a first reading. The session ended before further progress could be made and the bill was re-introduced in February 1817 with an important addition designed to meet the problem of the investment of funds by trustees. The bill would now require trustees to pay their balances to the Bank of England to a special account with the National Debt Commissioners. The Commissioners were to allow interest to trustees at the rate of 3d per cent per day or £4 11s 3d per cent per annum. This soon came to seem to be a high rate of interest, but for nearly 40 years the price of government stock had been sufficiently low for an average of £4 11s 3d to be earned easily by purchasing that security. An attempt was

[1] 33 Geo. III, c.54., *supra.*, p. 34.

made to delete this clause which would compel trustees to invest with the National Debt Commissioners on the grounds that there might be better ways of investing depositors' funds. It was suggested that mortgages might sometimes provide a better and more productive home for the money. But Rose's proposal was adhered to, most of the Commons apparently feeling that the safety of the investments ought to be the predominant consideration.[1]

Outside Parliament, a group of Radicals, among whom Cobbett was prominent, mounted a campaign against Rose and his bills. Cobbett described the campaign for founding savings banks as 'a project to get from labourers a part of their present income in order to collect it into a fund for their relief'. Rose himself who was Treasurer of the Navy and had held various other offices was said 'to smell pretty strongly of the immense sums of the public money which he has received'.[2] In spite of this criticism the Act of 1817 was effective in encouraging the formation of local savings banks on the trustee principle. This system of banking was defined as being 'to receive deposits of money for the benefit of the persons depositing the same, and to accumulate the produce of so much thereof as shall not be required by the depositors, their executors or administrators, deducting only out of such produce so much as shall be required to be retained for the purpose of paying and discharging the necessary expenses attending the management of such institution, according to such rules, orders and regulations as shall have been or shall be established for that purpose but deriving no benefit whatsoever from any such deposit or the produce thereof'.[3] Several sections of the Act were literally copied from the Friendly Societies Act of 1793 while certain of the privileges which the savings banks obtained—including the right to invest with the National Debt Commissioners and that of paying out small sums without letters of administration in cases of intestacy—passed from the banks to the friendly societies.[4]

The immediate effect of the Act was considerable. 132

---

[1] Lewins, *op. cit.*, pp. 46–52.
[2] Horne, *op. cit.*, quotes Cobbett's remarks from the *Register* of 7 Sept 1816.
[3] 57 Geo. III, c.130, s.1.
[4] P.P. 1874, XXIII, Pt. I, RCFS, Appendix No. 1, p. 10.

savings banks were founded in 1818, far more than in any other single year, and these included the savings banks in large centres such as Manchester, Leeds and Hull.[1] In the following year a further 39 banks were set up, including that at Sheffield.[2] The full government security offered by the Act to investments by trustees and, many assumed, to depositors, along with the favourable rate of interest undoubtedly made the banks increasingly popular. The rapid increase in the total sums lodged by local trustee banks with the National Debt Commissioners in the years following 1817 is shown by the figures in table 8.1. These figures reflect both fluctuations in the condition of the economy from year to year and special factors which concerned the savings banks as such. The prosperity of 1823–4 is shown in the comparatively large increase in the balances invested with the National Debt Commissioners and contrasts strongly with the figures for 1826, a poor year for the economy. The setback shown in the table for 1829 and 1830 was probably due in considerable measure to the reduction in the interest allowed by the Commissioners under the Savings Bank Act of 1828. It was argued by some supporters of the banks that this reflected a beneficial development since it was depositors from among the better off who were interest-rate conscious while working men thought most of the security offered. Accordingly, a welcome consequence of reducing the rate was said to be that 'the connexion which the higher classes had formed with the savings banks was now dissolved. Henceforth the returns may be looked upon as more than ever the result of habits of economy and thrift, and as representing the surplus money of the artizan and the lower portions of the middle classes.'[3]

One factor which may have had some influence on the growth of savings banks in the 1830s was the Poor Law Amendment Act.[4] Advocates of the new Poor Law claimed that it helped to

---

[1] Horne, *op. cit.*, pp. 80–1; J. H. Oates, *A Brief History of the Leeds Skyrac and Morley Savings Bank*, 1897, pp. 6 and 8.

[2] R. E. Leader, *A Century of Thrift—An Historical Sketch of the Sheffield Savings Bank 1819–1919*, 1920, p. 3.

[3] William Smart, *Economic Annals of the Nineteenth Century, 1821–1830*, 1917, p. 452; Lewins, *op. cit.*, p. 95.

[4] *Supra*, p. 69, for the possible impact of the Poor Law Amendment Act on Friendly Societies.

Table 8.1.

Balances due by National Debt Commissioners to trustees, 1817–41.

Year ending 20 November	Balance due	Increase (or decrease) over previous year*
	£	£
1817	231,028	—
1818	1,697,853	1,466,825
1819	2,813,023	1,115,170
1820	3,469,910	656,897
1821	4,740,188	1,270,278
1822	6,546,690	1,806,502
1823	8,684,662	2,137,972
1824	11,720,629	3,035,967
1825	13,257,708	1,537,079
1826	13,135,218	—122,490
1827	14,188,708	1,053,490
1828	15,358,504	1,169,796
1829	14,791,495	—567,009
1830	14,860,188	68,693
1831	14,698,635	—161,553
1832	14,416,885	—281,750
1833	15,324,794	907,909
1834	16,386,035	1,061,241
1835	17,469,617	1,083,582
1836	18,934,591	1,464,974
1837	19,711,797	777,206
1838	21,446,341	1,734,544
1839	22,486,553	1,040,212
1840	23,549,716	1,063,183
1841	24,536,971	987,255

* Including interest.

stimulate interest in thrift and that this could be seen in the expansion of savings bank activity in the years following 1834, particularly in some of the southern agricultural counties. The number of able-bodied paupers in Sussex was said to have been cut from 6,160 prior to the passing of the Act to only 125 in June 1836. The change was said to have involved 'the abolition and disendowment of the able-bodied pauper'. The able-

bodied population no longer subsisted on the rates but maintained itself and even proceeded to extend and consolidate the
system of saving. In his report to the Poor Law Commission on
the administration of the new law in the South-East, Tufnell,
an Assistant Commissioner, claimed that the welfare of the
labouring class had been steadily advancing since the enforcement of the new regulations and as proof he submitted a table
showing deposits in savings banks in Kent and Sussex from
friendly societies and from depositors of sums under £20 for
the period 1831–7. This is reproduced in table 8.2.[1]

Table 8.2.

Tufnell's abstract of savings bank deposits in Kent and Sussex,
1831–7.

Date	Kent Savings Banks	Sussex Savings Banks	Observations
20 Nov 1831	£ 93,694	£ 41,164	Years previous to passing of the Poor Law Amendment Act.
„ 1832	87,592	39,889	
„ 1833	91,317	41,686	
„ 1834	94,918	43,466	Poor Law Amendment Act discussed and passed.
„ 1835	97,613	45,897	Poor Law Amendment Act in partial operation.
„ 1836	106,156	50,148	Poor Law Amendment Act brought into universal operation.
„ 1837	110,156	51,409	

The overall national figures for sums deposited by trustees
with the National Debt Commissioners showed a moderately
larger rate of growth for the decade 1834–44 than for the
previous decade, but this was clearly influenced by such other
factors as changing the rate of interest and by fluctuations in the

[1] Charity Organisation Society, *Insurance and Saving: A Report on the
Existing Opportunities for Working Class Thrift*, 1892, pp. 8–11; P.P. 1837–8,
XXVIII, Poor Law Cssn 4th Annual Report, pp. 220–2.

national economy as well as by any change in the Poor Law. The extent of the influence of the new Poor Law on the growth of savings banks must have depended largely on the proportion of depositors who were labourers or other working men liable to be classed as able-bodied paupers. A further table submitted by Tufnell as evidence that the new law was bringing growth to the savings banks does itself seem to indicate that the number of potential candidates for 'able-bodied pauperdom' who became clients of the banks in the South-East was comparatively small. The table showed the increase in the various classes of depositors at Tunbridge Wells Savings Bank and is reproduced as Table 8.3. The enormous increase of 200 per cent for agricul-

Table 8.3.

Various classes of depositors in Tunbridge Wells Savings Bank, 1831 and 1837.[1]

	1831	1837	Increase per cent
Servants	361	483	34
Agricultural labourers	46	137	200
Children	857	388	9
Journeymen and apprentices	39	57	46
Charitable Societies	14	26	86
Benefit Societies	4	5	25
Small shopkeepers	8	16	100
Small farmers and others	54	68	26
Total	883	1,180	34

tural labourers represented an increase of only 91 while the two largest groups, servants and children, still accounted for three-quarters of the total number of depositors in 1837.[2] It is difficult to believe that the impact of the Poor Law Amendment Act on the savings banks was more than marginal.

The legislation of 1817 met with criticism from Joseph Hume

[1] *Ibid.*
[2] There is a fuller discussion of the membership of savings banks on pp. 228–31.

at an early stage. It appeared to Hume and to others who were by no means hostile to savings banks as such that the rate of interest paid by the National Debt Commissioners was leading to the better-off depositing money in the banks to take advantage of the good return available. The steady fall in interest rates generally and the rise in the price of government stock led to the guaranteed return of £4 11s 3d appearing increasingly attractive and, Hume argued, unnecessarily generous. The best way of ensuring that the savings banks served only the industrious classes for whom they were designed was to lower the rate of interest to the current market level. The government was unwilling to reduce the interest rate paid and sought to restrict the savings banks to their intended clientele by placing close limits on the total amounts that might be deposited by any individual. An Act passed in 1824[1] imposed a limit of £50 on deposits in the first year of an account, £30 in the second and subsequent years and a total of £200. Individuals were also prevented from depositing in more than one savings bank. The Chancellor of the Exchequer told the Commons that he 'should feel most reluctant to weaken the confidence which the public reposed in these banks, and which rendered them one of the greatest blessings ever conferred upon the country',[2] accordingly he did not propose to change the rate of interest. But the fall in interest rates continued and in 1828 Hume sought a return showing the dividends on stock held for savings banks received by the National Debt Commissioners and the amount of interest they had in fact paid to trustees. By 1827 the apparent annual loss was running at about £135,000 annually. Hume contended that the poorer classes ought to be placed in precisely the same situation as other people who had capital to invest and that it was quite wrong to attempt to subsidize thrift in this manner.

The argument now carried weight with the government and the Savings Bank Act of 1828[3] not only consolidated previous legislation but also lowered the rate of interest payable to trustees from 3d per cent per day to 2½d (or from £4 11s 3d p.a.

[1] 5 Geo. IV, c.62.
[2] *Parliamentary Debates*, New Series, XI, 602, 7 May 1824.
[3] 9 Geo. IV, c.92.

to £3 16s). The maximum permitted rate of interest which the savings banks could pay to their depositors was reduced to £3 8s 5¼d. Even the new rates were more generous than those prevailing in the market by this time and so the limits on individual deposits were also reduced to £30 a year and £150 in all; no more interest was to be paid once a depositor's total balance reached £200. The sanction and approval of the National Debt Commissioners was to be required in future—as well as that of the justices in quarter sessions—for the formation of new savings banks before they could become entitled to the benefits offered by the state. A copy of the proposed rules was to be submitted 'to a barrister at law to be appointed by the Commissioners for the Reduction of the National Debt, for the purpose of ascertaining whether the same are in conformity to law and with the provisions of this Act' and he was to certify them or point out any way in which they did not conform for a fee of one guinea.[1] This Act formed a turning point in the history of self-help organizations in the 19th century since the appointment of a barrister to register the rules of savings banks was the first step in the creation of the position of Registrar of Friendly Societies and the barrister who was actually appointed in 1828 was, of course, Tidd Pratt. Five years later the savings bank and friendly society were further assimilated by an Act which, among other things, gave the savings bank priority against the estates of deceased or bankrupt officers,[2] a privilege which had been vested in the friendly society by the first Friendly Societies Act.

Both the administrative and financial developments of 1828 were taken further by the Savings Bank Act of 1844.[3] In future, two copies of the rules of savings banks were to be submitted to the appointed barrister who, after inspecting and certifying them was to return one copy to the bank and send the other to the National Debt Commissioners. The justices in quarter sessions dropped out of the procedure. This same alteration was applied two years later to friendly societies.[4] The barrister was

[1] S.4.
[2] 3 of 4 Wm. IV, c.14, s.28.
[3] 7 & 8 Vict., c.83.
[4] 9 & 10 Vict., c.27.

given power to settle all disputes between the trustees of banks and individual depositors, their executors etc. and for that purpose to inspect the books of banks and to examine witnesses on oath. The rate of interest paid by the Commissioners to Trustees was further reduced to £3 5s per cent per annum. Both the centralization of the registration arrangements and the successive reductions in the guaranteed rate of interest payable by the Commissioners fitted in with the new political and social attitudes which came to predominate from the 1830s in government policy. While the trustee savings banks were of their very nature the most paternalistic of the institutions of self-help, the desire to persuade the industrious classes to fend for themselves penetrated even here.

It should be noted, however, that the continuing decline in long-term interest rates during the 19th century resulted in each of the levels of guaranteed rates of interest costing an apparently growing charge on the Treasury within a few years of a new rate being fixed—a position which led to a good deal of political friction between the many prominent supporters of the trustee banks and those government ministers who were intent on eradicating any vestige of a subsidy. The apparent loss to the state during the 40 years from the passing of the Act of 1817 to the setting up of the Select Committee of 1858 is shown in table 8.4. The losses shown in the table are described as 'apparent' since it could be—and was—argued by supporters of the banks that the free use of their deposited funds by the Chancellor of the Exchequer had saved the Treasury far more than the subsidy had appeared to cost it. When Goulburn was Chancellor, he used the money of the savings banks as a reserve from which to pay off dissatisfied fund-holders when he succeeded in reducing the rate of interest on government paper from 4 to 3½, then to 3¼ and finally to 3 per cent. The saving to the state from these manoeuvres amounted to £750,000 annually. Again the savings banks' funds were also useful as a way of avoiding the costs of loan raising in the Crimean War.[1]

While the state accepted responsibility for all funds deposited with the National Debt Commissioners, none of the legislation so far had extended the security of the state's guarantee to all

[1] Lewins, *op. cit.*, pp. 174–5.

Table 8.4.

Apparent cost to Treasury of guaranteed interest rates, 1818–58.[1]

Period	Rate of interest paid to trustees of of banks	Total interest paid in excess of open market rates	Average loss for each year of period
		£	£
1818–28	£4–11s–3d	744,363	67,669
1829–44	£3–16s–0½d	1,435,567	89,723
1845–58	£3–5s–0d	666,038	47,574
		2,845,968	69,414

funds deposited in the trustee savings banks. The impressive list of trustees which each savings bank possessed was intended to give confidence to those who placed their money in its care. Even so, many depositors found to their cost that the impression thus given did not mean that their confidence was well placed or that their savings were in fact safe.[2] A series of frauds in the middle years of the century served to moderate the overall growth rate of deposits and to indicate the shortcomings of the legislative framework within which the banks operated. Some of the earliest difficulties arose in Ireland where Cuffe Street Savings Bank, Dublin, finally collapsed in 1848. Depositors in the savings bank at Tralee were swindled of £36,000 by the Secretary; although he was sentenced to 14 years' transportation that did not restore their money to the depositors. Even

[1] Adapted from Scratchley, *op. cit.*, p. 128.

[2] Scratchley showed that it was not merely the depositors who falsely imagined that the state guaranteed the security of their money in the savings banks. He listed statements by many authoritative commentators in the 1830s who clearly shared this impression. G. R. Porter, for example, wrote in his *Progress of the Nation*, 'The savings banks, on the contrary, can never involve those who there deposit their savings in any risk or expense: the safety of the money is guaranteed by the State.' The Act of Parliament itself was said to be misleading, 'That it is expedient to give protection to such institutions, and the funds thereby established'—9 Geo. IV c.92. s.2.

while Tidd Pratt was sorting out the wreckage at Tralee, it became known that Killarney Savings Bank had stopped payment. Here the actuary had decamped and the deficiency was found to amount to £20,000 out of total liabilities of the bank of £36,000.[1]

One of the difficulties which faced the Government in considering how to strengthen the position of the depositors in savings banks was that if trustees were made fully responsible personally for any losses in their bank, then very few persons would be willing to act as trustees. Following these Irish bank frauds, the Government introduced a bill in 1848 which proposed to make trustees responsible for such losses up to a maximum of £100 each. It was hoped that this would be a large enough sum to make trustees cautious and vigilant but not so large as to frighten them into resigning. The bill met with a strong opposition from those who represented the interests of English savings banks who claimed that there should be no interference with the running of the banks. On the other hand, many Irish members and the trustees of Irish banks wanted the measure passed as a matter of urgency, for without it they feared that the savings bank movement in that country would be unable to survive the recent blows. Consequently, the government agreed to limit the application of the bill to Ireland, and it was passed.

The argument that the need for this bill was really due to conditions in Ireland and that it would have reflected unfairly on the management of English banks if it had been applied to banks in England was one which would have carried less conviction a few months later. The death of George Howarth of Rochdale in 1849 led to a series of revelations which indicated that depositors in English savings banks were quite as exposed to fraudulent practices as those in Ireland. Howarth was a member of the Society of Friends, had a cotton spinning factory, was a land agent and had many other business interests. He was also actuary of Rochdale Savings Bank. He was a pillar of local society, the first to be called on to aid any charitable or philanthropic cause. As William Lewins explained in 1866, 'It is true that some persons now and then expressed their surprise

[1] Lewins, *op. cit.*, pp. 184–93.

that George Howarth should act as actuary to a Savings Bank,
and moreover attend so closely to his duties there when his
hands were otherwise so full; but Howarth deceived even these
people by putting his connection with the bank on the ground
of charity, and an anxious desire to promote the happiness of
his poor fellow-tradesmen,—for whom indeed he was each day
laying up increased stores of untold misery. Clever to the last
. . . he escaped his justly merited punishment in this world, and
by an unscrutable providence was allowed to die unmolested
on the 19th of November, 1849.'[1] An audit of the books following Howarth's death revealed liabilities of £100,403, assets of
£28,686 and a deficit of £71,715. Most people in Rochdale
imagined that the loss would fall on the Government and that
depositors would be safe. Indeed, for some weeks 17s 6d in the
pound was offered for Rochdale Savings Bank books by local
speculators. The Government had, of course, no liability. A
sum of £17,000 was subscribed by the trustees and their
friends and a further £17,000 was realized from Howarth's
estate. In the end depositors were paid off at 12s 6d in the
pound. Howarth's mechanism for defrauding the bank had been
by keeping two sets of accounts, one of which was accurate and
the other a sham to deceive the public. The impact of this affair
on confidence in savings banks in the Rochdale area—and more
widely—was considerable.[2]

Further cases of fraud in other parts of the country added to
the urgency of the need to improve in some way the security
offered to depositors. In the same year as the Rochdale affair, a
fraud involving a loss of £4,000 came to light in Brighton
Savings Bank. In the following years the defalcations included
£12,932 at St Helens, £8,156 at Newport, Isle of Wight,
£10,000 at Mitcham, £6,221 at Poole and £3,213 at Spilsby.
The total of frauds made public amounted to £229,000. But
there were numerous instances of fraud which arose out of the
absence of a proper system of audit and inspection, which were
not given publicity. The trustees sought in such cases to avoid
destroying the confidence of depositors in their bank, and 'they
have very naturally preferred the personal sacrifice necessary

[1] *Ibid.*, p. 197.
[2] Scratchley, *op. cit.*, pp. 65–8.

to make good the deficiency, to incurring the censure that would justly have been passed on the laxity of management which had rendered such frauds possible'.[1]

III. The crisis of the 1850s

These continuing difficulties over the security of the banks and the almost constant series of clashes between the Treasury and Government spokesmen on the one hand and the trustee savings bank interests[2] on the other culminated eventually in the appointment of a select committee to 'inquire into the Acts relating to Savings Banks and the operation thereof' with Sotheron Estcourt as its chairman. The committee took much evidence on both of the main issues of contention: the security which could be offered to depositors and the way in which the Government invested the funds belonging to the savings banks. Virtually all the witnesses agreed on the need for a Government guarantee for the security of deposits. The disagreement lay rather in the degree of control which the state might need to exercise over trustees before it could be expected to give such a guarantee. The position was put clearly by Spearman, Controller of the National Debt Office, who told the committee that 'There will be no satisfactory amendment of the law unless the security of government is given to depositors. I think it is impossible that the present state of things should be allowed to continue. The question has often been discussed, and depositors in many cases have believed that they had the security of government, and found to their cost that they had not; complaints are constantly arising; applications are constantly made to know whether they have the security of the government or not. I think myself that depositors are entitled to have the real protection of a government security, but I think also that it will be quite impossible to give this security without at the same time giving to the officers of government a very different power of dealing with the management of savings banks. It would be idle to talk of one without the other.'[3]

---

[1] *Ibid.*, p. 58.
[2] For an account of these *cf.* Horne, *op. cit.*, pp. 129–40 and 145–50.
[3] P.P. 1857–58, XVI, S.C. on Savings Banks, Spearman, Q. 4,368.

The select committee accepted that Parliament should offer some security for the money of depositors who had no share in the management of the bank. The committee accepted that in the case of the large banks there was very little danger of fraud or error, but in the smaller banks there was a need to make arrangements which would provide checks against any misconduct. The solution proposed by the committee took the form of a supervisory Commission which was to be set up consisting of five members including the Chancellor of the Exchequer and the Governor of the Bank of England. This Commission was to control all investments and might invest up to one-third of the savings banks' funds in securities other than those currently authorized for this purpose. If the earnings of the invested funds did not meet the current cost of interest paid to the banks, then the rate should be reduced. The Commission was to be empowered to make regulations for the keeping and auditing of accounts and only banks which complied with these regulations were to call themselves savings banks, while security for deposits in such institutions was to be guaranteed by Parliament.[1]

The proposals from the committee did little to solve the actual problems. In the summer of 1859 Gladstone again became Chancellor. He introduced a measure which would have had the effect of widening the powers of investment of savings bank funds, but it was clear that he did not accept the main recommendations of the committee. Its members attacked Gladstone's bill and defeated it in a division on 20 July 1860. A minor measure was passed a few months later concerned with the investment powers of the National Debt Commissioners,[2] but by this time Gladstone and the Treasury were paying increasing attention to another way of providing working people with a reliable and secure savings bank system, namely by creating a state savings bank operated directly by the Government through the Post Office.[3]

[1] *Ibid.*, Report, pp. xi–xii.
[2] 23 & 24 Vict. c.137.
[3] When giving evidence to the Select Committee on Savings Banks in 1888, C. R. Wilson, Comptroller General of the National Debt Office was asked 'You attribute the establishment of the Post Office Savings Bank rather to the difficulty which the government met with in trying to exercise greater control over the

The deadlock between the trustees and managers of the existing savings banks on the one hand and successive governments on the other over the whole issue of security deposits and supervision of the banks at a time when there was a series of well-publicized frauds meant that from the mid-1840s the rate of growth in the total capital of the banks was much slower than earlier in the century. In 1847, 1848, 1849 and 1850 withdrawals exceeded deposits by a considerable margin. This was partly due to economic difficulties but was also the result of distrust and lack of confidence among depositors. In 1844, the total capital of the savings banks stood at £29,000,000. Fifteen years later, at the time of the select committee of 1858, the total had only reached £38,000,000. Writing in 1860, Samuel Smiles noted that 'although the balances to the credit of the depositors in savings banks have increased on the whole during the last 17 years, this result would not have been attained, not withstanding the increase of population and of wages, but for the accumulation of interest—the deposits in England during that period having been 93 millions and the withdrawals about 95½ millions. Thus there is an actual decrease in the capital sums deposited of 2½ millions.'[1]

Considered as a system, the trustee savings banks had grown up in a haphazard manner, the products of local paternalistic or philanthropic feelings. On this basis, it was not possible to plan any regular national distribution and in any case the difficulties of the 1840s and 1850s removed any impetus to found more of these institutions. The facilities for deposit offered by the existing banks were hardly encouraging for would-be depositors. In 1861, of the total of 638 savings banks, 355 only opened once a week, 54 only once a fortnight and 10 once a

---

trustee savings banks ?' He replied 'Very much so; and I think it is very important that the Committee should be aware of these facts. The committee will find that upon no less than four occasions in the few years preceding the Act of 1861, important measures were introduced by the government, one in 1848, another in 1853 and another in 1857, all having for their object the establishment of some efficient control over these banks. Upon the occasion of every one of these measures being introduced, the government were met by such opposition that the Bills had to be withdrawn.'—P.P. 1888, XXIII, Q.902.

[1] Samuel Smiles, 'Workmen's Earnings and Savings', *Quarterly Review*, vol. 108, 1860, p. 92.

month. Most of the remainder were open two or three times a week. Of the whole group, 50 banks were open for only four hours monthly, 124 for only one hour each week and 150 for two hours per week. Only in most of the larger cities was anything like an adequate service provided—even in some of these the idiosyncracies of trustees could have a limiting influence. This was the position in Liverpool for many years where Archdeacon Brooks insisted on paying everything personally with the consequence that the bank was only open two days a month for the repayment of money.[1]

Smiles thought it was 'curious' that the inhabitants of Wiltshire and Dorset lodged more money in savings banks per head of population than the more highly paid operatives of Lancashire and that rural parts of Yorkshire were apparently more thrifty than the 'highly favoured manufacturing classes of the West Riding'.[2] Smiles illustrated his argument with the material in table 8.5 which serves to illustrate the comparatively greater use made of trustee savings banks in agricultural than in industrial areas. In the agricultural counties the trustees were drawn

Table 8.5.

Savings bank statistics in certain counties in 1858.[3]

Counties	Number of accounts	Owing to depositors	Number of depositors to every 100 of population	Average deposit per head of population		
AGRICULTURAL		£		£	s.	d.
Berkshire	16,393	442,257	9·64	2	12	7
Devonshire	61,558	1,671,713	10·33	2	18	11
Dorset	14,134	480,898	7·67	2	12	2
Oxford	14,164	380,348	8·31	2	4	7
Somerset	29,115	857,147	6·55	1	18	7
Wilts	14,856	477,712	5·45	1	17	6
INDUSTRIAL						
Lancashire	117,927	3,285,522	5·80	1	12	4
West Riding	63,334	1,691,006	4·77	1	5	6

[1] Lewins, *op. cit.*, p. 239.
[2] *Quarterly Review*, 108, 1860, p. 93.
[3] *Ibid.* (based on the Parliamentary Return of 1858.)

from the same groups of society as those who established the county type of friendly societies. In the social conditions existing at the time, thrift organizations established by the landlord, squire, parson or other notable figures were clearly more attractive in rural than in industrial areas.[1]

Doubts as to the extent to which the trustee savings banks really succeeded in attracting and meeting the needs of working men are of long standing. As early as 1860 Scratchley suggested that not more than one-third of the total number of depositors could be described as 'workingmen'. On the basis of details given in the select committee report of 1858 and returns which he obtained from some of the largest banks, he showed that more than one-half of the total amount of deposits were from women and children.[2] Few detailed studies exist of the occupations of depositors of individual banks but G. C. Holland studied the occupations of the 5,022 depositors of Sheffield Savings Bank in 1840. He found 2,716 were males of whom only 967 were engaged in manufacturing trades. He calculated that there were more than 5,000 cutlers in the town, yet only 221 of them were depositors, while of 450 to 500 workmen in the silver-plate trade, 89 were depositors. Of the female depositors, only 5 were employed in works; the two largest groups were servants (650) and widows (213).[3] The situation at Bradford Savings Bank contrasted strongly with this for a classification of the bank's 6,225 depositors in 1852 showed that this included 598 female factory workers as compared with 541 domestic servants.[4] In Bradford special efforts were made to attract mill workers.

Some work has recently been published by scholars on this question.[5] Fishlow in his article showed that depositors were predominantly holders of small balances and that they were very probably of the wage-earning class. Yet the two large iden-

[1] *Supra* p. 33; Gosden, *op. cit.*, pp. 52–5.
[2] Scratchley, *op. cit.*, p. xxviii.
[3] G. C. Holland, *Vital Statistics of Sheffield*, 1843, pp. 131–37.
[4] *Transactions of the National Association for the Promotion of Social Science* 1859, 1860, p. 730.
[5] Albert Fishlow, 'The Trustee Savings Banks, 1817–1861', *J. of Economic History*, XXI, 1961, pp. 26–40; Peter L. Payne, 'The Savings Bank of Glasgow, 1836–1914', *Studies in Scottish Business History* (ed. P. L. Payne), pp. 152–86.

tifiable groups appeared to be domestic servants and children.
The industrial wage-earner was not attracted and 'the concep-
tion of the banks as an instrument of social policy must appear
naive.'[1] A similar conclusion was suggested by another recent
investigator who has suggested that while the savings banks had
their origin in the dissatisfaction of the influential classes with
the condition of the poor, the banks were not of use to the really
poor but appealed rather to the 'healthy' elements in society
which were not dependent on the poor law in any case.[2] These
studies have been based mainly on the few national statistics
that are available concerning such matters as the distribution of
deposits and depositors by size of deposits and the occupations
of depositors as shown by Report of the Select Committee of
1858. The much more detailed study by Payne of the Glasgow
Savings Bank has shown quite clearly that that particular large
bank attracted and retained the support of the manual workers
and it is also claimed that such a statement would be justified in
the case of Aberdeen Savings Bank.[3] There may have been a
difference between experience in Scotland and England or it
may simply have been that those savings banks in industrial
cities which set out to provide working men with the sort of
service they wanted were well supported by them.

One attempt to meet the needs of the poorer groups who
might, nevertheless, become depositors was sponsored by the
vigorous Glasgow bank at an early stage, namely the penny
bank. The first penny bank in the city was opened in one of the
poorest districts in 1850. The Committee of Management of
Glasgow Savings Bank believed that it was in the poorest
districts that the greatest proportion of people's earnings were
misspent and therefore crusaded for the establishment of penny
banks, conveniently situated for ease of access by depositors.
By 1860 36 penny banks had been opened in and around
Glasgow, by 1881 there were 213 penny banks with some
60,000 depositors and these penny banks were transferring to
Glasgow Savings Bank about £20,000 a year.[4] The savings

---

[1] *J. of Economic History*, XXI, p. 37.

[2] N. J. Smelser, *Social Change in the Industrial Revolution: an application of theory to the Lancashire Cotton Industry, 1770–1840*, 1959, p. 375.

[3] Payne, *op. cit.*, pp. 165 and 184.

[4] *Ibid.*, p. 156.

banks themselves would usually not accept any deposit of less than one shilling; thus, there was plenty of scope for penny banks where enthusiasts were prepared to operate them. The first penny bank is usually held to be that opened as a sort of feeder for Greenock Savings Bank in 1847. In the first year about 5,000 depositors placed £1,580 in this institution. Another early penny bank was that opened by the Reverend Queckett at St George's-in-the-East. In 1849 14,513 deposits were made in this bank. Queckett explained that this bank also acted as a recruiting agency for the larger savings bank in that depositors were themselves passed on to it when their weekly payments grew large enough. There was no expense apart from the purchase of stationery since all the assistance required was gratuitous.[1] Considerable numbers of penny banks were established in the 1850s often centred on a church or chapel, a club or a factory. The contemporary temperance movement supported savings banks strongly as a means of preventing intemperance. Temperance societies sometimes established penny banks. The Small Savings Society at Banbury, for instance, was founded in 1847 to accommodate the savings of those who could not rise to the savings bank but who might otherwise have turned to the publican.[2]

A considerable impetus was given to the penny bank movement in the North of England by Charles Sikes of the Huddersfield Banking Company who was later to become a leading advocate of the setting up of the Post Office Savings Bank. Like others who were convinced of the value of saving and thrift, Sikes believed that the frittering away of their wages by the working class was one of the great evils of the age. He put forward the idea that every mechanics' institute should appoint a preliminary savings bank committee which should attend weekly for the purpose of receiving deposits from members.[3] In

[1] *Quarterly Review*, 108, 1860, pp. 110–11.
[2] Brian Harrison and Barrie Trinder, 'Drink and Sobriety in an Early Victorian Country Town: Banbury, 1830–1860', *English Historical Review*, Supplement 4, 1969, p. 48.
[3] These proposals were first put forward in a letter published in the *Leeds Mercury*, 23 February 1850. They were subsequently published in pamphlet form, Charles W. Sikes, *Mechanics Institutes as Preliminary Savings Banks*, 1850.

advocating penny—or to use Sikes' term, preliminary—savings banks, he wrote that 'If a committee at each institution were to adopt this course taking an interest in their humble circumstances, and in a sympathizing and kindly spirit suggest, invite nay win them over, not only to reading the lesson, but forming the habit of true economy and self-reliance (the noblest lesson for which classes could be formed), how cheering would be the results!' The preliminary banks were simply to be feeders to the savings banks and when the money standing to the credit of any single depositor reached a guinea, this was to be paid into a savings bank.

The Yorkshire Union of Mechanics Institutes commended this plan to its member institutes and a considerable number of 'preliminary' banks were set up by them in the West Riding. One of the more successful of those penny banks was that opened at Halifax Mechanics Institute. This opened in 1856, by 1860 it had 4,000 accounts and received about 850 deposits each week. The total balance to the credit of depositors amounted to £10,029.[1] The growing importance of penny banks was reflected in an Act of 1859 which conferred on penny banks the privilege of investing all their proceeds in savings banks without regard to the general limitation on deposits which applied to individuals.[2]

One of the most successful if untypical ventures in the penny bank movement was the foundation of the Yorkshire Penny Savings Bank which opened in 1859 and which by the end of the century had more than £12,000,000 standing to the credit of its depositors. The founder of this bank was Colonel Akroyd of Halifax, an employer and philanthropist of note in the West Riding who was impressed by the financial insecurity of both the trustee savings banks and of friendly societies. He thought it not surprising that many working men were improvident since they argued that 'save and scrape as we can, we have no assurance of mending our condition. If we put our savings even into the Government Savings Banks they are not secure.'[3]

[1] *Quarterly Review*, 108, 1860, p. 112.
[2] 22 & 23 Vict. c. 53.
[3] Circular of 1856 from Akroyd to 'the nobility and gentry of the county' printed in H. B. Sellers, *Memoranda from a Notebook on the Yorkshire Penny Bank*, 1909, p. 8.

Akroyd proposed that the local philanthropists should sponsor the bank and that they should put up £10,000 as a guarantee fund. 'In such manner can the monied classes best evidence the sincerity of their desire to benefit the industrial classes.' This was to be the solution of the Yorkshire Penny Savings Bank to the problem of security posed in the trustee banks by the unwillingness of trustees to accept a personal obligation to meet losses.

The energy and financial acumen shown in establishing and running the bank in its early years largely account for its success. Within the first year the bank opened 24 branches and had 9,546 depositors. By 1863 there was a small profit of £226 on the year's business. Deposits were actively sought out and some enmity towards this aggressive newcomer was displayed by the trustee banks. From the beginning the bank invested depositors' funds at a higher rate of interest than that allowed to the trustee banks. At the end of 1859 most of the funds were invested in the preference shares of railway companies and in the Leeds Permanent Building Society. The Savings Bank Act of 1863[1] faced the bank with the problem of whether to register as a trustee bank or whether to register as limited company under the Joint Stock Companies Act. Registration under the savings bank legislation was 'considered most objectionable, on account of the many restrictions which the Act of 1863 imposed on the savings banks . . . as to the investment of funds, the amount of business to be done yearly and the aggregate with each depositor.'[2] Steps were taken to register the Yorkshire Penny Bank as a company limited by guarantee i.e. without shareholders since it was not being established for the making of profit. The word 'savings' had to be dropped from its title since after 1863 this could only be used to describe a bank registered under the provisions of the Act of that year.

The considerably greater measure of freedom which the bank now enjoyed enabled it to expand more rapidly than trustee banks could do. In 1872 it introduced cheque facilities and sought larger as well as small accounts. From 1874 school banks were established in order to encourage penny savings among

[1] *Infra* p. 242.
[2] Sellers, *op. cit.*, p. 33, quoting from a report to the Board.

children and their parents. These Yorkshire Penny Bank School Transfer Banks received a considerable impetus with the coming of free elementary schooling in 1891, the balance due to depositors rising from £3,313 in 1890 to £11,348 in 1892 while the number of depositors rose from 16,000 to 55,000. Its wide freedom for profitable investment enabled the bank to accumulate funds for further expansion of its branch network. By the end of the century about 40 per cent of funds were invested in British and Indian railway securities, 25 per cent in harbour, gas, water and corporation stocks and 16 per cent in mortgage loans on property. Table 8.6 gives some idea of the growth of this independent institution.[1]

Table 8.6.

Growth of the Yorkshire Penny Bank.

Year	No. of accounts	Balance due to depositors £
1860	—	23,313
1870	46,072	229,609
1880	120,657	1,115,008
1890	280,495	5,021,169
1900	438,100	12,840,902

Another development in the middle years of the century and one which is also interesting in that it closely involved the central government in running a savings bank for the first time was the military savings bank. The question of establishing such a bank was raised in 1827 by the commander of a regiment of Cameronians and brought to the attention of the Duke of Wellington. The Duke felt that any soldier could use existing savings banks if he so desired and that nothing more was needed. He added, 'Has a soldier more pay than he requires? If he has, it should be lowered, not to those now in service, but to those enlisted hereafter.' The topic was allowed to drop for a while, but a few years later it was raised again and was now

[1] *Ibid.*, Appendix.

supported by the Secretary of State for War. Parliamentary authority was given[1] and the scheme began to operate under regulations made by the War Office in 1842. The sums accumulated were deposited by the War Office with the National Debt Commissioners in a separate account known as the Fund for Military Savings Banks and the sums in this account were expressly exempted from the regulations of the Savings Bank Acts. The amounts that could be deposited were unlimited, but sums in excess of £30 received in one year would not bear interest for that year and when the total in an account reached £200 it ceased to yield any interest. The rate allowed to individual depositors was not to exceed 3½ per cent.[2] By 1860 a total of £227,299 had been accumulated.[3]

IV. The Post Office Savings Bank

In the difficult situation in which the savings banks found themselves in the 1850s it was not surprising that some enthusiastic supporters of the cause of thrift among the industrious classes came to suggest ways in which the Post Office might be used as an agency for collecting savings. Since Whitbread's bill of 1807 which proposed to use it as an agency for remitting contributions to a Poor's Fund, little attention had been given to the use of the Post Office for savings. After 1850 a number of proposals connected with the Post Office began to come forward again. In 1856 John Bullar, a prominent lawyer, suggested in a memorandum that the answer to the defects of the existing system with its lack of security, lack of facilities and general ineptitude would be to make the Money Order Department of the Post Office into a National Savings Bank, receiving money from all comers, investing the deposits in government securities and paying a moderate rate of interest (2½ per cent). He claimed that the principle of a National Savings Bank had already been admitted in the Military Savings Bank while the principle of the government acting as

[1] 5 & 6 Vict. c. 71.
[2] Scratchley, *op. cit.*, pp. 21–2.
[3] P.P. 1860, XLI, p. 637. Return of all Savings Banks established in Regiments etc.

banker to the nation had been admitted when the Money Order Department of the Post Office had been set up. Bullar calculated that the Post Office would earn a surplus on the investment of depositors' money which would be more than enough to meet the cost of operating the scheme.[1] The Money Order Department had been established within the Post Office in 1838 and within 20 years was handling about 7,000,000 transactions annually. Bullar's scheme met with a cool reception at the official level and he did not pursue the matter.

Charles Sikes of Huddersfield apparently arrived at much the same idea as Bullar's in 1859. Sometime after he had given evidence to the select committee in 1858 he set to work on the idea of using the Post Office organization as a means of extending savings bank facilities. Sikes had his scheme printed in the form of a letter and got in touch with Edward Baines, member for Leeds. He brought the scheme to the notice of Rowland Hill, Secretary to the Post Office, who considered it it to be practicable. Sikes then had his scheme printed as a pamphlet in the form of a letter addressed to the Chancellor of the Exchequer.[2] In the pamphlet Sikes contrasted the progress of savings banks with money order offices. Between 1846 and 1858 the business of the former had increased at the rate of $7\frac{1}{2}$ per cent and that of the latter at 79 per cent. The superior organization of Post Office money order offices which accounted for this development ought to be extended to the field of savings. Wherever the local Post Office inspector believed five money orders might be issued in a week, the practice was to make the local branch of the Post Office a money order office. These offices were open daily, receiving money and giving vouchers for the amounts transmitted through them. The Post Office held the money until it was drawn on presentation of a valid voucher elsewhere. Hence the Post Office was already in fact a bank for the transmission of money, sometimes holding it

[1] John Bullar's memorandum is printed in Lewins, *History of Savings Banks*, pp. 280–1.

[2] Charles W. Sikes, *Post Office Savings Banks. A letter to the Right Hon. W. E. Gladstone, M.P., Chancellor of the Exchequer*, 1859. Sikes presented a paper outlining his scheme at the annual meeting of the National Association for the Promotion of Social Science at Bradford in 1859. A summary was printed in *Transactions*, 1860, pp. 730–31.

for months until a money order was cashed. There was no reason why this system could not be extended and interest allowed so that there would be a national bank of deposit with 2,481 offices established all over the country. The details of Sikes' plan were that money order offices should transmit deposits to a chief savings bank in London. Savings bank interest notes bearing interest at 2½ per cent should be issued to depositors for sums of £1 to £30—the latter being the maximum for any single depositor in one year while individual deposits could not be less than £1.

A number of Liberal newspapers supported the ideas behind Sikes' proposals and petitions were sent to the Government from such towns as Liverpool, Leeds and York. Gladstone replied encouragingly to Sikes. While the difficulties were serious, there was so much of promise in the plan that it would be carefully examined.[1] The work of examining the scheme fell to the Post Office and Treasury officials. Chetwynd of the money order section and Scudamore, Accountant-General, were largely responsible for evolving the practical details of the scheme which came to be accepted. It was much simpler than Sikes' scheme and provided for a minimum deposit of a shilling instead of a pound. Each depositor was to have a book in which any money order office could enter a deposit, reporting all deposits daily to a central office in London. Withdrawals were to be by application by post to the central office which would issue a warrant payable at the nearest post office.[2]

Once a practical and acceptable scheme had been settled, Gladstone introduced a resolution in the Commons on which the general issues involved were debated. Reflecting his own experiences, Gladstone explained that while it was the wish of the Government to improve the constitution of the existing savings banks so as to make them more useful to the humbler classes, the way of doing this was a problem which they found extremely difficult to solve. 'Under those circumstances, they proposed to avail themselves of another description of machinery already in existence, simple in form, and recommended by

---

[1] Gladstone to Sikes, 30 November 1859; printed in Lewins, *op. cit.*, p. 288.
[2] P.P. 1897, XXIV, 43rd Annual Report of the Postmaster General, App. I, pp. 32–3.

its incomparable convenience, for the purpose of carrying out more effectually the objects for which savings banks had been set on foot.' He went on to compare the six hundred savings banks, most of them open for only a few hours each week, with the two to three thousand money order post offices, every one of which was open six days in the week for not less than eight or ten hours each day. 'Now, there was a machinery ready to hand and admirably adapted for extending the usefulness of the savings bank system.' After brief discussion, the House accepted the resolution giving a government guarantee to deposits in the new Post Office Savings.[1]

When the bill establishing the Post Office Savings Bank was debated on its second reading, some of those particularly concerned with the trustee savings banks expressed their fears concerning the possible impact of the new agency on them. Sotheron Estcourt, who had been chairman of the select committee of 1858, thought the new banks would be much more convenient to many people than the old were and that in a short time the new banks would absorb 'not only all future deposits, but also a great part, if not all, of those which had been made in the existing savings banks.' He went on to suggest means by which the challenge to the old banks by the Post Office might be checked. Despite these warnings, the measure was warmly supported by such speakers as W. E. Forster and Edward Baines.[2] The Post Office Savings Bank Act[3] received the Royal Assent on 17 May 1861.

The success of the new institution was both immediate and lasting and its history during the rest of the century indicated that its creators gauged accurately the extent of an existing need which was not being met by other institutions. The Post Office claimed in 1897 that its 'Savings Bank rapidly became an important factor in the general development of thrift in the country, not only by the assistance which it rendered to thrifty individuals, but also as the ally of the associations for self-help.'[4] It began business in September 1861, by the end of the

---

[1] *Parliamentary Debates*, Third Series, CLXI, 262–66, 8 February 1861.
[2] *Ibid.*, 2189–93.
[3] 24 Vict. c. 14.
[4] P.P. 1897, XXIV, p. 33.

following year 180,000 accounts had been opened and a total of £1,750,000 stood to the credit of depositors. Its history was one of steady expansion as may be seen from table 8.7. The Post Office believed that its savings banks reached a poorer class of

Table 8.7.

Growth of the Post Office Savings Bank, 1863–95.[1]

	Average number of accounts	Average total of deposits	Average balance in each account			Average number of offices open
		£	£	s.	d.	
1863–68	663,000	7,000,000	11	3	5	3,390
1869–74	1,373,000	18,000,000	13	5	3	4,498
1875–80	1,889,000	29,000,000	15	12	5	5,742
1881–85	3,088,000	42,000,000	13	11	3	7,348
1886–90	4,248,000	59,000,000	13	16	10	9,025
1891–95	5,776,000	83,000,000	14	7	0	10,887

depositors than the trustee banks did and that the very convenience of the facilities offered for the frequent deposit of small sums increased the 'inducements to Frugality, and removed the temptations to wastefulness'. As more branches were opened in post offices in rural districts and in the poorer and most densely populated districts of the cities, a gradual reduction in the average size of each deposit took place in the early years—thus apparently supporting the claims of the Post Office.[2] Thirty years later the Post Office attempted to determine what classes of the community chiefly used its savings bank by recording for three months the occupations of all depositors, assuming that these would give a typical sample of the total distribution. The results are reproduced in table 8.8. These details are of considerable interest but the classifications employed were too broad and general to enable any useful contrast to be drawn with the membership of comparable thrift organizations. Women and children concealed within all the classifications were believed to amount to 60.59 per cent of depositors.

[1] *Ibid.*, based on material from pp. 33, 34, 36.
[2] P.P. 1864, XXX, p. 587; Urquhart A. Forbes, *The Law relating to Trustee and Post Office Savings Banks*, 1878, pp. 7–8.

A considerable additional impetus was brought to the efforts of the Post Office in 1880 when the blind Henry Fawcett became Postmaster General in Gladstone's Government. He was a noted opponent of state action or 'interference' in social questions. His biographer, Leslie Stephen, wrote of him as

Table 8.8.

Occupations of all depositors in the Post Office Savings Bank in 3 months of 1896.[1]

Occupation	Percentage
Professional	1·55
Official	2·81
Educational	1·01
Commercial	3·88
Agricultural and Fishing	1·83
Industrial	18·43
Railway, Shipping and Transport	2·96
Tradesmen and their assistants	8·14
Domestic service	8·61
Miscellaneous	0·37
Married women, Spinsters, Widows, Children	50·41
	100·00

'a faithful Abdiel upholding true Radical theory, from which modern Radicals are too apt to depart'.[2] But vigorous support for savings bank facilities by the state appealed to Fawcett as the kind of interference which might stimulate rather than depress the tendency to self-help. As Postmaster General he increased rapidly the number of post offices in small villages which handled savings bank business. Special attention was paid to providing facilities for 'bodies of navvies and workmen' at their place of employment. Perhaps the most significant innovation was the arrangement he inaugurated for making very small deposits by slips on which postage stamps could be stuck. By

[1] P.P. 1897, XXIV, p. 14.
[2] Leslie Stephen, *Life of Henry Fawcett*, 1886, p. 169.

March 1881 576,000 completed slips had been received and 223,000 new accounts had been opened by this means. Fifteen years later, in 1896, 1,741,000 stamp slips were deposited with a value of £95,000.[1] Fawcett also arranged for the Post Office Bank to buy government stock for persons of small means and debit the cost to their accounts. The Post Office collected the dividend payments and credited those directly to savings bank accounts. By 1900, £10,468,000 of stock was held in this way through the Post Office Savings Bank Register, the average holding being £111.[2] In the winter of 1880 Fawcett prepared a pamphlet entitled *Aids to Thrift* of which about 1,250,000 copies were distributed free of charge. His aim was to translate into simple language the technical phrases of the *Post Office Guide*. In 1884 he noted the very considerable increase in the number of young persons who had become depositors and commented that by thus encouraging the habit of saving in early life the Post Office was doing more to assist than to retard private enterprise.[3]

The appeal to the young received special emphasis in 1891. The Education Act of that year abolished the small fees charged in elementary schools which amounted on average to ten shillings per child annually. The Post Office and the Education Department worked together to inculcate thrift by getting parents and children to save what they would have spent in school pence. School managers were urged in a circular to press the matter on all concerned, special stamp slips were prepared, stamps were supplied to managers on credit, and clerks attended schools to open accounts and to receive deposits. 3,000 schools adopted the scheme within three years. A sum of £14,000 was deposited within five months and £40,000 in the first year.[4]

A further useful service was added by the Post Office in 1893 when arrangements were made for more rapid withdrawals by telegram. The system of telegraphic withdrawals from savings

---

[1] P.P. 1897, XXIV, p. 36.
[2] *Ibid.*, p. 37; P.P. 1914, Cd. 7573, XLIV, p. 73. Similar facilities for the purchase of government stock were made available through the trustee banks at the same time.
[3] Stephen, *op. cit.*, p. 432.
[4] P.P. 1897, XXIV, p. 35.

banks had been used in other countries for some time, but the authorities had hesitated to introduce it here because 'it was strongly held that the cause of thrift was sometimes served by interposing a delay between a sudden desire to spend and its realisation.' This method of obtaining a withdrawal more quickly took two forms; a depositor could have the money telegraphed for and await the warrant by post or he could have the warrant telegraphed back also. The former cost the depositor the charge of a single telegram, 9d, the latter the charge of a reply-paid telegram, 1s 3d. The use made of the new service indicated the need for it. Within three years there were 8,000 telegraphic withdrawals by return of post and 94,000 by return telegram.[1]

V. Trustee banks after 1863

The principal effects on the trustee savings banks of the competition from the Post Office were strongly contrasting. The trustees of many of the smaller banks closed their institutions on the grounds that the new Post Office Bank could provide a far superior service which they could never hope to match. On the other hand some of the larger trustee savings banks were stimulated to improve the service they offered, lengthening their hours of business, facilitating deposits and withdrawals and opening more branches. Within twelve months the trustees of 35 of the older banks had closed their institutions. In order to facilitate the transfer of depositors' accounts and assets from closing trustee banks to the Post Office Savings Bank, a further Act was passed in 1863.[2] This Act relieved trustees of banks which were closing from liability with regard to the accounts of depositors who had not applied for repayment of their money, who were 'thenceforth to be considered to be depositors in the Post Office Savings Bank',[3] and made the transfer of accounts of minors compulsory. The trustees were also empowered to compensate their paid officials for loss of office out of their banks' surplus funds. This was an important provision and meant that

[1] *Ibid.*, pp. 35–6.
[2] 26 Vict. c. 14.
[3] S. 3.

employed officers of the banks no longer had quite the same sort of vested interest in trying to get the trustees to continue their bank.

By 1866 nearly 100 of the trustee banks had closed, transferring their business to the Post Office. Many of these had only been opening for one or two hours each week and few had more than £10,000 in deposits. The only large savings bank to close and transfer its assets was Birmingham Savings Bank which had been established in 1827 and had capital assets of £583,461. It was transferred in 1863, the trustees having resolved by a majority of two not to carry on. Even a savings bank as large as Birmingham had only been opening for a total of twelve hours each week. Its defection to the Post Office provided some reassurance to other trustees who were wondering whether to take similar action themselves. It was argued that if a majority of the trustees of such a well-managed and flourishing bank as Birmingham could decide that the right course was to close their institution and transfer its business to the Post Office, then any bank might do so.[1] The next largest bank to close and transfer its assets at this time was Canterbury which did so after it was found that this saving bank's actuary had defrauded it of £9,300. In 1865, the offender—a man of 70—was sentenced to 6 years' penal servitude.

A bigger blow to confidence in some of the smaller trustee savings banks immediately following the setting up of the Post Office Savings Bank was the scandal over the fraudulent practices which came to light at Bilston, Staffordshire, in 1862. Bilston Savings Bank was established in 1838 and the Revd Horatio Fletcher was prominent among those who set it up. In 1839 he added to his work as trustee the honorary office of secretary to the bank and in 1849 also undertook the office of treasurer. Shortly after this he also took upon himself the office of actuary. Thus he held all the offices which were supposed to provide some check on each other. But as incumbent of the parish and a justice of the peace clearly Fletcher was a man in whom all reposed confidence. In 1861 Tidd Pratt gave a lecture in Bilston on 'Benefit Societies' and referred to the 'irregular manner' in which returns were sent from the local savings bank.

[1] Lewins, *op. cit.*, p. 324.

Tidd Pratt at that time knew nothing of the circumstances of the local bank, but some of the trustees were roused to enquire into the affairs of their bank and in due course a new actuary was appointed. By the beginning of 1862 it had become clear that the frauds amounted to £8,840. When the frauds became apparent, Tidd Pratt was called in to investigate. Fletcher's duty as actuary required him to furnish weekly returns of transactions to the National Debt Commissioners; the correctness of these returns being checked by the treasurer—an office which Fletcher also held. Thus he was able to send in false returns and steal the amounts he excluded from the returns without fear. Tidd Pratt attended a meeting of depositors at Bilston in January 1862 and brought Fletcher's returns with him from London. 'The whole of the Returns he held in his hand were signed by Mr Fletcher as actuary and manager. In the statement dated January 1, 1859, the amount received was returned at £234. On looking at the books for that day, he found it should have been £334, therefore £100 had been abstracted on that day (cries of 'Shame', and sensation). On 8th January, he found payments were set down at £174, whereas they had been only £74, thus showing that the Treasurer had put another £100 in his pocket that week. In the return dated January 29, the receipts were set down at £183, and the payments at £148, whereas the former ought to have been £283 and the latter £48, thus taking to himself £200 (renewed sensation).'[1]

In the wake of these revelations, the leading supporters of trustee savings banks in the Commons obtained leave in March 1862 to introduce a bill which would have enforced on all trustee banks the regulations of the well-managed ones, to require every bank to have an auditor and to provide for the safety of depositors by requiring that no transactions should take place except at the office, during stated office hours and in the presence and with the signature of more than one person. Once again, an attempt at legislative reform made no progress, for various bodies of trustees and managers got in touch with Sotheron Estcourt, who was sponsoring the measure, claiming

[1] *Birmingham Daily Post*, 16 January 1862. Report of depositors' meeting reprinted in Lewins, *op. cit.*, pp. 214–15.

that it was unnecessary. In May Estcourt and his friends withdrew this bill and a group of trustees and managers undertook to attempt to devise another. The new bill, which was enacted in 1863,[1] was largely a consolidating measure repealing the various acts governing the banks and bringing their provisions together. Few substantial alterations were introduced. The accounts of every bank were to be audited at least twice a year, the trustees were to meet not less than twice a year, and not fewer than two persons were to be present on all occasions of public business.[2] Trustees were only to be personally liable for losses if they failed to see that these three conditions were complied with. The intractable issue of guaranteeing the security of depositors without increasing the liabilities of individual trustees to such an extent that no one would have been a trustee was really only successfully dealt with much later when the Inspection Committee of Trustee Savings Banks was set up in 1891.

In their struggle for survival and growth after 1861, the trustee savings banks had some competitive advantages. Perhaps the most obvious of these was the higher rate of interest which trustee banks could offer. The Post Office paid only 2½ per cent. The trustee banks themselves continued to receive £3 5s per cent from the National Debt Commissioners and were permitted to offer depositors up to £3 0s 10d per cent. Most of them were able to pay £2 15s per cent after meeting their own costs of management. This comparatively advantageous rate was abolished in 1888, but it was clearly an important factor in sustaining them in the years immediately following 1861.

The second facility which helped the more energetic trustee banks was the freedom which they possessed to adapt their institutions to meet particular local or specialized needs. Where they extended their hours, provided conveniently sited branches, offered more rapid withdrawal facilities than the Post Office and sponsored enterprising groups of penny banks, the trustee banks might hope to flourish. This was what happened in some of the larger cities. In Sheffield Savings Bank, for instance, there was no drop either in the number of depositors

[1] 26 & 27 Vict. c. 87.
[2] S. 6.

or in the balance due to depositors; in 1861 the balance due stood at £331,938 while ten years later it had reached £523,537. The balance due to depositors in Leeds Savings Bank amounted to £364,901 in 1860 and to £382,457 ten years later.[1] In Glasgow the local Savings Bank was, perhaps, exceptionally active and the Post Office did badly. In 1890, for example, the total transactions of the Post Office Savings Bank in Glasgow amounted to £102,705, or only 3½ per cent of the comparable figure for the ordinary department of Glasgow Savings Bank.[2]

Apart from the strong position trustee savings banks established in some of the large cities, there was a degree of regional variation between different parts of the country. By the 1870s it had become clear that trustee banks were less able to stand up to the new competition in the South-Eastern counties than in the North or Scotland. By 1872 the assets of the trustee savings banks in Middlesex totalled £5,136,016. The other counties whose trustee banks held assets totalling more than a million pounds were Lancashire with £4,705,130, Yorkshire £3,583,834, Devon £1,780,007, Cheshire £1,075,309 and Northumberland £1,033,374.[3] Following the closure of the Canterbury savings bank in 1865, five large banks closed in the next ten years, all but one of them being in the South East, namely: Portsmouth £146,241, Norwich £125,236, Paddington £124,902, Maidstone £119,385 and Chichester £107,147. Some of these developments are apparent from the figures given in table 8.9. There was a steady and continuing reduction in the total number of savings banks. Both the total number of depositors and the amount due to them declined in the years immediately following the establishment of the Post Office Savings Bank but from about 1870 both of these figures began to increase again, giving some indication of the capacity which many of the remaining banks showed for adapting themselves to the new competition. The far smaller average sum per depositor shown for the Post

---

[1] R. E. Leader, *A Century of Thrift—An Historical Sketch of the Sheffield Savings Bank, 1819–1919*, 1920, p. 34; J. H. Oates, *op. cit.*, Appendix I.

[2] P. L. Payne, *Studies in Scottish Business History*, p. 186, cites these details from J. Nicol, *The Vital, Social and Economic Statistics of the City of Glasgow, 1885–1891*, 1891, p. 299.

[3] P.P. 1888, XXIII, Report of Select Committee on Trustee Savings Banks, Appendix I.

Office Savings Bank in table 8.6 led many to conclude that the latter bank was 'carrying provident habits into a lower stratum of society than that reached by the ordinary savings banks'.[1]

Table 8.9.

Trustee Savings Banks, 1862–1887.[2]

	Number	Depositors	Total Amount due	Average per depositor
			£M	£
1862	622	1,558,189	40	26
1867	539	1,385,788	36	26
1872	484	1,425,147	39	27
1877	458	1,509,847	44	29
1882	430	1,558,983	44	28
1887	400	1,604,610	47	29

One direction in which some of the larger trustee banks moved from about 1870 was towards setting up special investment departments. Their aim in setting up these departments was partly to make provision for depositors who had reached the statutory limit of deposit in the ordinary branch. It was also believed that the higher rate of interest such a department could offer would deter the withdrawal of larger deposits in quest of higher returns—quite apart from the obvious competitive advantage such a facility would offer over the Post Office Savings Bank. Trustee banks were able to do this under section 16 of the Act of 1863 which permitted trustees to apply sums received from depositors for purposes other than investment with the National Debt Commissioners.[3] This clause was certainly not included in the 1863 measure in order to facilitate the

[1] *Ibid.*

[2] P.P. 1888, XXIII, Appendix II.

[3] 'The following appears to be the effect of this section, which of late years has begun to be largely acted on:—Whilst savings banks have no power to invest their collective funds, otherwise than with the Commissioners, their trustees may, from any persons already depositors in the bank receive deposits without limit, and, so long as they do not pay such sums to the account of the Commissioners, they may apply them in any manner, provided it be for the benefit of the several depositors i.e. those depositing under the section.' Urquhart A. Forbes, *The Law relating to Trustee and Post Office Savings Banks*, 1878, p. 57.

setting up of special investment departments. It was carried
forward from the Act of 1828 where it seems to have been incorporated to regularize the position of Exeter Savings Bank
which had always offered facilities for the purchase of Consols
for its depositors. In 1857 over £21,000 in Consols was held
for 118 depositors.[1]

In April 1870 the trustees of Bradford Savings Bank resolved
'that a department called the Bradford Investment Savings
Bank be forthwith opened and that the rate of interest allowed
at present be 4 per cent per cent per annum.'[2] Later the same
year, Glasgow Savings Bank, then the largest in the country,
decided to open a separate department in which ordinary
department depositors might deposit funds 'to be invested on
mortgages of the Glasgow Corporation Water or Gas Trusts, or
in equally secure investments. In this way they will also parti-
cipate in the higher rate of interest allowed by these trusts, an
advantage hitherto confined to capitalists.'[3] Apart from Bradford, which invested a good deal of money in private mortgages,
most of the banks confined their investments to local authority
or public board securities and occasionally ventured into railway debentures—all of which offered a better return than gilt-
edged or the National Debt Commissioners. Examples of the
distribution of the investments of the special departments of the
Bradford, Glasgow and Leeds savings banks may be seen in
table 8.10. Within the legal framework of section 16 of the Act of
1863, the savings banks usually adopted a rule which permitted
them to exercise general powers of investment at the sole risk
of the depositor. The nature of the securities purchased was
generally such that there was in fact little risk. The relative
importance which the special investment departments came to
assume in a few trustee banks may be judged from the position
of the Leeds Savings Bank where the amount due to depositors
in the ordinary department amounted to £619,248 by 1890,
while no less than £527,275 was due to depositors in the special
investment department.[4]

[1] Horne, *op. cit.* p. 222.
[2] *Ibid.* p. 223.
[3] Payne, *op. cit.*, p. 176, who quotes this from the 35th Annual Report of
Glasgow Savings Bank, 1870.
[4] Oates, *op. cit.*, App. I.

Table 8.10.

Analysis of Investments under section 16 (Special Investment Departments)[1]

Savings Bank	Security	1876 £	1887 £
Bradford	Loans to corporation	207,000	136,000
	Loans to school boards	—	292,000
	Mortgages	157,000	231,000
	Reserve	—	25,000
	Uninvested balance	3,500	25,000
Glasgow	Loans to Gas and Water Commissioners	137,000	103,000
	Loans to Police, School etc. Boards	50,000	371,000
	Glasgow General Stock	—	5,000
	Uninvested balance	—	18,000
Leeds	Corporation Bonds	54,000	137,000
	Debenture Stocks	35,000	166,000
	Loans to School Boards	—	134,000
	Loans on property	—	1,000
	Reserve	—	5,000
	Uninvested balance	—	7,000

In spite of the renaissance in the fortunes of many trustee banks in the 1870s and early 1880s, the opposition of trustees to more drastic legislative reform which had rendered the Act of 1863 a comparatively ineffective measure was to produce one of the most serious crises the savings banks ever encountered. In 1886 the actuary of Cardiff Savings Bank died and was found to have embezzled £30,000 of depositors' money. The trustees tried to persuade depositors to accept 17s 6d in the £ by way of settlement, but it appeared that many depositors had deposited their money irregularly—in excess of the statutory limit or out of office hours. It was also apparent that some of the committee of management had themselves been irregular depositors. The

[1] P.P. 1888, XXIII, Select Committee, App. 3.

question of the personal liability of trustees now came to the fore and some aggrieved depositors appealed to the Registrar of Friendly Societies for a ruling. The Registrar made an award for payment in full to depositors but the trustees decided to ignore this finding. It was quite clear by now that the collapse of the Cardiff Savings Bank at so late a date in the 19th century was bound to have considerable political consequences.

Some of the trustee banks themselves formed an association in an effort to protect their interests as they saw them. The Manchester bank took the initiative and a constitution was formally adopted at a meeting of the representatives of 26 savings banks in Manchester in 1887. Among the 26 were many of the largest banks in the North of England and Scotland. On the other hand the impact of the Cardiff scandal led to the closure of many savings banks and in the five years following 1886 over 100 were closed by their trustees; by 1891 only 303 trustee banks remained. One of the largest to close was Bristol Savings Bank which was financially sound and had assets of more than £500,000, but the trustees were alarmed by events in nearby Cardiff and transferred their business to the Post Office.[1] The Government passed a bill giving the Treasury power to apply to the high court for the appointment of a commissioner to inquire into and settle the affairs of a trustee bank when it had to be closed. E. L. Stanley was appointed as commissioner and set about investigating the Cardiff frauds. He submitted his report in 1888 and chronicled the story of defalcations.[2] He also offered two general conclusions about the trustee system which opened up the whole question of whether it should continue. These were, firstly, that it was not possible to go on relying permanently on the honorary supervision of trustees and, secondly, that there was no reason why 'the nation should pay an additional subsidy to these private banks where the depositor has less security than in the banks now established by the Nation itself'—the Post Office Savings Bank.

A select committee was set up to inquire into the trustee

[1] An account of the Cardiff Savings Bank frauds is given in Horne, *op. cit.*, pp. 236–45.
[2] P.P. 1888, XLIV, Interim Report of the Commissioner appointed to inquire into the affairs of Trustee Savings Bank in Cardiff.

banks' position with Shaw Lefevre as chairman. Of the witnesses from whom the committee heard, Ludlow as Chief Registrar and Brabrook as Assistant Registrar took strongly contrasting standpoints. Ludlow told the Committee that if the security of depositors were the only object to be considered then he thought the whole business of the trustee banks should be handed over as soon as possible to the Post Office. But if this were too strong a step to take, then depositors should at least be given a share in the government of the banks. At present they could claim that they were 'handed over bound hand and foot' into the hands of trustees who by their gross neglect might allow the funds to be squandered and then use the resources of their banks to screen themselves. 'That, I say, is a scandal which ought not to be possible.' Depositors should at least have power to examine the accounts of trustee banks and the banks themselves should be put fully under the Friendly Societies Acts.[1]

Brabrook, on the other hand, told the committee that in his opinion it was expedient 'that trustee savings banks should be retained very much as they are and in their present organization.' He was entirely opposed to merging them with the Post Office Savings Bank. The total transactions of the banks over 70 years had amounted to £1,050,000,000 and of this the total loss did not amount to £250,000. Moreover the local management and encouragement for institutions of this kind had in some respects advantages over central management, 'and as they exist, it would be a great pity to determine their existence until some more solid ground for doing so has been presented.'[2] The third major official witness was C. R. Wilson, by now Comptroller General of the National Debt Office who told the committee that his officers made 'constant remonstrances' but added 'we have no legal power of enforcing our warnings.' If the powers of the National Debt Office were to be increased, 'it should be a real and effective control.'[3] Wilson complained particularly of the wide powers given to the special investment departments of banks by section 16 of the Act of 1863. Now

[1] P.P. 1888, XXIII, Select Committee, J. M. Ludlow, QQ. 57–8.
[2] *Ibid.*, QQ. 595–97, E. W. Brabrook.
[3] *Ibid.*, QQ. 899, 901, C. R. Wilson.

that there were facilities for the purchase of government stock in small quantities under the arrangements introduced when Henry Fawcett was Postmaster General, the need for this section no longer existed.

The select committee also took evidence from representatives of the savings banks and reported in 1889. It concluded that there was room for both trustee and Post Office banks even although it was probable that many more of the smaller trustee banks might be merged in the Post Office. The committee felt that the audit and financial supervision of the trustee banks should not be undertaken by the National Debt Office since this would make the trustee banks as much a branch of the public service as the Post Office Savings Bank 'and we do not recommend this'.[1] The trustees ought to be empowered to form a board of audit of six or seven members for all affiliated banks and be authorized to apply part of their surplus funds for this purpose. The board could then appoint auditors as it wished in each locality.[2] The committee noted that 18 trustee banks had special investment departments under section 16 whereas in 1863 only one bank made use of this section. It commented that a very heavy responsibility lay on the trustees of a bank where money was advanced on mortgage as at Bradford where £292,000 was invested in this way.[3] But no recommendation was made concerning the banks' powers under this section.

The new bill which the Government proposed went a good deal further than the select committee had suggested. For example, it proposed to repeal section 16 and make special investment departments illegal. A large deputation which included 70 Members of Parliament went to see Goschen, Chancellor of the Exchequer, and he agreed to make some modifications in his measure. The Savings Bank Act of 1891[4] provided for the regular inspection of the trustee banks by means of an inspection committee, made the continuance of the office of trustee of a savings bank conditional upon the actual discharge of duties and adjusted the limits of deposit from £150

[1] P.P. 1889, XVI, Select Committee, Report, p. iv.
[2] *Ibid.*, p. vii.
[3] *Ibid.*, p. viii.
[4] 54 & 55 Vict. c. 21.

to £200—in the face of strong opposition from commercial banks. Finally, those banks which had special investment departments on 1 June 1891 were permitted to continue operating them but no more were to be set up and severe limitations on the powers of investment were placed on the funds held in existing special departments.

The Inspection Committee was not a Government department but rather a statutory body with independent standing. Three of its members were to be chosen by the larger trustee banks, one by the Bank of England, one by the Law Society, one by the Institute of Chartered Accountants and one by the Chief Registrar of Friendly Societies. The first chairman was Albert Rollit, representing the Hull Savings Bank and a champion of the trustee banks in the Commons. Apart from the formal inspection of the banks by accountants appointed by the Committee, which soon came to be made annually, the committee prepared a set of model rules which it recommended savings banks to adopt and generally watched over the enforcement of the law. The impact of the inspection committee was beneficial in that boards of management became more active and energetic.[1] During the first four years of the Inspection Committee's activity, another 42 banks closed but from 1894 the total due to depositors in the ordinary branches of the banks began to rise again following the decline that had set in after the troubles at Cardiff in 1887. An additional factor was almost certainly the reduction in the rate of interest allowed to the banks. This was reduced to £2 15s per cent from 1888 and the banks themselves were therefore only able to offer depositors in their ordinary departments £2 10s per cent.[2]

The severe limitations imposed on investment departments by the Act of 1891 did no good at all. Even those departments that could continue in business were virtually obliged to switch their investments to government stocks. Investments in loans to school boards and local authorities with rating powers had proved to be entirely safe and moderately profitable, but these were now forbidden. This led to several banks closing their special investment departments and by 1897 only 14 still

[1] E. W. Brabrook, *Provident Societies and Industrial Welfare*, 1898, pp. 171–2.
[2] Alexander Cargill (ed), *The Centenary of Savings Banks*, 1910, p. 145.

possessed these with about £5,000,000 invested.[1] Glasgow
Savings Bank eventually found the most satisfactory solution to
this difficulty in 1896 by transferring much of its special investment business to an investment trust registered under the
Companies Act but conducted in close association with the
bank. By 1901 the investment trust had just over £1,500,000 to
its credit. The trust took over all those mortgages and loans
which had to be realized by the Glasgow Savings Bank.[2] The
amendment to the Trustee Act for Scotland offered the
Glasgow Bank an opportunity to wind up its investment trust
and bring its assets back into a special investment department,
but south of the border the restrictions on investments continued until the Savings Bank Act of 1904 was passed.[3] This
permitted trustee banks with ordinary deposits over £200,000
without investment departments to open them and restored to
these departments power to invest in any security issued under
the Local Government Loans Act or loans on the security of
local rates. It also extended to the trustee banks the simple pro-
cedures for amalgamating which friendly societies already enjoyed. The restoration of the right of trustee banks to open
investment departments and to invest their funds more widely
was to prove extremely important for the future development of
these banks, for the total amount held in special investment
department deposits has now come to exceed that held in the
deposits of the ordinary departments.

VI. Railway Savings Banks

Quite distinct from both Post Office and Trustee Savings Banks,
some railway companies established savings banks for their
employees. The earliest such bank to be established was that
set up by the London, Brighton and South Coast Railway
Company in 1852. It was followed by others such as the London
and North Western in 1859, the North Eastern in 1860, the
Manchester, Sheffield and Lincolnshire in 1860, the Glasgow
and South-Western in 1865, the South-Eastern in 1869, the

---

[1] *Ibid.*, pp. 173-4.
[2] Payne, *op. cit.*, p. 179.
[3] 4 Ed. VII. c. 8.

Lancashire and Yorkshire in 1882, the Great Eastern in 1890 and the Great Western in 1892. By the end of the century there were sixteen railway savings banks with nearly 40,000 depositors and about £3,500,000 in assets. As with the trustee banks, the initiative for establishing railway savings banks did not come from the depositors but from those anxious to encourage thrift —in this case the directors of the companies.[1]

Those admitted to deposit in these savings banks were the employees of a company and their near relatives. Their children were often encouraged to start accounts, for instance. Accounts were also sometimes opened by benefit and social clubs established among the railwaymen. Unlike the state-supported savings banks, there was usually no restriction on the amount of each depositor's holding. The average amount due to each depositor was over £84 by 1898 in contrast with the average of £15 15s in the Post Office at the same time.[2] The main advantage to depositors in the railway banks was the higher rate of interest than the trustee or Post Office banks offered. In the 1860s the rates paid varied between $3\frac{1}{2}$ and 5 per cent while in 1898 the average interest rate was an attractive $3\frac{5}{8}$ per cent.[3]

The creation of savings banks was in effect an extension of the borrowing powers of a company, for the funds were deposited with the company and were secured on its profits ranking in terms of priority immediately after debenture stock. The banks were authorized in railway company acts and to ensure that reasonably secure conditions were enforced, a model clause was drawn up by Ludlow as Chief Registrar in 1876 and inserted thereafter in every private act promoted by a railway company for the establishment of a savings bank. The effect of the clause was to compel companies to register proper rules and to furnish annual accounts to depositors and the public. It also conferred on depositors certain privileges such as the nomination for sums payable at death and of the settlement of disputes by the Registrar of Friendly Societies.

---

[1] P. W. Kingsford, *Victorian Railwaymen: The Emergence and Growth of Railway Labour 1830–70*, 1970, p. 170; M. Riebenack, *Railway Provident Institutions in English Speaking Countries*, 1905, pp. 238–9.

[2] Brabrook, *op. cit.*, p. 193.

[3] *Ibid.*; Kingsford, *op. cit.*, p. 170.

Table 8.11. Trustee and Post Office Savings Banks, 1861–1900.[1]

| Year | Trustee Savings Banks | | | Post Office Savings Bank | |
	Accounts 000s	Total due to depositors in ordinary department £000s	in special investment department £000s	Accounts 000s	Total due to depositors £000s
1861	1,609	41,546	188		
1862	1,558	40,562	197	178	1,698
1863	1,556	40,951	208	319	3,377
1864	1,492	39,277	233	470	4,993
1865	1,468	38,745	258	611	6,526
1866	1,404	36,382	279	746	8,121
1867	1,385	36,533	279	854	9,749
1868	1,371	36,867	285	965	11,666
1869	1,377	37,553	290	1,085	13,524
1870	1,384	37,958	316	1,183	15,099
1871	1,404	38,819	449	1,303	17,025
1872	1,425	39,679	574	1,442	19,318
1873	1,445	40,525	684	1,556	21,167
1874	1,464	41,466	837	1,668	23,157
1875	1,479	42,387	1,098	1,777	25,187
1876	1,493	43,282	1,255	1,702	26,996
1877	1,509	44,237	1,410	1,791	28,740
1878	1,515	44,255	1,621	1,892	30,411
1879	1,506	43,797	1,806	1,988	32,012

1880	1,519	43,975	2,006	2,184	33,744
1881	1,532	44,137	2,261	2,607	36,194
1882	1,552	44,611	2,592	2,858	39,037
1883	1,566	44,986	2,898	3,105	41,768
1884	1,582	45,840	3,098	3,333	44,773
1885	1,592	46,355	3,318	3,535	47,697
1886	1,590	46,842	3,602	3,731	50,874
1887	1,604	47,261	3,833	3,951	53,974
1888	1,579	46,401	4,029	4,220	58,556
1889	1,551	44,930	4,220	4,507	62,999
1890	1,535	43,613	4,375	4,827	67,634
1891	1,510	42,858	4,056	5,118	71,608
1892	1,501	42,385	4,349	5,452	75,853
1893	1,470	42,225	4,534	5,748	80,597
1894	1,470	43,474	4,640	6,108	89,266
1895	1,516	45,312	4,744	6,453	97,868
1896	1,495	46,699	4,722	6,862	108,098
1897	1,527	48,463	4,599	7,239	115,896
1898	1,563	49,995	4,587	7,630	123,144
1899	1,601	51,404	4,600	8,046	130,118
1900	1,625	51,455	4,530	8,439	135,549

[1] H. O. Horne, *A History of Savings Banks*, 1947, App. II and III, pp. 386–92. Prior to 1891 the special investment department figures are incomplete but the amounts omitted are inconsiderable.

Trustee Savings Bank figures relate to the year ending 20th November and the Post Office Savings Bank figures relate to the year ending 31st December.

There were other savings arrangements made by employers for their employees but they did not attract the public notice as did the railway savings banks, since the railway industry was unique in the extent to which it was regulated by act of Parliament.

Chapter Nine

The Crisis at the End of the Century

At the end of the 19th century the Chief Registrar wrote that 'it remains as one of the great glories of the Victorian era that . . . welfare has been established in a very large degree by the labours and the sacrifices of working-men themselves, and by the wise and judicious legislation which has permitted and encouraged their endeavour in the direction of self-help.'[1] By the beginning of the 20th century the total funds of the various provident institutions amounted to nearly £400,000,000 —the most rapid rate of increase in funds in the last years of the 19th century being in the friendly societies and the retail co-operatives.[2] During the period when this country came as near as it has ever done to a full acceptance and application of the doctrines associated with economic individualism, the provident societies were the instruments of widespread material benefit to the 'industrious classes'.

[1] Brabrook, *op. cit.*, pp. 219–20.
[2] Brabrook, 'On the Progress of Friendly Societies and Other Institutions connected with the Friendly Societies Registry Office', *J. Statistical Society*, LXVIII, 1905, p. 341.

I. The problem of old age

Before the end of the century it was becoming clear that one particularly pressing need was not being adequately met by voluntary associations and it looked increasingly unlikely that it could or would be—that need was for reasonable provision for old age. The difficulties in relying on working men to make such provision for themselves and the consequent need for the state to concern itself with this aspect of social life were coming to be recognized by 1900. While movements in social philosophy are never easy to measure, it has been said of the 1880s that 'In the exceptions and alternatives to economic individualism in practice and in new statements of philosophy a two-fold idea was gaining wide-support. In modern industrial society individuals in isolation, unsupported by the social structure, can achieve neither material welfare nor positive freedom; and it is the function of the state actively to promote a social basis for welfare and freedom.'[1] It was against this background that the need for better provision for old age came to attract increasing attention and that various schemes for old age pensions were publicly discussed and inquired into by official commissions and committees.

The problem which faced friendly societies in particular was not whether they should enter the field of old age insurance in addition to their existing areas of insurance against sickness and death; they already found themselves in that field paying old age benefit in the guise of prolonged sickness payments and therefore virtually shouldering a liability which had not been met by appropriate contributions. In 1879 a competition was held for essays suggesting possible ways in which superannuation might be provided by the societies. The first prize in the Forster Prize Essay competition was awarded to R. W. Moffrey, then Past Provincial Grand Master of the North London district of the I.O.O.F.M.U., whose essay incorporated many of the main features of the various schemes for dealing with the matter which came to be advanced in the next twenty years. Moffrey favoured the organization of any superannuation scheme being undertaken by the friendly societies for two

---

[1] H. Lynd, *England in the Eighteen-Eighties*, 1945, p. 155.

reasons, firstly the people who needed it were already members and it could easily be brought to their notice, secondly the additional expenses of management which would be needed for a second organization would be avoided.

Moffrey described how many of the aged in the Oddfellows and other societies drew sick pay—full, then half and finally quarter pay—during the last years of their lives when they were not so much sick as senile.[1] This practice was leading to difficulties with the calculations on which contributions for sick pay were based and the only safe principle to adopt was that of sickness pay ceasing at a certain age and a life annuity then commencing. He recognized that the main difficulty would be the cost for most men simply could not afford the necessary 17s 6d a year from the age of 25 to provide 5s a week from 65 onwards. A possible solution would be to have a combined sickness and superannuation subscription. For a sickness benefit of 10s per week for one year and 5s per week for the remainder of the sickness the cost was 21s 8d annually, superannuation would be another 17s 6d. If sickness benefit always ceased at 65 a combined contribution of 36s 9d would cover the whole package of benefits. Moffrey admitted that the large contribution would make his plan currently impracticable since members needed to be 'educated up to that point of present self-denial to secure a certain but far distant benefit'. Solvent branches of the affiliated orders might lead the way by applying surpluses thrown up by valuations to the establishment of superannuation funds. When annuity funds came to be established they should be common funds in connection with several branches. In the orders the district seemed to be the right unit to take to secure that the members of each fund were sufficiently numerous to ensure the average duration of life among them. Bringing all this to pass was a matter for persuasion, not com-

---

[1] The high rate of frequency with which elderly members of societies drew sickness benefit was illustrated by the evidence of William Sutton to the Royal Commission on the Aged Poor. The official Actuary's figures showed that on the basis of the quinquennial returns from registered societies for the period 1861–70, 804 members out of 8,991 living at the age of 65 had been in receipt of some amount of continuous sick pay for 2 years; 849 out of 4,289 living at the age of 70, and still higher proportions at later ages.—P.P. 1895, XIV, Report of R.C. on Aged Poor, pp. lvii–lviii.

pulsion, 'at present our duty lies in educating the members up to meeting the conditions necessary.'

The impact on the financial position of friendly societies of the burden of continuous sick benefit in old age came to be remarked upon with increasing frequency. It was the younger members whose interests were most damaged by liberality towards the old. Yet the societies themselves could hardly follow the Court of Queen's Bench which decided that 'natural decay' was not 'sickness'.[1] In clubs which preserved the notion of brotherhood among the members the cause of humanity naturally triumphed so that aged and frail brethren were not left to become altogether destitute. One suggestion that was put forward to deal with this problem was that the Friendly Societies Act of 1875 should be amended to make it illegal for registered societies to offer sickness contracts running for the whole of life but that they should be closed at 60 or 65.[2] The Royal Commission on the Aged Poor in its Report of February 1895 also recommended a change in the Friendly Societies Act so that after a certain date members joining a society should be able to insure for sick pay up to 65 only and not for sick pay throughout life. They should also be able to insure for an annuity beyond that age. The hope of the Commissioners was that this would both ensure provision for old age and secure the financial stability of the societies.[3] It would have represented a complete change from the system of freedom of contract then permitted and would have been very difficult to enforce. If it had been made a condition of registration, the main effect would probably have been to encourage registered societies to become unregistered. There was no apparent way of forcing such a condition on unregistered societies.[4]

Quite apart from changing social ideas and the improvement in the standard of living over the century, the greater longevity of members began to have a noticeable impact on the financial position of friendly societies in the 1880s and 1890s. In deciding their rates, many societies relied upon Farr's Life Table No. 1

---

[1] Wilkinson, 'Friendly Society Finance', *The Economic Journal*, vol. II, p. 725.
[2] *Ibid.*, 727.
[3] P.P. 1895, XIV, Report of R.C. on the Aged Poor, p. lxiii.
[4] Brabrook, *op. cit.*, pp. 113–14.

which was based on mortality data for the years 1836 to 1854. Yet by the end of the century the average age at death of males in their late teens had been extended by about 2½ years. The fevers and infections which had been the scourges of communities in the early part of the 19th century had been checked by sanitary reform, municipal improvement and so forth. There was a greater tendency to live longer and eventually to suffer from a chronic and lingering malady such as bronchitis or cancer. Thus members not only lived longer on average than the contribution tables made provision for, they also tended to suffer from longer and more persistent illnesses than had earlier, shorter living, generations.[1] The extent to which the proportion of older members was increasing in the societies in the later 19th century may be illustrated from the experience of the Manchester Unity. In 1846–48 only 0.20 per cent of the total sickness risk represented members over 65 years of age but by 1893–97 this had increased to 4.66 per cent.[2] This trend was, of course, still continuing in the last decade. In 1892, 4.40 per cent of the members of the Manchester Unity were over 65; by 1897 that figure had crept up to 4.71. In the Hearts of Oak the development became marked a little later, in 1892 only 0.70 per cent of the membership was over 65; by 1900 the comparable percentage was 1.09, and by 1910 this had reached 3.82.[3]

If any solution to the problem were to be found by the friendly societies it would have necessitated the refusal of sick pay over a certain age by all of them. Competition for members was such that no society could have risked acting on its own.

[1] A. W. Watson, 'Some points of interest in the operations of friendly societies, railway benefit societies and collecting societies', *Journal of the Institute of Actuaries*, XLIV, 1910, p. 216, commented that 'the claims in old age, compared with the expectations grounded on the early standards, are known to be remarkably heavy'.

[2] Bentley B. Gilbert, 'The Decay of the 19th century Provident Institutions and the Coming of Old Age Pensions in Great Britain', *Economic History Review*, 2nd Series XVII, No. 3, 1965, pp. 553–4; A. W. Watson, *An Account of an Investigation of the Sickness and Mortality Experience of the I.O.O.F.M.U. during the five years 1893–1897*, 1903, pp. 16–20; for further discussion of this question Bentley B. Gilbert, *The Evolution of National Insurance in Great Britain*, 1966, pp. 171–4.

[3] E. C. Snow, 'Some statistical problems suggested by the sickness and mortality data of certain of the large friendly societies', *J. Statistical Society*, LXXVI, 1913, p. 447.

Moreover the constitutional government of the societies clearly made it impossible for any of them to go against the apparent wishes of the vast majority of their members. As it was, the societies 'do undertake to pay sick pay during the whole of life, and practically that comes to this, that it is a pension'.[1] In spite of the probable lack of demand for separate superannuation schemes, both the Oddfellows and the Foresters introduced such arrangements whereby members might subscribe for pensions from the age of 65. Since they were not able to cut off sick pay at that age, the schemes failed to attract more than a handful of members even though the contribution was paid to the local secretary along with the normal lodge contribution and it was the secretary who transmitted it to the central office.[2] The friendly societies which offered superannuation schemes presumably hoped that they would gradually build up support so that in the end it would prove to be possible to separate the sickness and annuity insurances. The Chief Registrar was firmly opposed to any state action on this issue and made no secret of his belief that friendly societies themselves needed to face the problem of continuous sick benefit in old age squarely and say 'That is not the thing which we are providing for. If you want to provide for that you must pay for it by a separate contribution, and you must pay for it to a pension fund, not the sick fund'.[3] Details of some of the schemes available in 1894 to friendly society members who might wish to secure an annuity of 5s per week from the age of 65 are set out in table 9.1.

In the last decade of the 19th century the Chief Registrar frequently returned to the inadequacy of the existing provision for old age by the friendly societies. He continued both to urge the societies to undertake the task themselves without state aid and to oppose the introduction of any form of state pensions. The basis of his belief that a satisfactory solution could be found in this direction he set out in his evidence to the Royal Commission on Labour. He argued that the members of affiliated orders paid about one week's wages each year to their friendly societies for sickness and death benefits—taking mem-

[1] P.P. 1893–4, XXXIX, R.C. on Labour, Q. 1329.
[2] Wilkinson, *The Friendly Society Movement*, 1886, p. 188.
[3] P.P. 1893–4, XXXIX, R.C. on Labour, Q. 1329.

Table 9.1.

Payments necessary to secure a pension of 5s a week from age of 65.[1]

Society	Contributions not returnable	Contributions returnable	Single premium payable between ages 24 and 25 Contribution not returnable	Single premium payable between ages 24 and 25
Manchester Unity Oddfellows	11d every 4 weeks from 16 or 11½d every 4 weeks from 18	1s 3d every 4 weeks from 16 or 1s 4d every 4 weeks from 18	£17 14s 6½d	—
Ancient Order of Foresters	12s 4d a year at 18 (or 2¾d per week)	£1 2s 2d a year at 18 (about 5d a week)	£16 8s 5d	£34 0s 10
Berkshire Friendly Society	10d every 4 weeks under 15 1s every 4 weeks at 18 (2½d and 3d a week)	—	—	—
Hampshire Friendly Society	A payment of £1 a year from 14 (or 4½d a week), or of £1–4s a year from between 17 and 20 (or 5½d a week), secures sick pay of 10s a week for one year, 5s for the following half year, 2s 6d a week during remainder of illness, and a 5s weekly pension after 65.			

[1] Geoffrey Drage, *The Problem of the Aged Poor*, 1895, p. 302.

bers of the affiliated orders to be earning 30 shillings a week or so on average. It seemed to him that there was room for the ordinary member of an affiliated order to pay another week's wages to get himself a pension in old age. He believed it was entirely practical for friendly societies 'if they will only take up the question earnestly and really mean to do it', to require their members to save a little more for the purpose of providing for old age.[1] The type of provision likely to prove most attractive was where the pension began not at a fixed age such as 65, but rather when a man felt unable to work any longer. The Friendly Societies Act of 1875 had defined old age as 'any age after 50'. A man who was still capable of earning £1 or 30 shillings a week was unlikely to give it up for the sake of 5s; his annuity would be left to go on accumulating and if a few years delay enabled him to gain a pension of 7s or 10s or more, he might be left to seek his own time for retirement. The Chief Registrar went on to express his dislike for the various forms of state or state-aided pension schemes that had been proposed. There was no other way of providing for old age than by 'thrift, self-denial and forethought in youth'. Any plan for relieving the working man of that which ought to be a charge on his wages was bound to be disadvantageous to him. 'It is for his friendly society to fix what he ought to pay, and for his trade union to see that he has the means of paying it.' It was much better that a man should be paid proper wages than that a deficiency should be made up by doles of any kind from the general body of taxpayers.[2]

II. *Schemes for state pensions*

The various schemes which were advanced for providing pensions through state action fell into three broad categories, viz.:
—that the state should compel every citizen to buy a pension through a contributory system,
—that the state should assist every citizen who wished to buy a pension,
—that the state should grant a free pension to every citizen.
A pension scheme of the first type was put forward by Canon

[1] *Ibid.*, Q. 1327.
[2] P.P. 1892, LXXIII, Report of the Chief Registrar for 1891, p. 23.

Blackley in an article in 1878.[1] Everyone was to be required to contribute £10 by the age of twenty-one to a fund controlled by the state and this would be sufficient to entitle each contributor, when physically unable to earn, to weekly sick pay of 8s and to an old age pension of 4s from the age of seventy. The National Providence League was established to promote Blackley's plan andit was able to stir sufficient interest for the Commons to set up a select committee in 1885 to examine this scheme along with a number of subsequent similar proposals. The dissolution of Parliament in 1885 and in 1886 meant that the committee was twice re-appointed and it was only in 1887 that it made its final report.[2] The sick pay portion of the scheme was condemned, but the old age provision met with a generally favourable reception even although the committee indicated that it would rather wait for a further development of public opinion before recommending the general adoption of a compulsory system of old age pensions.

The National Providence League and Blackley dropped the sick pay proposals and incorporated the notion that the state should pay half of the necessary old age contributions. Blackley believed that this would overcome one of the great objections to his scheme, namely that many of the population could never have afforded it. Supporters argued strongly that the scheme would have to be compulsory if it were to meet the needs of the situation since the people could not be relied upon to provide for their own future. While the plan would not encourage thrift, 'if you make a man provided in early life there are possibilities of thrift, but not necessarily consequences. In some people thrift will follow, in a great many it will not, but it is no blame to the Scheme as proposed that it should fail to make all men thrifty.'[3] One positive recommendation that the select committee had made was that there should be compulsory teaching of thrift in the elementary schools.

The second approach, that of offering state assistance to persons to encourage them to buy annuities, found its most

[1] W. L. Blackley, 'National Insurance, a cheap, practical and popular means of abolishing poor rates', *The Nineteenth Century*, IV, 1878, pp. 834–57.

[2] P.P. 1884–85, X, 41; P.P. 1886, XI, 1; P.P. 1887, XI, 1, Report from Select Committee on National Provident Insurance with Proceedings etc.

[3] G. Drage, *The Problem of the Aged Poor*, 1895, p. 237.

powerful advocate in Joseph Chamberlain. He suggested at a bye-election in 1891 that the state might offer the concessionary rate of five per cent on sums deposited by individuals towards the cost of annuities in a publicly sponsored scheme. Shortly after this he took the initiative in forming an unofficial committee of about 80 members of the Commons. From the committee came a number of suggestions for a subsidized voluntary scheme to be administered through the Post Office. It was said that this body could carry out all the administrative work involved for as little as $\frac{1}{4}$ per cent on the total of contributions that would be deposited. Chamberlain recommended to the Royal Commission on the Aged Poor a scheme by which a man who saved enough to buy an annuity of 2s 6d a week should have the sum doubled by the Government.

The principal advocate of the third approach was Charles Booth whose studies of poverty and its causes led him to believe that the only practical way of dealing with the problem of the aged poor was by paying everyone who attained the age of 65 a pension of 5s per week financed by the Treasury. Booth was able to show that old age itself was the most potent cause of pauperism. While the percentage of paupers to population under the age of 60 amounted to only 4.6 in 1890, the percentage over the age of 65 amounted to no less than 38.4. Of all who died over 65, not less than 40 per cent and probably more received public relief in one shape or other during the last years of their life, but of these not more than $\frac{1}{8}$th would have been chargeable to the poor rates before they were 60. While it could be argued that all pauperism was to some extent the fault of the pauper—he might have drunk less, or worked harder, or saved more, or brought his children up so that they would have taken more care of him in old age and so on—yet 'the popular sentiment, which accounts as misfortune the lapse into pauperism of any who have up to old age kept clear of relief, is perhaps more just'. Consequently the giving of outdoor relief to the elderly was popular and common. Moreover it was cheaper than workhouse maintenance. But out-relief lacked the one virtue of confinement to the workhouse. 'If desirable, it is not deterrent, and it is only on the side of deterrence that our poor law encourages economic virtue.' Hence the need for a pension scheme which for most of the aged poor would take the place of outdoor or indoor relief and which, 'if it does not positively encourage thrift, shall at least not discourage it, by making the exhaustion of all savings a first qualification for aid as is the case under the present law'.[1]

The main argument against the state pensions in this form was the political impossibility of imposing the burden this involved on the Treasury. Booth claimed that a universal pension list at £13 per annum each would only amount to £17,000,000 for the 1,300,000 men and women aged over 65. Since the total national income stood at £1,000,000,000 and assuming that the necessary taxation could be arranged to fall in proportion to income, then the charge would only amount to 1.7 per cent of each person's income. In return those whose annual income was above about £150 would get back less than they paid but those who earned less than this would benefit. If it were assumed that tax were to fall in proportion to income, the working classes would pay about the same contribution towards these annuities as their German contemporaries were paying under Bismark's scheme where employer, workman and the state each contributed about one-third.

Booth believed that any plan would be disastrous if it disturbed in any way the bases of work and wages, discouraged thrift, or undermined in the slightest degree self-respect or the forces of individuality, 'upon which morality as well as industry depends'. He believed it could hardly be claimed that what old men were already doing they would cease to do; the small fixed income from 65 might encourage them to turn to such work as that of watchman or caretaker. The absence of the means test— that essential precursor of poor relief—would encourage thrift since every shilling saved would bring more comfort. The greater certainty of the enjoyment of saving might well make thrift more attractive. Self-respect would hardly be undermined by the receipt of a pension which all old people, regardless of their means, would draw. Given these likely consequences of universal state pensions, it followed that industrial

[1] Charles Booth, 'The enumeration and classification of paupers, and state pensions for the aged', *J. Statistical Society*, LIV, 1891, pp. 600–43, but s ee especially pp. 629–41; Charles Booth, *Pauperism and the Endowment of Old Age*, 1892, gives more detail and further evidence.

energy and all the forces of individuality were much more likely to be stimulated than checked by the security afforded to old age.

The attention which schemes such as those of Blackley, Chamberlain and Booth attracted was the greater because of developments in other countries. New Zealand was to be the first of the English speaking nations to adopt a universal old age pension scheme while in Europe, Denmark and Germany both adopted schemes which came into force as early as 1891. The German plan was widely studied for any guidance it might offer. It was incorporated in a law adopted by the Reichstag on 23 May 1889 for insurance against invalidity and old age. This law was described by a Vice-President of the Institute of Actuaries as 'one of the most daring social and economic experiments in modern history'.[1] The Bismark-sponsored law was said to have been the product of a mixture of militarism and protection. In 1879 Bismark announced the change of policy away from free trade to protection, industry was to be unconditionally protected and steadily increasing tariffs followed. The Chancellor had expressed the hope that the state would come to possess a monopoly of the German insurance industry and the law for compulsory insurance against old age fitted into this context. Moreover there was a tradition of compulsory insurance against sickness in Prussia where from 1854 workmen had been required to join sick relief societies. The Sickness Insurance Law of 1883 enforced a similar principle of compulsion throughout the German Empire.

The law for old age insurance applied initially to about 12,000,000 persons, that is to say, to all whose wages did not exceed 2,000 marks or about £100 annually. Contributions were payable by the employee and his employer in equal shares with the state adding a subsidy of 50 marks to each annuity actually paid. Benefits were paid at any age in cases of confirmed incapacity for work provided that contributions had been paid for five years. The old age pension for those remain-

[1] T. E. Young, 'The German Law of Insurance against invalidity and old age: a history, analysis and criticism', *J. Institute of Actuaries*, XXIX, 1891, pp. 269–364; See also W. H. Dawson, *Bismark and State Socialism*, 1890; further development of this scheme is discussed in Dawson, *Social Insurance in Germany 1883–1911*, 1913.

ing in good health was payable from the age of 70 and the minimum period of contribution for this benefit was 30 years. The actual method of collection of the premiums was by sticking stamps on insurance cards, the stamps being purchased from post offices by the employer who deducted the employee's share from his wages. The administration of the scheme was put in the hands of specially created state insurance institutes, each with a conveniently sized territory. A State Commissioner and supporting officials were appointed by the government for the district of every institute. The size of the pension payable was related to the average wage on which contributions had been paid and the lowest scale produced a pension of little more than 2s weekly.

The interest in the pensions question as illustrated by the proposals being made at home and the plans being implemented abroad led to pressure for a full enquiry into the condition of the elderly and of the poor law administration. The Royal Commission on the Aged Poor began its work in February 1893 and issued its Report in 1895.[1] The chairman was Lord Aberdare and the membership included persons of such diverse views as Joseph Chamberlain, Charles Booth, and C. S. Loch, the secretary of the Charity Organization Society. Although a member, Chamberlain gave evidence to the Commission in favour of his own scheme of offering public money to encourage persons to contribute throughout their lives for the purchase of annuities. He condemned the compulsory German scheme as inapplicable to English habits and feelings. The cost of its administration was proving very heavy and it would be very unpopular with the working class. As for Booth's scheme, it would be very expensive and the Commons would never provide the money. On the other hand a scheme such as he himself suggested would enable industrious, temperate and thrifty workmen to make provision for themselves. A sharpening of the deterrence of poor law administration was impossible while the worthy were still obliged to seek parochial aid. Chamberlain's views are of particular interest in that he was the leading political figure to associate himself with the cause of old age pensions in the 1890s. At all times he showed a politician's

[1] P.P. 1895, XIV, XV.

sensitivity for the feelings of the friendly societies. In his evidence to the Royal Commission he said that he attached great importance to them. 'They are in touch with the thriftily minded section of the working class. Their criticism of any scheme would be very damaging: their opposition might be fatal. They have very great Parliamentary influence and I should myself think twice before attempting to proceed in face of hostility from so important and dangerous a quarter.'[1]

The Royal Commission heard evidence from representatives of every point of view. The majority of members in their report recommended no major changes in the existing system of dealing with the elderly. It would be undesirable to interfere with the existing discretion of the guardians as to how relief should be given since it was essential that guardians should keep the power to deal with each case on its merits. Having examined the various schemes for old age pensions, the Royal Commission felt unable to recommend the adoption of any of them. It did recommend that the law should be changed to oblige friendly societies to end sick pay at 65 and to pay only separately funded pensions thereafter. Provision for annuity or pension arrangements should in fact be through the friendly societies, or possibly through the existing Post Office annuities, and should continue on a voluntary basis without either compulsion or state aid.[2]

The Gladstone Government lost the election of 1895 and the Unionist Government that was victorious had given the impression of being favourably inclined towards social reform even although it had not promised to introduce old age pensions. Chamberlain had by this time become Secretary for the Colonies and his energies were increasingly occupied by imperial affairs, but his influence on social policy might be seen in the appointment of a Treasury committee in 1896 with Lord Rothschild as chairman. The committee's terms of reference required it to consider any schemes that might be submitted to it for encouraging the industrial population to make provision for old age. Schemes for compulsory provision lay outside its terms of reference. The Rothschild committee consisted mainly

---

[1] Quoted in A. Wilson and G. S. Mackay, *Old Age Pensions*, 1941, pp. 26–9.
[2] P.P. 1895, XIV, R.C. on the Aged Poor, pp. lxxxiii–lxxxvii.

of civil servants, including the Chief Registrar of Friendly Societies along with A. W. Watson, actuary to the Manchester Unity and Alfred Chapman who was parliamentary agent to the Ancient Order of Foresters. The committee found itself unable to agree on any scheme which would be free from grave disadvantages.[1] The outcome was not really surprising in view of the membership of the committee and its terms of reference. The Government's sincerity in setting up the committee has recently been questioned and it has been suggested that the Cabinet never intended that the committee should find old age pensions feasible.[2]

The exasperation at this turn of events shown by those who saw an urgent need for pensions was typified by Lionel Holland, a Conservative member of the Commons, who expressed his dissatisfaction in a letter in *The Times*. He pointed out that the Report of the Royal Commission had given the Government all the information needed if it had the will to act; the Rothschild committee had since wasted a further two years. It remained for the Cabinet to show that 'they are not content to falsify the expectations they aroused at the general election, that they realize the occasion for trifling has gone by and possess not only the "heart to resolve" but a "head to contrive" and "a hand to execute".'[3] The next year Holland introduced a pensions bill and in moving the second reading he claimed that the latest figures showed that only 18 of the 800,000 members of the Manchester Unity were contributing to that society's superannuation scheme and only 3 of the 720,000 Foresters had joined the superannuation scheme of the A.O.F.[4] Following the debate a select committee was set up 'to consider and report upon the best means of improving the condition of the aged deserving poor, and of providing for those of them who are helpless and infirm, and to inquire whether any of the bills dealing with old age pensions and submitted to Parliament during the present session can with advantage be adopted either

---

[1] P.P. 1898, XLV, Report of the Committee on Old Age Pensions, pp. 9–10.
[2] Gilbert, *The Evolution of National Insurance in Great Britain*, 1966, p. 187.
[3] *The Times*, 11 July 1898, p. 10 quoted by Ronald V. Sires, 'The Beginnings of British Legislation for Old-Age Pensions', *Journal of Economic History*, XIV, 1954, p. 237.
[4] *Parliamentary Debates*, Third Series, LXIX, 62, 22 Mar 1899.

with or without amendment'. This select committee, known after the name of its chairman as the Chaplin committee, was notable as being the only official body to consider the question which made positive recommendations and it made them within only three months of its appointment.

The select committee decided to review the improvement of poor relief as well as the institution of old age pensions. It studied the Danish and New Zealand systems and put forward a plan which would have made the poor law authority responsible for providing a pension of 5s to 7s a week depending on the local cost of living, up to half the cost being refunded by the Treasury and the pensions being paid through Post Offices. Pensions should be paid to all men and women over 65 whose total income did not exceed 10s a week and who had neither been sent to prison nor had received poor relief during the previous twenty years. At an early stage the committee had excluded from further consideration schemes involving compulsory contributions.[1] These recommendations were referred to a departmental committee by the Government to report on their financial implications. The South African War had just begun. By January 1900 the committee had reported and costed the scheme on the alternative bases of pensions starting at 65, 70 and 75 giving the total cost in each case for the three dates 1901, 1911 and 1921. By this time the Boer War had developed into an expensive undertaking and this was to prevent any movement towards legislation for a plan for old age pensions for a further period of some years.

III. Friendly societies and the coming of old age pensions

It has been pointed out that the pensions issue had clearly been more than adequately investigated. The failure to legislate was due both to the lack of a sufficiently strong desire for such legislation on the part of the Government and the absence of a powerful and well-organized public opinion or lobby in favour of it. On the other hand the strong opposition to pensions legislation which trade unions and cooperative societies as well as friendly societies had shown in the 1880s and early 1890s had

[1] Wilson and Mackay, *op. cit.*, p. 34.

been quite enough to make politicians very cautious. In 1891 the president of the T.U.C. admitted his own inclination towards 'self-help'. The next year's president commented that there was a 'catchy sound' about old-age pensions and added that 'It seems essential before adopting such a system that we should utilise the agents that presently exist.' From 1896 there was a shift in trade union opinion and the parliamentary committee was instructed to work towards old-age pensions for all workers.[1] By the turn of the century the cooperative societies had moved to a position favouring pensions from their earlier attitude of silence. The position taken by the friendly societies, particularly by the affiliated orders and their spokesmen, clearly had an important braking effect on the pensions campaign. Although a government-operated contributory pension scheme would relieve them of the increasingly heavy financial burden of virtually continuous sick pay for many of their older members, yet it would also have the effect of bringing the Government into direct competition with them for the workingman's savings. Many friendly society leaders did not believe that workmen could afford both a contribution for a pension and their existing friendly society dues. If the former were to be compulsory, the latter would in many cases be abandoned and the societies would go down. If the societies themselves undertook the administration of state-subsidized schemes for annuities on the lines suggested by Chamberlain, this would be bound to involve close governmental control of their affairs—if only to ensure solvency. Essentially, the only thing the societies had ever sought from the state was the protection of the law which they gained through registration. Even by the end of the century very many societies were still not prepared to have this minimal amount of contact with the public authorities; the members valued their independence, their freedom to do as they pleased with their own, much too highly to accept registration.[2] Thus the suspicious attitude of the friendly societies to any form of Government 'interference' in the field of pensions was

[1] Sires, *op. cit.* p. 240 quoting from T.U.C. *Annual Reports* for 1891, 1892 and 1896.
[2] As late as 1892 the Chief Registrar believed that there were still probably some 3,000,000 members of unregistered friendly societies—P.P. 1893–4, XXXIX, Q. 1331.

deeply rooted in the history and tradition of the friendly society movement.

The opposition of the friendly societies to the various pensions proposals was made manifest in connection with each of the different official inquiries. The select committee which sat from 1885 to 1887 to examine the plan put forward by Canon Blackley heard the very strong objections from the leaders of friendly societies to such a scheme. The committee commented in its report that 'The objections resolved themselves mainly into apprehension, lest operation of compulsory national insurance should interfere in the numerical increase of their own organizations. So keenly apprehensive are the officials of some of the societies of this effect, that Mr Reuben Watson, Actuary of the Manchester Unity of Oddfellows, did not hesitate to reply to Q 909, "If you could devise some scheme which would be for the welfare of all classes in this country, but which would be to the detriment of the friendly societies, you would not object to it on that ground?" Answer, "Well, I think I should object to it. I consider that friendly societies have voluntarily done a very great deal of good in this country, and I think they ought not to be interfered with by the establishment of any system which would be injurious to them".'[1] The next year Reuben Watson put his argument in rather more general terms arguing that 'state subsidisation appears likely to be appealed to in some cases to accomplish that which intelligent men in these dominions seem determined to do for themselves without unnecessary state or other interference or aid.'[2]

This wider, philosophical objection to state interference in the affairs of the individual was of course bound to evoke widespread support. T. E. Young whose interest in the German attempt to deal with the problem of old age had led him to write a long, and initially sympathetic detailed analysis of it for the Institute of Actuaries, felt obliged to close his account by expressing certain reservations on the moral and philosophical implications of the scheme. He feared that a government which by detailed and elaborate supervision held itself out as possess-

---

[1] P.P. 1887, XI, Report of the Select Committee of the House of Commons on National Provident Insurance, pp. vi and vii.

[2] Reuben Watson, *An Essay on Friendly Societies and Sick Clubs*, 1888.

ing the sole remedy for all social ills, demoralized and impeded national life 'by confirming and widening the social habit of appealing to the State at every crisis, real or imagined'. So far as the government subsidy was concerned, people too often regarded the state as a distinct entity with funds of its own quite apart from those it drew in from its citizens. 'State funds are viewed as external reservoirs of opulence; the financial rains, whose descent is implored, are not observed to be simply the accumulation, as in nature, of financial currents ascending from the earth.'[1]

The critical attitude of the friendly societies accorded entirely with the views of most liberal politicians. Henry Fawcett was one of the most energetic and far-sighted Postmasters-General of the 19th century, and his reaction to an approach on this issue from postal employees is of interest. Some postmen and sorters asked him in 1884 to establish a system of compulsory deductions from their wages with a view to securing annuities. Fawcett declined to have anything to do with the suggestion observing in particular that it would not encourage *self*-help. He went on to suggest that individuals might make provision for their old age by using the Post Office Savings Bank. By putting a penny stamp on a card every week and depositing it when filled at a savings bank, a lad of 15 would have money enough for an annuity of £2 10s a year at the age of 60. By saving 2s a week from 20 to 50 an annuity could be secured of £18 a year to commence at the age of 50.[2]

This same emphasis on the moral and ethical value of personal effort and forethought as contrasted with the human decay and perpetual pauperism that would result from any sort of state pension was vigorously sustained by the Charity Organization Society well into the 20th century.[3] This influential body campaigned vigorously in support of the friendly societies' standpoint in the 1890s. What society needed was not that each man should find that when he reached the age of 60 the state like a fairy godmother had put an adequate balance at his bankers, but rather that during life he should have learned

[1] T. E. Young, *op. cit.*, pp. 348–51.
[2] Leslie Stephen, *Life of Henry Fawcett*, 1886, p. 435.
[3] C. L. Mowat, *The Charity Organisation Society 1869–1913*, 1961, p. 144.

to limit his responsibilities so that at 60 he found himself with enough for his old age. 'The valuable thing is not £ s. d. but the character and capacity for further progress which is created by this wholesome discipline. To remove the necessity of providing for old age would be to remove one of the most potent influences of civilization.' There was nothing in the various proposals for state-aided pensions which differentiated them in any way from the existing out-door relief and they would have exactly the same demoralizing effect on the 'thrifty instincts' of the people.[1] The secretary to the Society, C. S. Loch, argued that the large percentage of the population who died as paupers (put by Booth at 42.7 per cent) was not a reason for introducing pensions, but rather for applying rigorously the remedial measures proposed by the Poor Law Commissioners of 1832. Above all no outdoor relief should be given to the able-bodied. In unions where this principle had been enforced all pauperism had decreased including that of old age. The people to whom outdoor relief had been refused had not been forced into workhouses but had managed to provide for themselves or had been provided for by their relations in their old age.[2]

In his history of the Charity Organization Society, C. L. Mowat has shown how this attitude governed policy until the end of the 19th century but that the position was then on the point of changing. 'For the moment the dykes held; but soon only the C.O.S. would be manning them.'[3] Even in some of the friendly societies a slow change of attitude was becoming perceptible around 1900. Chamberlain's efforts to win them over to his idea of a partnership with the state subsidizing a pensions plan which would have operated through the societies was unsuccessful at the time it was made. In support of his plan he argued that the societies would very soon have to face the financial problems arising out of their practice of giving what amounted to old-age benefit in the form of sick pay. He set out his arguments in a speech to friendly society representatives in Birmingham in December 1894. The substance of the speech

[1] T. Mackay, *Insurance and Saving: A Report on the existing opportunities for working-class thrift*, 1892, p. 33.
[2] C. S. Loch, *Old Age Pensions and Pauperism*, 1892, p. 40.
[3] Mowat, *op. cit.*, p. 144.

was published as an article in the *National Review* which printed a reply two months later by J. L. Stead, assistant secretary of the Foresters, claiming that friendly societies had given a great deal of consideration to Chamberlain's plans in 1892 and 1893. But the proposals involved suggestions for state aid and were therefore unacceptable, the scheme had been rejected by the National Conference of Friendly Societies in 1893.[1] J. L. Stead became Chief Secretary of the A.O.F. in 1897 and his personal influence certainly played its part in ensuring that the Order maintained a persistent and unyielding opposition to old age-pensions into the early 20th century.

The financial problems to which Chamberlain had pointed may well have been influential in bringing eventually a shift in the attitude of some friendly societies. The A.M.C. of the Manchester Unity passed in 1896 by 290 to 244 a heavily qualified resolution apparently favouring pensions in certain conditions:

'that any well considered and suitable scheme propounded by the legislature for the relief of the aged and infirm, benefiting our unfortunate brethren, will receive the cordial support of the Manchester Unity, provided that the pension is independent of the Poor Law and does not create any power of government interference in the general management of the affairs of this Unity'.

Leading and influential officials of the Manchester Unity such as Alfred Watson remained strongly opposed to any of the schemes for old age pensions which had, in fact, been put forward and the Unity's influence continued into the present century to be exerted against the early enactment of pensions legislation.

Some of the other friendly societies adopted a more conciliatory attitude about the turn of the century. In 1901 the Hearts of Oak resolved at its annual meeting that the state should pay a pension to every person of 65 who had been a member of a provident society for twenty years or more. The National Conference of Friendly Societies passed a resolution against some opposition in 1901 similar to that of the Hearts of Oak and

[1] Joseph Chamberlain, 'Old Age Pensions and Friendly Societies', *National Review*, XXIV, 1895, pp. 592–615; J. L. Stead, 'Friendly Societies and Old Age Pensions, A Reply to Mr. Chamberlain', *National Review*, XXV, 1895, pp. 59–71; these articles are referred to by Bentley B. Gilbert who discusses fully Chamberlain's efforts in his *Evolution of National Insurance in Great Britain*, pp. 180–88.

appointed a committee to prepare possible legislation on pensions.[1] The strength of the opposition to old-age pensions which continued to be felt among the societies showed itself frequently. After the committee on old-age pensions had reported to the National Conference, the representative of the North London district of the Manchester Unity at the Cheltenham A.M.C. proposed that the Oddfellows should withdraw from membership of the National Conference as a protest against the 'notorious scheme' put forward by the committee. The A.M.C. decided not to withdraw but it did show its irritation by suggesting that meetings of the National Conference should only be held 'when necessary' instead of annually since much mischief could come from regular meetings.[2]

The Boer War and the financial demands which it brought with it made it impossible for the government to introduce a pension scheme for a few years. Balfour was later to argue that it made it impossible for either party to introduce old-age pensions any earlier than they were in 1908.[3] The large increase in the representation of the labour and overtly working-class interests in the House of Commons in 1906 undoubtedly played an important part in bringing Asquith and the leaders of the Liberal party to take an altogether more urgent view of the matter. The gradual development of the Government's policy between 1906 and 1908 has been traced very fully.[4] By 1908 Asquith's scheme had taken shape in the form of a non-contributory pension of 5s weekly for men and women over 70 of limited income. He had concluded that contributory schemes were impracticable. Such a scheme on a voluntary basis would not have brought help to those most in need of it, only the better-off and thriftily-inclined would take advantage of it. Any scheme involving compulsory contributions would lead to a clash with friendly societies, collecting and similar organizations which would find themselves competing with the state from a position of considerable disadvantage. For reasons of

---

[1] Sires, *op. cit.*, pp. 238–40 where the shift in attitudes in a number of friendly societies is traced.

[2] *The Times*, 5 June 1903, p. 4.

[3] Wilson and Mackay, *op. cit.*, pp. 37–8, quoting from *The Times*, 17 Dec 1912.

[4] Gilbert, *op. cit.*, pp. 202–21.

cost, the non-contributory pensions would only start at 70 and would be confined to those with an income of less than £26 annually—or £39 total income in the case of married couples whose joint pension was limited to 7s 6d.

Certainly, a non-contributory scheme would serve to help relieve friendly societies of the financial problems caused by continuous sick benefit for the elderly. But the societies, strongly wedded to the notion of self-help and independence, remained divided, some opposing the bill, others approving of it and yet others declining to take an attitude. This divided condition was illustrated by the replies which the Chief Registrar received to a question he circulated to the societies early in 1908. In this he asked whether they considered the passing of a non-contributory bill conferring old-age pensions would have an injurious effect on friendly societies. 151 reply forms were received back. Twenty of these came from societies which refused to answer this question directly, of the rest there were 67 positive and 64 negative answers.[1] Even before the old-age pensions actually began to be paid from 1 January 1909, private discussions had started between some leading members of the societies and the Government on the possibility of involving the societies in a future national health insurance scheme.

The continuing importance of the voluntary provident associations in the first half of the 20th century was recognized by the place accorded them in the administrative machinery for the state's insurance system until after the Second World War. The principle of recognizing the voluntary efforts of members of friendly societies and kindred institutions had already found expression in the Old Age Pensions Act itself. Exemption from various disqualifications for a pension was granted provided that the applicant 'has continuously for 10 years up to attaining the age of 60, by means of payments to friendly, provident, and other societies, or trade unions or other approved steps, made such provision against old age, sickness, infirmity, or want or loss of employment as may be recognised as proper provision for the purpose by Regulations under this Act'.[1]

[1] P.P. 1908, LXXXVIII, p. 367, Circular letter issued by the Chief Registrar to the principal Friendly Societies with reference to the proposed non-contributory scheme of Old-Age Pensions, with abstract of their replies.

Under the National Insurance Act of 1911, friendly societies, collecting societies and industrial insurance companies were all enabled to become agents for the operation of the state insurance scheme. The friendly societies were thus able to offer their members a 'package' of benefits, partly paid for by contributions to the state scheme and partly by their own contributions. The industrial insurance concerns were more interested in using their position as operators of 'approved' societies to gain introductions and contacts for the purpose of selling more 'life' insurance.

In this way the friendly societies themselves, which might have seemed to be the thrift organizations most vulnerable to the introduction of a state welfare system, not only survived but apparently flourished until the 1940s and the changes which were then made in the administrative structure of the national insurance system. In 1899 the registered friendly societies had 5,217,261 members with total funds of £5,672,659; the comparable figures for 1945 were 8,719,972 members and funds of £192,829,305. Individual societies tended to be larger since the number decreased from 27,000 to 18,000. Collecting societies were shown in the Chief Registrar's returns as having 5,922,615 policies in force in 1899 as compared with 29,644,895 in 1945, their funds having increased from £5,207,686 to £116,552,688.

Other types of voluntary provident associations were not so directly concerned with the entry of the state into the field of social welfare and both in terms of membership and funds they

Table 9.2.

	Members		Funds	
	1905	1945	1905 £	1945 £
Building Societies	612,424	2,065,324	70,348,997	823,954,621
Cooperative Societies	2,375,903	9,230,240	49,941,142	357,283,973
Trustee Savings Banks	1,730,331	4,438,160	60,632,468	603,079,997

The details set out in table 9.2 illustrate this growth.

[1] 8 Edw. VII, c. 40, S. 3.

continued to show very considerable growth in the changing circumstances of the 20th century.

The change in the social background against which these various associations developed in the present century has meant that while they remained mutual aid organizations, were still grouped under the surveillance of the Friendly Societies' Registry, and remained expressions of the 'spirit of self-help', they nevertheless gradually ceased to be the various means by which that portion of the population which was 'within the risk of pauperism' endeavoured to escape from it.

Bibliographical Note

The most directly relevant of the sources consulted in preparing this volume are mentioned in the references and no attempt is made here to set out a full bibliography. It may be helpful, however, to bring together in this note some of the material useful in studying the main topics discussed in this book.

I. General

E. W. Brabrook, *Provident Societies and Industrial Welfare*, London, 1898.

J. Frome Wilkinson, *The Mutual and Provident Institutions of the Working Classes*, London, 1888.

Bentley B. Gilbert, *The Evolution of National Insurance in Great Britain*, London, 1966.

Reports of the Registrar of Friendly Societies, annually from 1856 to 1875.

Reports of the Chief Registrar of Friendly Societies, annually from 1876.

(These reports constitute the most considerable single source of statistical and other contemporary material relating not only to friendly societies but to all classes of mutual aid associations.)

Royal Commission appointed to inquire into Friendly and Benefit Building Societies, 1871–1874.

—First Report, 1871, XXV

—Second Report and Evidence, 1872, XXVI

—Third Report, 1873, XXII

—Fourth Report with Appendices, 1874, XXIII Pt I

—Reports of Assistant Commissioners, 1874, XXIII, Pt II

(The Royal Commission gathered a great deal of evidence

about contemporary friendly societies, burial and collecting societies, and building societies.)

II. Friendly Societies

J. M. Baernreither, *English Associations of Working Men*, London, 1889 (original German edition, Tubingen, 1886).
E. W. Brabrook, *Friendly Societies and Similar Institutions*, London, 1875.
Paul Davis, *The Old Friendly Societies of Hull*, Hull, 1926.
Margaret D. Fuller, *West Country Friendly Societies*, Reading, 1964.
P. H. J. H. Gosden, *The Friendly Societies in England 1815–1875*, Manchester, 1961 (pp. 245–58 contain an extensive bibliography on friendly societies).
C. Hardwick, *A History of Friendly Societies*, Manchester, 1893.
E. J. Hobsbawn, 'Friendly Societies', *The Amateur Historian*, III, 3, 1957.
F. G. P. Neison, 'Some statistics of the affiliated orders of friendly societies', *Journal of the Statistical Society*, XL, 1877, pp. 42–81.
J. Frome Wilkinson, *Mutual Thrift*, London, 1891.

III. Building Societies

E. W. Brabrook, *Building Societies*, London, 1906.
E. J. Cleary, *The Building Society Movement*, London, 1965. (pp. 313–15 contain an extensive bibliography on building societies).
Oscar R. Hobson, *A Hundred Years of the Halifax*, London, 1953.
J. M. Ludlow, 'Building Societies', *Economic Review*, III, 1, 1893.
S. J. Price, *Building Societies: their origin and history*, London, 1958.
A. Scratchley, *Treatise on Benefit Building Societies*, London, 1849.

IV. Cooperative Societies

Board of Trade, Report on Workmen's Cooperative Societies in the United Kingdom, 1901, Cd. 698.

C. R. Fay, *Cooperation at Home and Abroad*, London, 1908.

G. J. Holyoake, *The History of Cooperation*, London, 1908.

G. J. Holyoake, *The History of the Rochdale Equitable Pioneers*, London, 1900.

S. Pollard, 'Nineteenth Century Cooperation, from community building to shopkeeping', *Essays in Labour History*, (ed. Asa Briggs and John Saville), London, 1960, pp. 74–112.

Percy Redfern, *The Story of the C.W.S.*, 1863–1913, Manchester, 1913.

V. Savings Banks

Alexander Cargill (ed.), *The Centenary of Savings Banks*, Edinburgh, 1910.

A. Fishlow, 'The Trustee Savings Banks, 1817–1861', *Journal of Economic History*, XXI, 1961, pp. 26–40.

H. Oliver Home, *A History of Savings Banks*, London, 1947.

William Lewins, *A History of Banks for Savings*, London, 1866.

Peter L. Payne, 'The Savings Bank of Glasgow, 1836–1914', *Studies in Scottish Business History*, (ed. P. L. Payne), London, 1967, pp. 152–86.

A. Scratchley, *A Practical Treatise on Savings Banks*, London, 1860.

H. B. Sellers, *Memoranda from a Notebook on the Yorkshire Penny Bank*, Leeds, 1909.

Index

Index

Gourley's Bill, 162–3
Government Annuities, 48
Grand National Consolidated Trades' Union, 182
Great Eastern Railway Company Savings Bank, 255
Great Western Enginemen and Fireman's Mutual Assurance, Sick and Superannuation Society, 61
Great Western Locomotive and Carriage Department Sick Fund Society, 60
Great Western Railway Company, 60
Great Western Railway Company Savings Bank, 255
Greenford, 181
Greenwich, 159

Halifax Building Society, 165, 166, 177
Halifax Equitable Building Society, 165n
Halifax Industrial Cooperative Society, 188
Halifax Permanent Building Society, 165n
Halifax School Board, 166
Hampshire, 13, 33
Hanwell, 181
Hardwick, Charles, 69
Harle, William, 156
'Harmony', 182
Harrington Colliery, 32
Hartlepool, 157
Heart of Honesty Lodge, I.O.O.F.M.U., 88
Hearts of Oak Benefit Society, 62–3, 104–5, 263, 279
Hereford, 13
Herefordshire Friendly Society, 26n
Hertford (Sunday bank), 210
Heyrood Street Ragged School, 118
Higham, James, 154
Highland Society, 19, 212
Hill, Rowland, 236
Hole, James, 185
Holland, G. C., 229
Holland, Lionel, pensions bill, 273
Holloway, George, 107–8
Holloway Societies, 107–8
Holyoake, George, 32n, 181, 182, 190
Hosking, Josiah, 148, 149
Howarth, Charles, 183
Howarth, George, 223–4
Huddersfield Banking Company, 231
Hughes, Tom, 73n
Huguenots, 6
Hull, 215
Hull Savings Bank, 253

Hulme Philanthropic Burial Society, 118
Humane Sick and Burial Club, Ashton-under-Lyne, 119
Hume, Joseph, and savings bank interest rates, 218–19
Huskisson, 31

Incorporation of Carters (Leith), 6
Ideal Benefit Society, 108
Industrial and Provident Societies Acts, 203;
  1852, 192, 195
  1862, 193–5, 201; and the C.W.S., 194, 199–200
  1867, 194
  1871, 194
  1876, 195
  1893, 195
Industrial Permanent Building Society, 159
Infants' Funeral Friendly Society, Doncaster, 117
Ingoldby, Frederick, 155
Inspection Committee of Trustee Savings Banks, 245, 253
Institute of Chartered Accountants, 253
Instructions for the Establishment of Benefit Building Societies, 151

Jennings, William, 144
Joint Stock Companies Act, 1844, 193, 233

Kay, Justice, 99n
Kent, 13, 33
Kershaw, John, 184n
Killarney Savings Bank deficiency, 223
Kingsley, Charles, 76

Lancashire, 13, 14, 37, 40, 43, 44, 55, 56, 62, 110, 116, 144, 148, 159, 186, 188, 228, 246
Lancashire and Yorkshire Railway Company Savings Bank, 255
Lancet, 113n
Langford, J. A., 144
Lansdowne, Marquis of, 210
Law Society, 253
Leaseholders, right to vote, 153–4
Lecture on the Friendly Societies of Antiquity, 3
Leeds, 21n, 29, 58, 121, 144, 157, 191, 215, 236, 237
Leeds Amalgamated Friendly Societies Medical Aid Association, 113